PARLOR POLITICS

In Which the Ladies of Washington Help Build

a City and a Government

JEFFERSONIAN AMERICA

Jan Ellen Lewis and Peter S. Onuf, Editors

Catherine Allgor

PARLOR POLITICS

In Which the Ladies of Washington Help

Build a City and a Government

University Press of Virginia • *Charlottesville and London*

THE UNIVERSITY PRESS OF VIRGINIA

© 2000 by the Rector and Visitors of the University of Virginia

All rights reserved

Printed in the United States of America

Second printing 2001

♾ The paper used in this publication meets the minimum
requirements of the American National Standard for Information
Sciences—Permanence of Paper for Printed Library Materials,
ANSI Z39.48-1984.

Book design by Kachergis Book Design, Pittsboro, North Carolina

LIBRARY OF CONGRESS CATALOGING-IN-PUBLICATION DATA
Allgor, Catherine, 1958–
    Parlor politics : in which the ladies of Washington help build a city
and a government / Catherine Allgor.
        p.   cm — (Jeffersonian America)
    Includes bibliographical references (p.) and index.
    ISBN 0-8139-1998-3 (cloth : alk. paper)
    1. Women in politics—Washington (D.C.)—History—19th
century.   2. Upper class women—Washington (D.C.)—History—
19th century.   3. Entertaining—Washington (D.C.)—History—
19th century.   4. Washington (D.C.)—History—19th century.
5. Washington (D.C.)—Politics and government—19th century.
6. Washington (D.C.)—Social life and customs—19th century.
    I. Title.   II. Series
    HQ1236.5.U6 A45 2000
    305.42'09753'09034—dc21

                                        00-033415

To my husband, Jonathan Lipman—
who gave me his entire self, wholly and
without reservation.

Contents

෴

Illustrations

PARLOR POLITICS

In Which the Ladies of Washington Help Build

a City and a Government

Introduction

"A kingdom for a stage"
—WILLIAM SHAKESPEARE, *Henry V,* prologue, 3

STORIES ABOUT WOMEN IN POLITICS often carry the promise of behind-the-scenes intrigue, spiced with a whisper of the illicit. Cleopatra, Madame Pompadour, Pamela Harriman—fascinating women all, whose source of political power lay in their sexuality. The story of this book, also a story of women and power, has a different cast of characters. Rather than taking place behind the scenes, the action unfolds everywhere that politics happened in Washington City, the new capital of the new United States of America in the early nineteenth century.

The elite and middle-class white women of Washington City have long been studied by historians in the context of their relationships with "Great Men," and their observations have supplied background and color to more traditional history. Here Washington women—both well-known and not—appear as political actors in their own right, using social events and the "private sphere" to establish the national capital and to build the extraofficial structures so sorely needed in the infant federal government. Unlike their more lurid political sisters, these women acted not as femmes fatales but as mothers, wives, sisters, and daughters. Like other women on farms and in shops, they participated in the family business—in this case however, the family business was politics.

Politics incorporates many goals, including the allocation of resources and the assignment of values. In the uncertain years following the American Revolution, however, politics formed the core of a culture-wide discussion about how the new Americans wanted to be ruled. In 1801 Thomas Jefferson, the leader of the new and victorious Republican party, came to Washington determined to purge the federal government and the country of any Federalist tendencies and to constitute a government of "pure republicanism"—a political theory that stressed public virtue, reduced government power, and promoted the public good over private interests. Jefferson's goal was no less than to create a system of governance unlike any that had ever existed in the world.

Over the next decades Jefferson saw his goal achieved, but not in the way he and other members of the founding generation had envisioned. By the 1820s they noted with dismay the growth of a democratic government style, a political culture that included more voters than ever before and accommodated two political parties, and the beginnings of a powerful, centralized nation-state that had not been on their own Revolutionary agenda. In 1828, when Andrew Jackson, another new leader of a new party, the Democrats, rode into the capital for his inauguration, the United States was on its way to being the first modern democracy in the world, with a strong federal government and executive branch and a powerful capital.

How this happened in Washington City, and how it happened relatively smoothly, is the story the ladies of Washington have to tell. They tell it in unexpected ways—through private letters and diaries, with invitation lists and calling cards, with words and, above all, with actions. If we can listen to what they have to say, the narrative in these documents will alert us to the gap between political rhetoric and reality. It will demonstrate that a smoke-filled backroom and a lady's parlor are both political spaces. Ultimately, the story of the Washington women profoundly changes the political history of the early Republic.

As we begin this tale, remember that, though the general plot of this history may seem familiar, the specific events will not be. To understand how this drama develops, we must focus on what past historians have seen out of the corner of their eye, if they saw it at all. Wisdom, after all, can come from unexpected places. In *Pacific Overtures,* his musical play about the opening of Japan by Commodore Perry, Stephen Sondheim explains that truly to understand historical events, we must learn to read and consider not only official documents but also the seemingly peripheral characters and apparently irrelevant minutiae of daily life. In their reenactment of the 1858 treaty signing between the Americans and the Japanese from the point of view of an anonymous boy hiding in a tree, Sondheim's actors argue for including such frivolous factors as attitude, tone of voice, clothing, and beverage choice (and, by implication, musicals) to gain a true sense of "what really happened." So in that spirit, let us begin our journey to early Washington City, looking all the while for ". . . cups of tea / And history / And someone in a tree."[1]

President Thomas Jefferson in
Washington City

"O, brave new world that has such people in't!"
—WILLIAM SHAKESPEARE, *The Tempest* 5.1.183–84

WASHINGTON CITY, the new capital of the United States of America, Anno Domini 1801. The federal government under President John Adams had officially removed to the city the previous June. Almost immediately, people, then as now, engaged in the city's most popular unofficial sport—Washington-bashing. Disparaging comments came from new residents and visitors alike, focusing on the city's rural isolation and its lack of built environment. As one might expect, European travelers supplied some of the most colorful and pithy descriptions of the aspiring capital. One Englishman, told by his companion that they were entering Washington City, looked in vain for houses and public buildings. Sure that he had misunderstood his guide, the visitor asked where the city was, only to be told that he was standing in the middle of it. A fellow countryman, Augustus John Foster, arriving from England to serve as secretary of the British Legation, reckoned that if Congress had really meant this little town to be their capital, "they would have acted much more wisely than by settling in the swamp."[1]

Though Europeans took malicious glee in lambasting the upstart city, even patriotic Americans likened their capital to a mule, "without pride of ancestry or hope of posterity." The sight of early Washington inspired usually taciturn New England folks to heights of invective and wit. One of the first arrivals, Ebenezer Mattoon, representative from New Hampshire, wrote to his friend Thomas Dwight, "If I wished to punish a cul-

4

prit, I would send him to do penance in this place, oblige him to walk about this city, city do I call it? This swamp—this lonesome dreary swamp, secluded from every delightful or pleasing thing—except the *name* of the place, which to be sure I reverence."[2]

Raconteurs competed to render the wittiest and nastiest verdicts; indeed, some of the sharpest reactions became widely quoted clichés. In 1818 Thomas Hubbard, representative from New York, referred to old and accepted Washington wisdom in a letter to his wife, Phebe. He gleefully related that "Old Abbe Correa, the Portuguese minister (a monk)" and "a man of great powers and learning," had opined "that every man is born with a bag of folly which attends him through life." Although George Washington had been burdened with only a "small bag, which he kept to himself and never imparted any of it to the world," when "the metropolis of the nation was founded . . . he emptied the whole of it into this city."[3]

Many early descriptions have contributed to the general view of the new capital as a "fever-stricken morass," lacking society and civilization. Albert Gallatin, for example, wrote his spouse, Hannah Nicholson Gallatin, that the early congressmen were "discontented . . . living like a refectory of monks, with no other amusement or occupation." However, Washington City was one of the fastest-growing urban settings in the United States during the first three decades of the nineteenth century. New buildings were constructed throughout the era, and the population grew rapidly. The number of federal government employees grew as well, from 291 in 1802 to 625 in 1829.[4] Further, the geographical isolation and country setting that astonished and appalled some more cosmopolitan observers had quite a different effect on other new arrivals, an effect articulated by one of the chief players in early Washington City.

In 1800 Margaret Bayard Smith arrived in Washington as a newlywed. Her new husband, Samuel Harrison Smith (who was also her second cousin), had won not only her heart but her mind as well. Born into a distinguished Federalist family, Margaret changed her allegiance and became an enthusiastic supporter of Thomas Jefferson and the Republican party when she married. The couple came to Washington from Philadelphia under Jefferson's personal patronage. He wanted Samuel Smith to become the editor of the first national American newspaper, the *Daily Intelligencer.*

Samuel Smith justified his patron's trust; he attended Congress every day, recording its proceedings faithfully for his paper's pages.

Yet it was Margaret Bayard Smith who became posterity's ideal informant. First and foremost, she was consistently *there*—no mean feat in a city known for the transience of its inhabitants. By the 1840s a core of long-time residents made up a political and social elite in Washington, but no one could match the Smiths' forty-four-year residence. Both her continued presence and her social position assured Bayard Smith a front-row seat at all the events of the day. She quickly became a leader; as her husband rose in prominence and she became enmeshed in the community networks of the town, her entrée to places and people proved unparalleled.

Bayard Smith possessed one more qualification invaluable to anyone curious about Washington City in the early Republican era. She was a writer, with an artist's sense of the outside perspective. She could render descriptions of scenes and assessments of people with a few choice words or phrases, in effect a few well-chosen brush strokes. She wrote both reportage and fiction and possessed the writer's double ability to be both of a situation and outside it, the reason, according to Truman Capote, that writers are dangerous people to have around. Though Margaret Bayard Smith rarely wrote with malice, she could spot and dispose of pretension in a manner that bears Capote out.

Bayard Smith's pen supplied many of the most crucial scenes that comprise the historical narrative of the early Republic, yet political histories have not identified or individualized her, instead mentioning her only as a "society matron" or "doyenne." But the Margaret Bayard Smith who stepped upon the Washington scene in 1800 could not have been less doyenne-ish. Young, vibrant, and bursting with energy, she was eager to write to her sisters and family of the new world that greeted her on her arrival. Bayard Smith sustained this enthusiasm for sharing experiences with her female kin (both natal and marital) for the rest of her life.

Bayard Smith conscientiously recorded the raw aspects of her new home. Her description of their arrival echoes Abigail Adams's account of a woman who looked "in vain for the city." The planned avenues consisted of stone markers, and the roads were only footpaths, presenting an unforgettable image of the "ungraceful" Capitol, surrounded by "mud, shavings, brick," and other materials for completing it and the adjacent structures.[5]

But once they were settled in, Margaret and Samuel Smith discovered a different, more delightful side to the new city. The young couple spent long hours roaming through the countryside of the federal city, enjoying the sights, sometimes collecting herbs or flowers. "I seldom enjoyed a walk more than this," she declared after one such ramble, "and had scarcely resolution to return, although the sun had set." On another "delightful day," she "sallied forth" with a group of friends; "I will not say we walked along . . . , the elasticity of the air had given such elasticity to my spirits that I could not walk." She did not have to travel far to appreciate the natural beauty of the place. Samuel described their house to his sister as standing "on a commanding hill bounded by one of the handsomest streams in our country, now descending into a cool valley covered with wood and watered by gently flowing rills." He loved the "noble oaks" in the yard, and Margaret loved the sweetbriers.[6]

As an old woman she remembered with nostalgia the panorama from Capitol Hill in those early years, the "extensive and beautiful view" of the "wide plain, through which the Tiber had wound its way." Undisturbed by building and development, the riverbanks were shaded with trees "of every variety," most conspicuously "the Tulip-Poplar." The flowers she listed inhabit a scene of lush abundance, even a romantic bower: "The magnolia, azalea, the hawthorn, the wild-rose . . . violets, anemones and a thousand other sweet wood-flowers. . . . The wild grape-vine climbing from tree to tree hung in unpruned luxuriance among the branches of the trees and formed a fragrant and verdant canopy over the greensward, impervious to the noonday sun."[7]

Other commentators shared Bayard Smith's initial dismay at the lack of settlement and then subsequent praise for "the situation." Louisa Catherine Johnson Adams, wife of Senator John Quincy Adams, arrived in Washington in 1801, the year after the Smiths, to visit her parents. Her first impression consisted entirely of criticisms, "the city not being laid out; the streets not graduated, the bridges consisting of mere loose planks and huge stumps of trees cut down intercepting every path." At the same time she enthusiastically predicted to her husband, "I'm quite delighted with the situation of this place, and I think should it ever be finished it will be one of the most beautiful spots in the world."[8]

Even some of the European travelers proved susceptible to the charm of the upstart Republic's capital. In 1796 Henrietta Liston, who had come

to America with her husband, Robert Liston, the British minister, counted one hundred houses and thought the situation "noble and beautiful, strangely resembling Constantinople," their last posting. The Prince
d'Orleans also commented favorably on the countryside, marveling at the
peach trees already in bloom in early April. An Englishman, David Baillie
Warden, who may have wished to curry favor with those in power (he
dedicated his *A Chorographical and Statistical Description of the District of Columbia*
to Martha Washington), exulted, "It is scarcely possible to imagine a situation more beautiful, healthy and convenient than that of Washington."
He went on to describe the "rising hills" as "truly picturesque"; the "gentle undulated" topography threw the "water into such various directions,
as affords the most agreeable assemblage."[9]

Margaret and Samuel found more than the consolation of nature
in their new home. From her earliest letters the young bride described
herself as plunged into a whirl of activity, in which relationships with
women offered especially intense socializing and mutual support. Bayard
Smith shared her wedding cake with Mrs. Bell, who had brought her a
"large basket of sweet potatoes and some fine cabbages." Shortly after setting up housekeeping in the federal city, she detailed the companions who
treated her with familial affection: Mrs. Bell was like a mother; Miss
Thornhill and Eliza, her sisters; and "in Mr. English, a most attentive
brother." Local gentry joined with other official families, among them
"Mr. and Mrs. Law, Captain and Mrs. Tingey, Mr. and Mrs. Otis and Dr.
and Mrs. Thornton," to form an intimate circle for Bayard Smith only a
month or so into her residence.[10]

The Capitol area sometimes resembled a building lot, and wildlife
abounded, but the city was sited in a land of farms, plantations, and prosperous small towns, including Georgetown. Nearby Alexandria was a
thriving port. Some 500 Maryland and Virginia families with incomes of
a thousand or more pounds a year lived within a day's ride of Washington, and by one society watcher's estimation, in 1802 Washington City
contained 150 socially eligible ladies and gentlemen. The local gentry—the
Tayloes, the Ogles, the Custises, and the Laws—provided the city with a
ready-made select society. To be sure, the surrounding communities were
mostly rural settlements or plantations, but the landed families of the
area included Europeans of great refinement such as Rosalie Stier Calvert

and Anna Maria Brodeau Thornton. These elites functioned in a population of more than 14,000 souls in the federal district, with 3,000 white residents in Washington proper, along with 623 enslaved Americans and 123 free blacks.[11]

Washington society mixed cosmopolitan flair with rural neighborliness. Many foreign travelers spent time by the firesides of Bayard Smith and her neighbors, discussing intellectual subjects in English and French. On the other hand, the Smiths often dropped in on neighbors during their rambles, and on one of these visits Margaret was treated to a fine roast turkey and a viewing of the contrivance that cooked it, a stove called a Ranger. Often morning visits among these women turned into all-day sessions, in which visitors and hostesses performed such domestic tasks as hanging curtains. After Congress adjourned for the day and the legislators had their evening meals in the boardinghouses, they often went to households such as the Smiths' to drink tea and spend the evening talking politics.[12]

Women were everywhere in Washington City. The mixed and contradictory evidence about the presence of elite white women at any given time stems from the cyclical nature of their presence. There always remained a steady core of female residents, both official and local, but most women came to Washington for the social season, which roughly corresponded to the congressional session. Albert Gallatin may have felt he was living in a celibate community during those first years because, though the congressmen arrived in November, the "season" did not begin until after the New Year and ended before Congress rose in the spring.[13]

Though cyclical, the women's presence in Washington certainly appeared regular; that is, women began arriving for the social season the first year of Jefferson's term, and they never stopped. Many letters sent home from congressmen mention the arrival of other legislators' female relatives at their boardinghouses. Women attended Jefferson's inauguration, packed the House for church services, crowded the galleries in both houses of Congress, browsed the congressional library, and filled the houses and the streets. The socially indefatigable Harrison Gray Otis teased his wife that he had found "several really fine and fashionable" ladies to conquer at an otherwise dull party. A close reading of early sources reveals Washington to have been not "a pleasureless outpost," as one scholar has asserted, but a thriving, vibrant, growing community, populated by both women and men.[14]

Visitors and new residents from New England and the Middle Atlantic states, accustomed to residing in towns and cities of long standing, expressed their horror and disappointment more vociferously than southerners, but apart from regional prejudice the perceptions of Washington City depended on what the various observers and commentators wished or expected to see. Those who came with fixed notions of what should be there were much more likely to be disappointed. In contrast, visitors and new residents who focused on the location's potential, as suggested by the first row of fine brick houses or the lush natural environment, were much more positive about the future and more accepting of the current rough conditions. In 1801 Washington City seemed more potential than place. The prospects challenged, excited, and alarmed everyone who came there, not the least of whom was the first president to begin his term in the new capital.

THE REPUBLICAN DREAMWORLD

Washington City was born of the imaginations of two men: George Washington, who sited and laid out the city, and Thomas Jefferson, the first national leader to take up full-time residence there. In striking contrast to all future presidents, these two men poured their hearts and souls into the creation of the capital. Washington City's biggest booster and "leading spirit" from the beginning, Jefferson gave more attention to the formation of the capital than any other government official. Some see this to be his "first major effort of statesmanship" as a cabinet member in Washington's administration. Because George Washington began the project, he devoted his attention mostly to geographical and surveying matters, while Jefferson absorbed himself in architecture and landscaping for the selected site.[15] Much as he did with his beloved Monticello, Jefferson expended a great deal of energy on the aesthetics of the new federal city. Unfortunately, again as in the case of Monticello, he paid less attention to practical matters such as roads and drainage than to a comprehensive vision. That Washington City and the grounds around the President's House looked so unfinished for much of his administration echoed Monticello's state of perpetual process.

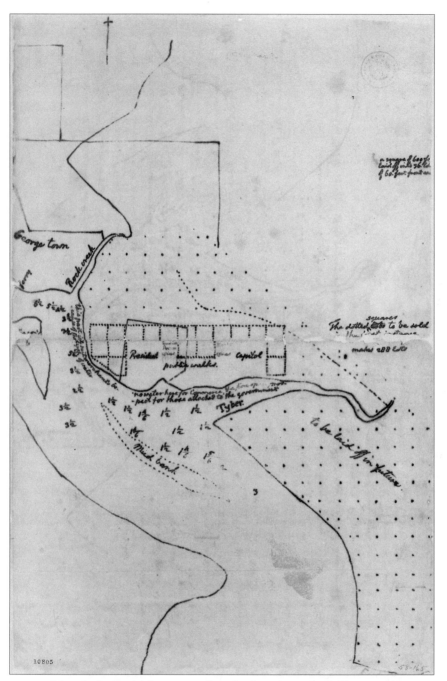

Untitled, undated map of Washington City, drawn by Thomas Jefferson, probably in March 1791.
(Courtesy of Manuscript Division, Library of Congress, Washington, D.C.)

Thomas Jefferson, by Mather Brown, 1786. (Courtesy of the Adams Family Collection; photograph, Corbis, New York)

Jefferson, as the first president actually to live in the federal city, concerned himself deeply with the philosophic implications of the embryonic capital. Though his political motivations were evident in his "Notes and Calculations" on the siting of the capital in 1783, by the time the House elected him the new leader of the nation in February 1801, he was primarily concerned that the city give "physical form to his vision of what the Republic should be."[16] Jefferson entered the infant capital fully determined to make in this landscape a new kind of "city upon a hill," a shining example of a republican society for the world to emulate.

Like many influenced by the Enlightenment, Thomas Jefferson was a man with utopias on his mind. His fascination with states of nature, where fundamental humanity might stand revealed, combined the scientific bent of John Locke with the romantic vision of Jean-Jacques Rousseau. The desire to create his own perfected society may also have been something of a family tradition. His father, Peter Jefferson, had carved his own materially advanced and eminently civilized estate, Shadwell, out of what was then a wild frontier of Virginia. In doing so, Peter Jefferson followed a pattern set by a minority of rich southerners: building a comfortable and luxurious mansion ex nihilo in uncultivated wilderness.[17]

With his background in this high-living culture of country seats, Thomas Jefferson likely saw no incongruity in the plan of building a classical capital in the countryside. As his father had surveyed and laid the boundaries for a new Eden, so the son would do the same with his own frontier, and he brought considerable zeal to the task. Jefferson scholars who assess him as a man with a "polygonal mind," one for whom "nothing that promised the ultimate physical or moral improvement of mankind was alien," only echo the opinions of Jefferson's contemporaries. Augustus John Foster, the British secretary, tagged him as a "visionary," one who "loved to dream with his eyes open."[18]

Jefferson's predisposition to see America as a land of limitless possibilities had strong roots in his belief in a golden age, a pre-Norman, Anglo-Saxon utopia, evident in his Revolutionary justifications of the colonies' rebellion against the Crown. His 1774 pamphlet, *A Summary View of the Rights of British America*, contrasted the current state of affairs with a past in which people lived in freedom and harmony, unhampered by government or king. Jefferson's arguments for independence predicted that once purged of the corruption of the present, America could recapture the perfect past for its future. This was not a pose affected for strictly political reasons; it reflected something deeply rooted in Jefferson's character.[19] In the classical worlds to which Jefferson constantly referred, nature provided metaphors and commentary on human actions, and it might have seemed that he stood at the edge of a more natural and moral world as, in January 1801, a large comet fired the sky over Washington City.

But Jefferson would not be free to pursue his plan of utopia in peace. He began his reign at a time of great turmoil and division. Almost from the end of the Revolutionary War, Americans feared that the whole experiment, based on the political theory of republicanism, would fall apart, and that anxiety pervaded the political atmosphere. Undoubtedly the political culture of the 1790s and early 1800s embodied in particularly virulent form the postulate that politics is always personal. This "Age of Passion" was marked by inflammatory rhetoric, vicious public and private attacks, and a fear of conspiracy which scholars have labeled paranoid, in all of which Jefferson participated fully.[20] In an era before party systems, power sharing was not an option; it was all or nothing for the two protoparties, the Federalists and the Republicans, and they justified their right to rule by casting the opposition in the blackest hues.

The election of 1800 focused and concentrated the free-floating apprehension. Power had never passed peacefully from one faction to another, and that it would in 1801 was not at all certain. Jefferson's Federalist enemies viewed his assumption of power as the signal for a reign of Jacobin terror. "There is scarcely a possibility that we shall escape a civil war," gloomily predicted the *Connecticut Courant*, a newspaper located deep in the heart of Federalist country. "Murder, robbery, rape, adultery, and incest" would not only be practiced but taught; the very "air will be rent with the cries of distress," the soil soaked with blood, "and the nation black with crimes."[21] With so much at stake, the rhetoric was high-flown and low-down—bitter, vicious, and personal.

In his turn, Jefferson hated Federalists and viewed his success in 1800 as the last, best hope of the Republic. It had been a close call. The Federalist "barbarians" had "really flattered themselves they should be able to bring back the times of Vandalism, when ignorance put everything into the hands of power and priestcraft." But the ship of state survived the previous years of federalism; "put on a republican tack," she would sail free. His "fellow-citizens" had been "hoodwinked," but now that "the band is removed," they would see and appreciate a government of perfect republicanism.[22] It was morning in Jefferson's America.

Part of the Federalists' anxiety lay in uncertainty; they worried that

Jefferson intended a thorough overhaul of the government, but they did not know the exact process or goals. Neither did Jefferson. Until they swept the election of 1800, the Jeffersonian Republicans had always cast themselves as an opposition, tracing their origins to the "Country Party" of England, a group of late seventeenth- and early eighteenth-century disaffected gentry. Theorists such as John Trenchard and Thomas Gordon developed their version of "pure republicanism" in opposition to what they saw as the danger to liberty posed by the English court's corruption. In their vision, centralized power had caused the disintegration of the government institutions and social practices that ensured English freedom. This philosophy of radical reform had supplied the colonists with a Revolutionary ideology—especially warnings against standing armies and other signs of arbitrary power—but after the war disagreement over interpretations of Country Party doctrine split the founders. First the Anti-Federalists and then Jefferson and his followers co-opted its tenets to define themselves against the Federalists.[23]

Republicans, the Country Party of the United States, like its counterpart in Great Britain, had positioned themselves as a critical minority; in Britain, elites who led the faction actually were few in number. By electing their leader president, however, the American Republicans had ascended to the majority position, and the opposition, in the person of Thomas Jefferson, had become the Establishment.[24] No doubt fed by the Anglo-Saxon myths of a lost golden age, Jefferson's political rhetoric had always been couched in terms of restoration, sweeping away present corruption to re-create some simpler past. When it came to positive formulations of what he was for, however, Jefferson proved a little hazy on the details. In 1801, as he took office, he found himself in an ironic position: he had railed against the danger of consolidated government and abuses of power, and now he held the reins.

History did not provide Jefferson with any models for constructing the first large, modern, republican government. The only successful republics either had existed in ancient times or were small and easily governed. But, as suited his contrary mind, he had very definite ideas about what he did not want for a new social order: anything smacking of aristocracy, a danger he associated with federalism.[25] As the Federalists feared that the "democratic demagogue" would destroy the Constitution and usher in his own Reign of Terror, so Jefferson saw federalism as the next step to a monarchy, bringing with it all the vice, luxury, and corruption inherent in aristocratic societies. Though Jefferson's warnings and anxieties seem almost paranoid at times, ample evidence exists that talk of monarchy did not end with the rejection of John Adams's proposals about titles.

Even some Federalists shared Jefferson's fears of aristocratic excess. Ironically, a few who worried about creeping royalism, like Mercy Otis Warren, fretted that capitals, such as Jefferson's Washington City project, constituted breeding grounds for the luxury that signaled a loss of republican values. Her particular concern was for the young, unborn at the time of the Revolution, who would abandon the "simpler paths" of "competence and felicity" to "follow the fantastic fopperies of foreign nations." Longing for the "distinctions acquired by titles," America's young citizens would eschew "real honor which is ever the result of virtue."[26] In Otis Warren's estimation, the seat of power seemed the place most likely for this to happen.

Not if Jefferson had his way. Not only was it paradoxical for a man who feared consolidated power to champion a national capital; Jefferson, Washington City's biggest promoter, also loathed cities of any kind. Like other Rousseauian romantics, he regarded urban centers along with courts as twin symptoms of civilized decadence. Echoing Rousseau's dictum that "cities are the abyss of the human species," Jefferson declared them "sores" on the body "of pure government." Having recently returned from Paris, from which he traveled to other European countries, Jefferson had himself borne witness to urban dangers. In a privately circulated document, "Hints to Americans Traveling in Europe," he warned that even the spectacular art and architecture of the great European cities served only to distract from the corrupt and depraved lives of their inhabitants. In his own country Federalists gathered together in cities to plot and plan, a circumstance which created the false impression that they reflected the will of the majority. Their proximity to urban areas enabled the Federalists to "act in a body readily and at all times."[27]

Washington City, rustic to a fault, seemed the ideal republican setting. Created in the negative space of Federalist fears, the blankness of Washington provided both challenges and promises. The fact that government was the only business of the place freed Washington City from the influence of bankers, shippers, and other persons associated with trade in more established settings. With few public buildings in any state of completion, no halls of power existed, no recesses where courtiers could hide and plot. The capital resembled Jefferson's "pure republicanism," undeveloped and untested enough to be ideal. That the rich and respectable wanted to go back to Philadelphia, the former capital, against the wishes of the "rough" majority, as Secretary Foster reported, only indicated to Jefferson that he had found the ideal spot to take his stand against the monarchical and aristocratic practices he saw threatening the young Republic.[28]

MANNERS, MORALS, AND REPUBLICAN WOMEN

In the quest to create a new republican world, no aspect of life was immune from worried self-examination and criticism. Many probably agreed with "Cornelia," who, in writing against levees and other monarchical distinctions during the George Washington administration, declared, "No character or place ought to be so sacred in a republican government as to be above criticism."[29] Moreover, an important part of the theory of republicanism did not assume matters of style and social affairs to be irrelevant, diversions from or mere reflections of the body politic, but rather considered them as crucial causes and symptoms.

English Country Party and Jeffersonian Republican critiques of government had always included catalogs of social ills thought to affect the character of the people and hence their rulers. Republicanism presumed a cycle of decay and renewal in human history, with the abuse of power passing from monarchs to legislatures and even to the people at different points in the cycle. A slothful and luxury-loving populace, lacking personal and civic virtue, endangered liberty when the wheel of power turned their way.[30] Republican theorists knew that for good or ill, they could not isolate issues of government completely from the realms of society and social life, from family life, material possessions, and issues of style. They strove instead to make that interdependency work for them, stopping the cycle of decay by ensuring simplicity and virtue at all levels of society.

Republicanism demanded the radical reform of all human institutions, so after the Revolution, when the leaders of the new government began to decide on the structure and scope of the federation of states, matters of

tone and style came to the fore. One of the first orders of business for the
new Congress in 1789 concerned the question of titles for government officials. A shared belief in republicanism and the assumed interdependency
of all human arenas created strong feelings on both sides. They both
wanted to preserve republican simplicity while establishing the new government's credibility with the public, perhaps even inspiring pride and
awe. These debates unfolded in a high-stakes atmosphere, for in a period
of creation, every major decision set a precedent, carrying future power
and resonance.[31]

Though Congress eventually quashed the proposals for titles, it could
not quell the general debate over how much aristocracy was too much.
The founding generation seesawed between the need to appear virtuous
and the need for the legitimacy gained from the only status symbols their
culture knew: the monarchy and a hereditary aristocracy.[32] Political and
cultural elites, women and men, groped toward what it meant to be elite,
and thus unquestionably the country's leaders, and what it meant to be republican, and thus unquestionably worthy of these roles.

Jefferson's experience as a government official in Paris reinforced his
understanding of the importance of manners and society in maintaining
the virtue of the Republic, as well as in civilizing the new nation. He considered the corruption and depravity of general society he had seen in
France as signs that the French government and culture had slipped onto
the downside of history's cycle. Arriving home from Europe in late 1789,
Jefferson had been startled and dismayed to hear monarchical sentiments
openly discussed with approval at dinner tables; he considered this license
characteristic of the Federalist administrations.[33] Under both Washington
and Adams, Jefferson continued to discover new portents that the young
nation had begun the downward slide he had observed in Paris. The
source of these trends seemed clear: they came from the parlors of the
rulers. With their capital located in the large cities of New York and
Philadelphia, Washington and Adams had created an elite-centered, stately form of society, centered around formal entertainments called "drawing rooms" or "levées."

Upon his arrival in New York (then the capital) in 1789, George Washington, though wanting to be available to all who wished to see him,
quickly discovered that an open-door policy allowed him little time to ac-

complish government business. In addition, the new president's concern for the "dignity of the office" led to questions of official protocol. These issues so worried President Washington that he wrote to Chief Justice John Jay, Vice President John Adams, and Secretary of the Treasury Alexander Hamilton for their advice. The president stressed the importance of the governors being accessible and available to the governed, while puzzling out his own role as the leader. Only Hamilton's and Adams's replies survive; the new president adopted the former's more restrictive recommendations. The new procedures handled the accessibility question by instituting an official weekly presidential reception, to be held on Tuesdays.[34]

Formality of body movement, position, and gesture stand out most clearly in descriptions of these weekly events. Before the guests arrived, George Washington, his cabinet, and "other distinguished men" positioned themselves before the fireplace, the focal point of the room. At three o'clock the doors of the dining room opened, and each visitor, after being announced, greeted the president with a bow. Though shaking hands among gentlemen was becoming a common custom in the United States, bowing prevailed at the president's house. At a quarter past three, the doors closed. The visitors, exclusively male, moved into a circle, and the president then went round, exchanging a few words with each one. When he reached his original position, the visitors approached him again, one by one in succession, bowed, and retired from the room.[35]

Not a participant in the official proceedings, Martha Custis Washington instituted her own levees, held on Fridays, beginning on May 29, 1789. In contrast to her husband's official receptions, Martha's events mixed the sexes, and there were always many ladies present. Though these events also contained elements of ceremony, they seem to have been more imbued with a spirit of informality and entertainment. At his own receptions George wore a sword and carried a cocked hat; on Fridays he appeared at Martha's levees in the capacity of a private citizen, signaling that he was not the host by sporting neither hat nor sword.[36]

The local elite of the capital (first New York and then Philadelphia), distinguished visitors, and foreigners attended Martha's events. The receptions were held not in a special receiving room but in the dining room, converted for the occasion. Clad in simple white, Martha seated herself

on a slightly raised platform, with the other official wives arranged hierar-
chically around her, mirroring the group around George at his receptions.
As Superintendent of Finance Robert Morris sat at Martha's right hand
at dinner, so Mary White Morris occupied that same place of honor at
the levees. According to Abigail Adams, the servants announced each lady,
and a gentleman then received her at the door of the drawing room. He
handed the lady up to Martha, "to whom she makes a most respectful
courtesy and then is seated without noticing the rest of the company."
George then approached the lady and spoke with her, "which he does
with a grace, dignity, and ease that leaves royal George far behind him."
The refreshments were almost austere—tea, coffee, lemonade, and plain
cake—though it is possible that ice cream made its appearance as well.
Martha Washington had established a definite ceremonial style, so later
First Lady Abigail Adams and other hostesses in Philadelphia and New
York copied her levees, thus creating the paradoxical institution of a "Re-
publican Court."[37]

Republican reactions to these events provide ample evidence of early
party activity and presage Thomas Jefferson's stunning election victory in
1801. In 1792 Jefferson's paper, the *National Gazette*, launched a six-month
campaign against the Washington administration by attacking these
events, especially Martha's levees. Though George and Martha Washington had tried to mark their events as public and private, respectively,
chiefly through the participation of women, the *Gazette* and the other
newspapers that picked up the story refused to make the distinction.
Though ostensibly a private lady, Martha bore the brunt of the criticism.
Republicans lambasted her levees as "tending to her a supereminancy and
as introducing the paraphernalia of the courts." The raised platform and
her decision to receive while sitting seemed "too queenly." "Mirabeau" in
the Republican *National Gazette* placed "Levees!" as number two in the ten
warning signs of creeping monarchy and aristocracy.[38]

Embittered and appalled by what he saw in Philadelphia, Jefferson
broke his own policy of public discretion and criticized even the revered
general. However, like his newspaper, he saved his most concentrated ven-
om for Martha Custis Washington, reading a darkly papist, hierarchical
message in her popularity: "They burn incense to her." To Jefferson these
entertainments embodied the European practices characteristic of the

court systems that republicanism meant to overthrow. The role of unofficial structures (such as social events) and unofficial players (such as women) in politics signaled the deep corruption of monarchies, a corruption that seeped down the social ladder. To be sure, Jefferson's issues with women were probably firmly rooted in his own inner life. His unusual decision not to remarry after his wife's death, his affair with Maria Cosway, his flirtatious/standoffish correspondence with female friends, his manipulative language with his daughters, even his choice of a sex partner who by her slave status had to remain hidden—all create the sense of a man uncomfortable with women, especially in close proximity.[39]

But from his experience of politics, Jefferson had ample evidence of just how dangerous women could be when close to the seat of power. During his tenure as minister plenipotentiary to France in the 1780s, Jefferson was appalled by the degree to which women in Paris involved themselves in the upheavals of the times. Elite European women participated in politics more intensely and in many more ways than their transatlantic sisters, resulting in a more frank debate among Europeans of Jefferson's day, one at which the more prudish American press only hinted. Political theorists such as Montesquieu and Rousseau discussed in print the deleterious effects of sexuality on public affairs; sexual caricatures depicting the French queen in congress with men, women, and domestic animals circulated widely; explicit satires on elite women appeared in respectable newspapers, replete with sexual puns and dripping with scorn.[40]

In the French capital Jefferson attended philosophic salons and became close friends with *salonnières,* women who were much more than mere hostesses. These educated and politically minded women played an active, public, and "masculine" role in the republic of letters. Jefferson was thus exposed to the most openly political women in the Western world. And he was not impressed, not favorably at least.[41]

Everything about female participation in politics shocked Jefferson— the conversations of the elite men and women, the speeches and marches of the female lower orders—but above all, he abhorred women who "mix promiscuously in gatherings of men." This "promiscuous mixing" extended from the dirtiest city streets to the most aristocratic drawing rooms. French women dominated social events, and in their capacities as social leaders they exerted a powerful and (to Jefferson's mind) destructive effect on the government's decisions, "their solicitations bid[ding] defiance to laws and regulations." In 1788 Jefferson wrote George Washington detailing the Notables' plans for reform and added, "In my opinion a kind of influence, which none of their plans of reform take into account, will elude them all; I mean the influence of women in the government." Women were allowed to "visit, alone, all persons in office" in order to obtain jobs for their "husband, family or friends." Female influence proved so powerful that it would negate any attempts at official reform. Jefferson could only rejoice that American women's "omnipotent influence" kept itself behind the "domestic line," thereby saving America from a similar "desperate state."[42]

In warning a young man about the dangers of Europe (an influence, Jefferson surmised, that would render men unfit for public office if experienced in any great quantity), he described the peril as consisting largely of contact with undesirable women. He did not merely warn against frequenting whores but also alerted the young man to "the spirit of female intrigue" into which elite women would entice him. Jefferson blamed the violence and even the very occurrence of the French Revolution on Marie Antoinette, declaring, "I have ever believed that had there been no queen there would have been no revolution."[43]

For this particular American politician, the issue of women in the polity was the crucible that contained and amalgamated all of his other apprehensions about Federalists and the corruption of aristocracy.[44] Not only were women, as Aristotle said, a "disorder" by their very nature, but also given the chance, even American women, led by their love of luxury, would practice the kind of aristocratic politicking Jefferson feared most. In his opinion, some of them had already come too close.[45]

Thomas Jefferson had barely arrived in the President's House in Washington City when he announced that there would be no formal receptions, except on New Year's Day and the Fourth of July. Early in Jefferson's first term, the ladies of Washington City, determined to have their levee even if there was no president's wife, presented themselves en masse at the President's House. Jefferson, equally determined they should not have their way, arrived at the drawing room in his riding clothes and, expressing surprise at the incredible coincidence of their all coming to visit at once, circled the room, charming everyone. According to one account of the event, the ladies laughed at the joke on them and went away. Jefferson abolished levees in his administration because (among other reasons) by dismantling the Republican Court created by the Washingtons, he deprived women of a way to project and exert public power.[46] Henceforth the presence of women at the President's House, except on the two official days, would be severely restricted to the companions of gentlemen invited to Jefferson's dinners.

SOCIAL WORK

Today the term *society* can convey anything from a vague notion of "high society" to a synonym for culture. In the eighteenth century, in contrast, *society* had a very specific meaning, as a realm separate from the political sphere but, though private in some ways, distinct from the intimate family. Theoretically, within this sphere people met on terms of social equality, in an environment in which the arts, elevated conversation, and highly structured interpersonal behavior could soften and civilize them. In reality, of course, this model of society contained many tensions and contradictions; obviously, it included only white people of a certain class. Though society demanded that women be the chief agents of civilization, they certainly were not regarded as occupying equal positions with men.

Like the good eighteenth-century liberal that he was, Jefferson believed in the edifying effects of society and was determined to establish such a realm in Washington City. By eliminating levees and the open participation of women characteristic of his predecessors' administrations, Jefferson did what he did best—stripping away the old. It remained, however, for him to create something to replace it. Jefferson may not have wanted a court, but he did crave society—republican society, of course, entirely separated from political function.

But politics cannot exist in a vacuum, and for all that Jefferson abhorred the openly political displays of earlier levees, he proved a master at using social occasions for political purposes. Thus, from its beginning society in Washington City unfolded in an atmosphere of denial, with social events serving as both private events and political arenas, often at the same time. The politicking necessary to government could be undertaken, as long as it did so in the guise of private entertainment.

Jefferson's dinner parties remain his best-known social events, small, intimate dinners that he gave regularly through the congressional season. To these gatherings Jefferson invited only the men of one party or the other, not mixing Republicans and Federalists. These dinners have come down in history as illustrations of Jefferson at his best. He appears generous, hospitable, and definitely democratic, expressing his casual, Virginian sociability. Seated at a round table, to promote both intimacy and equality, Jefferson presided over the dinner, serving guests with his own hands (also known as "being Mother") and urging them to help themselves. Jefferson sometimes used dumbwaiters to help with the serving, thus encouraging guests to speak openly, freed from the "tittle-tattle" of eavesdropping slaves. With food from the French chef, wine from well-stocked cellars, amusing stories shared over Madeira and nuts, these dinners seem the epitome of intimate graciousness.[47]

Historians have long recognized the political advantages of Jefferson's dinners, calling them part of his statecraft, a strategy Jefferson implemented to cope with an office lacking built-in mechanisms to influence others or make his views known. In the conventional formulation the extent of his politicking lay in getting to know his guests and letting them get to know him. Jefferson chose his guests for compatibility, steered them away from shoptalk, and "planted the seeds of his political philosophy by indirection," depending upon "his charm and the menu" to do the actual work. This was enough, in scholarly opinion, to render Jefferson extremely effective in the first chaotic years of the Washington community. The failure of Madison and Monroe to retain the presidential power Jefferson had won thus lay in their inability to duplicate his entertainments.[48]

However, a more aggressive, explicit connection existed between Jefferson's sociability and his success as a president. He had no intention of letting his charm do the work, though he might have appeared to, and these events, far from being casual expressions of friendliness, served him as vehicles for governing. Even the physical setting reflected Jefferson's need to seem easy while retaining perfect control. The round table, lauded as a democratic innovation in a world of ranked seating, also prevented any private conversations. The small number of guests, often seen as an indicator of intimacy, ensured that no one could discuss anything without

Jefferson's knowledge. The dumbwaiters, which participants thought merely spared them from slave gossip, also guaranteed that Jefferson had control of all sources of leaks among the company. Personal communications were impossible, let alone plots and schemes. Apparently Jefferson began his reign with "mixed" political events, including both Republicans and Federalists, then decided to invite only those of one political party at a time. Though this practice may have grown out of his hatred of contention, it also ensured a climate in which Jefferson could either rally the troops freely or create a space for picking up gossip and information among men who knew each other well.[49]

Jefferson's own notes, collected and later published as the *Anas*—one scholar rightly calls this little collection from his commonplace book a "gossip log"—certainly demonstrate that he used his table for politicking and collecting information. But he also put his dinners to a more active purpose. What one observer called his "Epicurean artifices" could be used to affect policy. Though Jefferson forbade political talk at table, on many occasions he invited particular members of Congress to linger after the rest of the company had departed, and the intimacy of the postprandial party enabled Jefferson to make his views known. He noted these occasions in his *Anas* and then appended notes as the congressional session proceeded, following the actions of the men he had singled out.[50]

Though historians tend to regard Jefferson's presidential dinners as unmitigated successes, the true results may have been more mixed and, as befits a Jeffersonian innovation, contradictory. Jefferson clearly instituted these parties to create political accord and to retain control over the development of the government, but the two goals were not always compatible. In fact, by trying to defuse the small conflicts that might erupt with members of both parties at the same table, he may have fostered a deeper division. Other politicians, like Federalist senator William Plumer of New Hampshire, knew that the way to unity lay in bringing people of different points of view together, as an "interchange of sentiments tends to correct one's own errors and lead us to think more favorably of others." Plumer saw the way his own party tended: "Their prejudices govern more than their reason," a situation made worse when the Federalists realized at one point that they were not being invited to dinner at the White House (a consequence, Plumer reckoned, of the president taking their speeches against him personally). Plumer decided that Jefferson used friendly conversation and good food and wine to bind congressmen to himself and divide them from one another. Instead, Plumer thought, Federalists and Republicans should borrow the same strategy to create bonds among themselves, thus furthering the goal of "amalgamation."[51]

But quite possibly calmness, not unity, was Jefferson's goal. He hated Federalists and looked forward to a time when they would no longer be a presence in the government. In his mind, the "good" ones would convert (as Plumer eventually did), and the recalcitrant elites would simply be voted out of office. Jefferson was more interested in defusing conflict and avoiding scenes than in bringing people together. Even among members of his own party, Jefferson determined to abort any attempts to create liaisons and coalitions among congressmen, for enmeshed legislators might create a new aristocracy built on family, connections, and favors. Such a privileged group not only would thwart republican government but also would bypass its leader's power. Political compromise and accommodation, the lifeblood of politics, translated to Jefferson as betrayal of principle. He worked to ensure that Washington City would have none of these structures and alliances, which encouraged intrigue and distributed power and booty.[52]

Jefferson used his dinners for political purposes, while hiding behind an invocation of private life. A former diplomat, accustomed to European courts, he certainly knew what he was doing. He called his parties "campaigns" and drew up master lists, indexed by event and name, of invitations sent and accepted, as well as seating charts (by state). At the same time Jefferson sent his presidential invitations as a private citizen, invoking the private sphere for his own agenda and exasperating and confusing some of his guests. How aware Jefferson was of these contradictions remains unclear. But as he played peekaboo between social and political spheres, Jefferson made some crucial discoveries. Ironically, the social sphere, so essential to the political life of monarchies, proved even more so in the new Republic. In an antipower atmosphere, where any meeting of politicians was decried as "cabal" and formal organizations as "factions," groups of republican men could meet over food and drink to make alliances and influence legislation. Political supporters, commonly called "friends," could then just be friendly. Led by Jefferson himself, the Republicans, having learned the danger and futility of open coercion from the Federalists' experience, became more practiced in the manipulative arts.[53]

DOMESTIC POLICIES

Jefferson was not the only one who used social events for political purposes. During his tenure in Congress, Senator William Plumer paid a series of calls on Jefferson, visits that he explicitly dubbed "social" but on which he embarked for political information.[54] Jefferson seems to have cooperated with Plumer, for he proved very forthcoming, perhaps as a way to communicate with Plumer's Federalist colleagues. He may also have felt a sympathy with the man, and indeed Plumer became a Jeffersonian Republican later in his career.

Plumer's narration of these events demonstrates their dual nature. He was not the only one to avail himself of this access to Jefferson, and the president kept track of his visitors, as Plumer noted, on a penciled list by his side. Plumer received amazing amounts and varieties of information during these calls, and he in turn—by "observing" and "enquiring"—imparted knowledge according to his Federalist point of view. He recorded these visits carefully, in detail and "in nearly his [Jefferson's] own language." These exchanges provide a precise instance of a social custom taking the place of any official communication. Jefferson did not make speeches to Congress, hold conferences, or distribute press releases. Instead, he disseminated his views on the happenings of the day during morning visits, under the pose of gossiping with friends.[55]

Politics and society proved to be one among several gendered dichotomies Jefferson adapted to serve his political ends; he also exploited the differences between the spheres of men and those of women, between public and private. In letters sent from the scenes of government to his grown daughters in Virginia, he consistently contrasted public life ("disgusting," "rancorous," "a constant sacrifice") with the "blessings of domestic society" ("serene," "pleasurable," filled with "contentment" and "felicities," "love and delight"), sighing for the time when he could abandon the former for the latter.[56] The presence of women comprised the crucial difference between the bitterness of public life and the sweetness of domesticity.

In Jefferson's vision the benign influence of women characterized private life, and they reigned as the undisputed monarchs of their domains. But they ruled like women, with grace, charm, and subtlety, wielding indirect influence rather than masculine power. Their self-effacement disarmed conflict, for they imposed their will by seeming to submerge it. Unlike strife-ridden public life, with its overt shows of power, home was a place of peace, harmony, and stability, presided over, according to Rousseau, by a ruler whose "commands were caresses; her menaces are tears." The harmonious homes of women provided for the larger society's economic and political stability.[57] Though women clearly had no place in public life and found their happiness fulfilling their true natures at home, Jefferson's black-and-white pronouncements hid a shifting, conflicted, gray reality, often invisible to outsiders because it was invisible to him.

In his longings for the "blessings of domestic society," Jefferson explicitly contrasted domesticity with the only public life he had ever known, dominated first by wartime violence, anxiety, and tumult and then by the bitter divisions of two Federalist administrations. In Washington City, Jefferson saw his chance to create a new style of governing, one appropriate to an antipower republic. He found his model in his idealization of private life. If home played an important role in transmuting political passion, as it did for many political philosophers of the era, or made modern politics possible by divesting it of its personalized bitterness, Jefferson went one step further. Though he did not believe in public affairs intruding on the home, he saw no contradiction in inserting home into public life. Home would become politics itself.[58]

Both Jefferson's contemporary Alexander Hamilton and later historian Henry Adams found Jefferson's ruling style to be "feminine." This suggestive adjective provides an important clue to the new republican power structures Jefferson brought to the capital. He had despised the overtly masculine, military styles of Hamilton and George Washington, the aggressive wielding of power that characterized the Federalist way of doing things. After all, the Federalists, in the person of President Adams, had attempted to control their enemies with the harshest demonstration of arbitrary power the new nation had yet seen: the various Alien and Sedition Acts.[59]

The Republicans contrasted the Federalists' courtlike intrigue and overt shows of power with their own political style, with its emphasis on open candor and reliance on the opinion of "the People." Jefferson would maintain and enhance this image, while proving himself a master manipulator. Like the female politicians of the home, Jefferson ruled in subtle, domestic, feminine ways, combining a spare and nonhierarchical ruling structure with a modern deployment of political power, one dependent on the appearance of consensus and eschewing outward shows of force.[60] In striking contrast to his predecessors, Jefferson's would be a "minimalist presidency," designed to make the executive appear not as a prime mover but as one cog in a perfect, noiseless machine that ran itself. Jefferson's contribution, as he saw it, did not lie in what he could add to the governmental structure but rather in what he could eliminate. In his estimation, progress came with a purgation of excess, with ridding the organism of "accumulated debris." The unnecessary power of the federal government was one kind of debris to be cast aside; the quasi-patriarchal, quasi-military political style of John Adams, George Washington, and European kings was another.[61]

Using the election of 1800 as a mandate for a thorough housecleaning, Jefferson implemented his philosophy in the structure of his cabinet and in his daily schedule. He surrounded himself with a "mass" of friends but with none of the "secondary characters" that had plagued Adams's administration. He succeeded admirably, his cabinet proving to be one of most stable and effective in American history. In keeping with his hands-off presidency, Jefferson rarely held full cabinet meetings. Department heads handled the business relevant to them, sending him written summaries of their decisions. Jefferson preferred the individual interview rather than the full-scale meeting, serving as "the hub of the wheel," the supervisor rather than the ruler. Unlike his enemies John Adams and Alexander Hamilton, Jefferson relied upon indirect expressions of authority and longed for at least the appearance of consensus, much as his ideal woman ran her household.[62]

In both his personal and public writings, Jefferson advised exactly the same behavior for both men and women, that they avoid conflict at all costs, which was an astonishing position in such a gendered world. Consensus and lack of open hostility provided the key to good relations in Jefferson's familial government. He conducted his public world like a well-run home, bonded by ties of love and loyalty. His cabinet, in a metaphor that both he and others often chose to describe it, became his family, and he used the language of the domestic fireside to discuss his advisory body. Stressing its harmonious atmosphere, Jefferson noted, "There never arose, during the whole time, an instance of an unpleasant thought or word between the members."[63]

Just as no shouts or threats (regularly featured on the floor of Congress) would mar the harmony of a household, Jefferson's cabinet endured no fiery scenes of the kind that had plagued John Adams and would plague almost every subsequent president. If dissension flared during a meeting, Jefferson reacted not by openly confronting the parties but by asking Secretary of State James Madison to go behind the scenes and indicate that such behavior was not to be repeated. "Separate consultations," he advised, would prevent "disagreeable collisions." Jefferson masked his feelings and refused to enter into political debates, valuing order and peace in his polity. For him good rulers were like women, using patience, deference to the wishes of others, flattery, and suppression of the will to obtain their ends.[64]

Real women also had an important place in Jefferson's vision, but not all women. Republican theory prohibited women from using social events for political purposes, but Jefferson's domestic-public mix not only accommodated female guests but even depended on them. His dinner parties promoted accord and hid political uses under a cover of sociability. Women, with their diversionary and harmonious qualities, proved perfect for these goals. Indeed, the more Jefferson used dinners for political purposes—the "hotter" they were—the more he needed women to provide cool heads and to forestall conflict.

Unlike Rousseau, who believed in the total separation of the sexes to preserve women's chastity and the purity of the republic, Jefferson believed demure women had a salutary effect; indeed, they were necessary for society. Their presence precluded any ugly political scenes; moreover, the very subject of politics had to be avoided as an inappropriate topic of conversation in their company. When a dinner party did not include women, Jefferson apparently seemed "stilted and subdued."[65] But, of course, a female guest had to be the right kind of woman, a republican woman.

The historical construction of the republican woman as friend and dinner companion shares important characteristics with her "Mother" and "Wife" versions.[66] She is an elite woman, without question, but not following European elite models. The perfect republican woman, though educated, was essentially a domestic being, able to be lively and articulate without calling attention to herself, and astute enough to appear politically null. Though ideally beautiful and witty, she did not occupy center stage; her place was beside her male companion, as the perfect dinner partner.

In his own way Jefferson (along with women of the upper and rising classes) was working out what being a woman meant in a republic, where all could share in the bounty previously reserved, in Europe, for the wealthy, powerful, and corrupt. Jefferson had an exemplar of this kind of woman in his daughter Martha, but she could only occasionally visit Washington City. Instead, Dolley Payne Todd Madison, the wife of the secretary of state, served as official hostess. In her early political naïveté, the young Margaret Bayard Smith adored Jefferson and exemplified the kind of loyal and sentimental presence he needed: friendly, sociable, and, perhaps best of all, a converted Federalist. Dolley Payne Todd Madison, Margaret Bayard Smith, and other women at Jefferson's dinner table cloaked power and politics in a context of sociable consensus.

THE LADYLIKE JEFFERSON

In this government-family, Jefferson played the role of mother, assuring peace through self-effacement. In keeping with this role, and in explicit contrast to George Washington, Jefferson determined not to be the visible manifestation of authority that the general had been. Many eyewitness accounts of the government under Washington's presidency demonstrate that the near-godlike status he enjoys in history books originated while he lived. The focus by ordinary folks and elites alike on his every move, his appearance, and his gestures reveals his status as a charismatic figure. The Federalists, well aware of the awe he inspired, projected him as a national symbol.[67]

From a political perspective that charismatic capacity proved not only beneficial but necessary for the new nation. The dignity, power, and transcendence embodied in the person of George Washington legitimized the new government, endowing it with his "gift of grace." Before the American people learned to adhere to the collective out of impersonal loyalty, they did so first out of affection for their leader. The early nineteenth-century elites, taking over from the Revolutionary generation, consistently invoked the charisma of General Washington to assure themselves of their new nation's identity. After George Washington's death in 1799, a British official noted the "evident effect" of the "hyperbolic amplifications" and "panegyrics" in praise of the late president in reassuring the younger, more uncertain politicians.[68]

In contrast, Jefferson represented the republican reverse, an anticharismatic figure. His contemporaries recognized the "ostentatious simplicity" of his inauguration as a political statement. One eyewitness described the rustic ensemble he donned for the ceremony, complete with green breeches and gray wool stockings, as what he felt "suitable for the head of a republic." According to this observer, "Everyone knew, of course, that he had a fine French wardrobe of damask waistcoats, frilled shirts, and silk stockings."[69] Whether or not this observer accurately described the contents of Thomas Jefferson's clothespress, he understood and acknowledged Jefferson's political statement.

Jefferson made few public appearances; if he allowed women few opportunities for display at levees and other social events, he also did not permit them for himself. He even began the custom of sending his speeches to be read in Congress. These republican innovations did not pass unnoticed. While "gentlemen of rank and consequence here [in Washington City] were usually attended when they ride," the sharp-eyed William Plumer noted, Jefferson rode either alone or accompanied only by his secretary. Plumer did not know the cause of this "singularity," but he suspected it was "affectation." Whatever the reason, he felt that it ill-fit the "dignity of the Chief of a great nation."

After the inauguration Jefferson continued to use his person to assert his essential republican simplicity, drawing on a tradition of slovenliness particular to Virginia gentry. Plumer never got over his initial meeting with the president, when Jefferson "was dressed, or rather undressed, in an old brown coat, red waistcoat, and . . . slippers without heels." If the general shabbiness were not enough, this man, whom Plumer took to be a servant, had the temerity to sport "old corduroy small-clothes, much soiled and woolen hose." Plumer was "surprised" to hear this person announced as the president and, as a consequence, often recorded details of dress after a visit to the White House, reporting with relief when Jefferson looked decent on more formal occasions.[70]

Margaret Bayard Smith's approval of all things Jeffersonian stemmed from such displays of simplicity, though she tended to stress inner factors over sartorial ones. In her eyes his legitimacy as a leader derived from his possession and use of women's weapons. She provides a perfect example of his self-effacing style, with its many feminine elements, in her account of their first meeting. Bayard Smith, unsure of the identity of the stranger standing in her parlor, began a conversation which almost instantly turned unreserved and intimate. With a "countenance beaming with an expression of benevolence and with a manner and voice almost femininely soft and gentle," the gentleman drew Bayard Smith into a discussion of the topics of the day and then made observations of a "more personal and interesting nature." His manner induced Bayard Smith to treat him as an intimate, and she "unlocked her heart," telling him frankly what she liked and disliked about what the gentleman called her "new home." She had quite forgot he was not "a friend of her own," when the door opened, and Samuel Harrison Smith walked in and introduced him as "Mr. Jefferson."[71]

Ceding the central place to her husband, cheeks burning and heart throbbing, Margaret Bayard Smith retreated to her corner to ponder the incongruity between the "vulgar demagogue" of whom she had heard and this "stranger whose deportment was so dignified and gentlemanly, whose language was so refined, whose voice was so gentle, whose countenance was so benignant." None other than Thomas Jefferson![72] "Soft," "gentle," "refined" were all words of approbation that her culture applied to women. Indeed, in this encounter Jefferson acted the part of the perfect lady: at first reserved and a bit distant, but after a very short time, as an implied compliment to his hostess, dropping his reserve. Ladies were known for their childlike ease and trust, qualities Jefferson demonstrated by opening his heart and waxing confidential, discussing personal feelings and domestic arrangements.[73]

In a discussion of Jefferson's deliberate evocation of powerlessness, it is important to remember the underlying paradoxical motive—power.

Plumer proved not far off when he labeled Jefferson's displays of humble simplicity as affectation. Jefferson developed an antipower persona in order to exercise complete control over the government. He was probably the most flagrantly hands-off president in American history and yet one of the most effective.[74] It would be a mistake to suppose that the one was a direct cause of the other; Jefferson only appeared not to be running the machine. Perhaps the surest evidence of the iron control he exerted beneath his casual velvet glove lay in the future, when his successors attempted to duplicate his outward shows only to find themselves rendered weak and ineffectual.

Jefferson's need to maintain complete control of any situation probably originated deep in his character, but in Washington City there existed good political reasons as well. He most emphatically did not want a court to develop in the capital of the United States. Fear of courts loomed large in theories of "pure republicanism," especially distrust of ministerial influence. Americans knew firsthand the dangers of royal advisers. Before the Revolution the colonists had been convinced that King George harbored only good intentions toward them but that designing ministers had led him astray. A court atmosphere bred ambitious, unscrupulous individuals, who gained power and influence by creating and participating in the kind of personal power structures that grew up around a monarch. Jefferson knew that the legislative community could tend that way, and he was determined to thwart any such developments by being the sole power of the place. Jefferson wanted to eliminate all of what is considered essential to the business of politics: namely, politicking and human relationships, the actions of individuals working together for their own interests. The new republican nation had to be guided only by pure ideals, and with that criterion Jefferson could guarantee only himself.[75]

Analysis of the symbiotic relationship between society and politics, taking into account the deep commitment Jefferson held to create a new world in which a pure republican government could exist, profoundly changes our view of the era. The participants in the political culture took seriously the strictures of etiquette and manners that later historians have felt it unnecessary to consider. The concerns about levees, Jefferson's dishabille, the debate over titles—all become more understandable when seen in this light. As a practical demonstration of how this new lens on the world of Washington City can illuminate the traditional narrative, let us examine one of the more flamboyant and mysterious events of Jefferson's first administration: the Merry affair.

THE MERRY AFFAIR

The story of the Merrys begins with the entrance of two weary and disgruntled travelers upon the Washington stage. Like the Smiths they, too, were newlyweds. Anthony Merry had been appointed the first minister to the United States from Great Britain on the recommendation of Rufus King, his American counterpart at the Court of St. James's. King described the career diplomat to Jefferson as a "plain, unassuming, and amiable man" and a much better choice than the other candidate for the post, Francis James Jackson.[76] Elizabeth Leathes Merry had been a wealthy widow, quite prominent in her Suffolk community, and she married Anthony Merry in 1803 only days before he heard of his new appointment to the United States.[77]

Upon arrival in Norfolk, Virginia, the Merrys took leave of their shipboard friend, the poet Thomas Moore, who continued on to Bermuda. The crossing had been full of delays and storms, and the couple and their entourage of people and possessions still had a substantial journey to reach Washington. Six days on another ship brought them to Alexandria, and the Merrys crossed to Georgetown in a "coachie." This primitive conveyance provoked Mrs. Merry's "mirth and risibility" and her husband's "quiet astonishment and inward groaning."[78]

Once at Washington City, the Merrys had a hard time settling in. Not for them Margaret Bayard Smith's raptures about wildflowers and gently flowing brooks. They found no residence completely habitable, so they put two together, though both were "mere shells of houses, with bare walls and without fixtures of any kind, even without a pump or a well." Before they had even unpacked, Anthony and Elizabeth Leathes Merry had floored the natives with their mountains of luggage and retinue of white servants. To their shock the Merrys discovered that provisioning their household, not only with the luxurious items required by a diplomatic establishment but even with staples, required repeated trips to Baltimore over wretched roads.[79]

With the Merrys safely (if not happily) ensconced in Washington

City, Anthony Merry readied himself for his presentation to the president, an occasion of crucial import in the diplomatic world. On November 28, 1803, accompanied by Secretary of State James Madison, he arrived at the President's House to be presented to Thomas Jefferson. That morning the British minister had attired himself in full diplomatic dress: deep blue coat with black velvet trim and gold braid, white breeches, silk stockings, ornate buckled shoes, plumed hat, and a large sword.[80]

In Anthony Merry's view, things did not go well from the first. Not finding Jefferson in the reception room, Madison left Merry in order to search for the president. Uncomprehending, the British minister followed him into the hallway. When both men were in the narrow passageway, Jefferson entered from his study, forcing the startled minister to retreat into the first room. Diplomatic etiquette required that Merry execute this maneuver without turning his back on Jefferson, despite his cumbersome regalia. Jefferson and Anthony Merry finally ended up in the same room, where, shaken and disconcerted, the minister gave the speech he had carefully prepared.

These clumsy bumblings were not the only cause of the minister's uncertainty as he struggled through his speech. The greatest shock of the morning was sartorial. According to Merry, the president of the United States was "not merely in an undress, but *actually standing in slippers down at the heels,* and both pantaloons, coat, and under-clothes indicative of utter slovenliness and indifference to appearances and in a state of negligence actually studied." The subsequent interview between the two men passed well enough, but Merry noted with horror that for the entire time the seated Jefferson tossed one of his down-at-the-heel slippers up in the air and caught it with his big toe.[81] The British minister withdrew in chagrin and confusion.

The second skirmish in this etiquette war occurred only three days later, at the first White House social event at which Mrs. Merry was to be present. By the time the couple arrived at the president's door, they were both feeling a bit at sea. Anthony Merry had barely recovered from what he perceived to be the president's insult to him and possibly to his country. In addition, after the presentation Madison had informed Merry that he was expected to make the first visit not only to him, the secretary of state, but also to all the other department heads. When Merry objected, stating that his predecessors, men of lower diplomatic rank, had the first call paid to them, Madison replied that the present administration was not bound to old rules of diplomatic etiquette followed in previous (and Federalist) administrations. An experienced diplomat who realized that official business required the personal contacts supplied by these calls, Anthony Merry swallowed his outrage and made the rounds. At least Elizabeth Merry was spared a similar affront. Cabinet wives were required to call first on diplomatic families, and Mrs. Madison led the way.[82] But this night Anthony and Elizabeth Merry might have expected things to proceed differently at what was, they assumed, a dinner in their honor.

Their first shock, upon entering the room, was discovering Louis André Pichon, the French chargé d'affaires. England and France were at war, after all, and diplomatic custom should have prevented the social and political awkwardness of their common presence. Jefferson's flouting of this convention, the Merrys would soon learn, originated not in unstudied ignorance but in deliberate planning. The president had gone so far as to press Pichon to cut short his business in Baltimore in order to attend.[83]

The spark that would ignite the flames of the etiquette war came when dinner was announced. According to social and diplomatic custom, Jefferson should have led the way, escorting the lady of honor, Mrs. Merry, followed by Mr. Merry and the lady of second rank, Mrs. Madison. Mrs. Merry would sit on Jefferson's right, Mrs. Madison on his left, and Anthony Merry would sit next to her, making him the closest male to the president. The rest of the company would follow and be seated in order of precedence.

Instead, at the announcement Jefferson took the arm of the lady next to him, Dolley Payne Todd Madison, and escorted her into dinner, though Dolley demurred, whispering, "Take Mrs. Merry." The other guests were dumbfounded. The wife of the Spanish minister, born Sally McKean of Philadelphia, declared to Dolley, "This will be the cause of war!" Madison led Elizabeth Merry into the dining room, leaving the flabbergasted Anthony Merry to scramble for a seat. As he reached for a respectable place near the wife of the Spanish minister, an agile congressman slid past him and claimed the spot. As distressing as this was, the president's refusal to step in or even to care if he got a seat distressed Anthony Merry more. The British minister called for his carriage as soon as the meal was over, and the couple left, one assumes, in the highest of dudgeon.[84]

In his official dispatch of December 7, 1803, Merry complained of this treatment and of his initial interview with Jefferson. Having made his displeasure known, the minister disclaimed any intention of taking official action and determined to carry out his mission in this place where "the excess of the democratic ferment in this people is conspicuously evinced by the dregs having got up to the top." The Merrys had accepted an invitation to the home of the Madisons for that evening. By the time they entered the Madisons' home, the gossip mill had already related the tale of the couple's encounter with the new form of etiquette Jefferson called "pêle mêle," a French wordplay that means "to mix." All were anxiously awaiting what would happen if the couple had to endure another such slight.[85] What ensued at the Madisons' dinner delighted the gossips and outraged the Merrys.

With the announcement of dinner, the host, James Madison, led the lady nearest him, Hannah Nicholson Gallatin, wife of the secretary of the treasury, into the dining room. As Merry watched and seethed, no one chose his wife. According to the Federalist newspapers, the two stood, both stranded, as the procession of guests passed them into the dining room. While the story may exaggerate their slighting by the other guests, the Merrys did escort each other into dinner. They would not, however, acquiesce in this social chaos. The angry British couple confronted Hannah Nicholson Gallatin at the head of the table, and she yielded her seat to Elizabeth Merry, who took the place of honor with little grace.[86]

Anthony Merry's initial suspicion of the motives behind all of this pell-mell grew when he and Elizabeth Merry discovered that Madison had never before followed this usage, and they viewed his adoption of it in their case as a deliberate insult. In a letter to George Hammond, a friend at the British Foreign Office, Anthony Merry concluded that this new etiquette proceeded "from design and not from ignorance or awkwardness (though God knows a great deal of both as to matters even of common etiquette is to be seen at every step)." According to Merry there was precedence at these events, the preference being given "in every respect to the wives of the secretaries (a set of beings as little without the manners as without the appearance of gentlewomen)."[87]

Merry requested instructions from the Foreign Office as to whether formal protests were in order, but the couple implemented their private retaliatory strategy immediately. They decided to refuse all invitations and persuaded the Spanish minister to join them. A banquet boycott followed, and though the British minister sometimes appeared at official functions, he refused to risk exposing his wife to a repetition of the same "want of distinction."[88]

In vain Madison protested that the British minister was in a republic now and could no more expect courtlike distinctions than he, Madison, could demand republican equality in the court of the British king. The Merrys just sat at home. Less than five weeks after their arrival, by the end of December, the boycott was total. As the French minister reported, "Washington society is turned upside down; all the women are to the last degree exasperated with Mrs. Merry."[89]

No business between the United States and Great Britain was possible without social interaction, and Jefferson and Madison soon realized that something must be done. When Anthony Merry appeared without his wife at the New Year's Day levee, which all the world attended, the president and his secretary of state began damage control. Jefferson inquired, through Madison, whether the minister would consider attending a dinner without his wife, ostensibly to spare that lady any impropriety. Madison thought he had discerned from the British minister that a compromise might be effected, but when Jefferson proffered the invitation, it was declined. Anthony Merry justified his refusal on the grounds that he needed to await official instructions from his government, a reply that sent Thomas Jefferson into his own fit of pique: "I shall be highly honored when the king of England is good enough to let Mr. Merry come and eat my soup."[90]

In January, Jefferson and his cabinet, perhaps feeling that the new rules needed the legitimacy of print, drew up the "Cannons of Etiquette" (the misspelling making a lovely martial image for an etiquette war). This remarkably short document declared that equality among persons was the basic principle. The residents would pay the first call to visitors and earlier comers to later arrivals, except in the case of foreign ministers, who were expected to make the first call. There would be no distinctions of degree or rank among foreign ministers and American or other officials at social events. The canons decreed, to encourage the growth of pell-mell, that public officials should follow in their own homes "the ancient usage of the country, of gentlemen in mass giving precedence to the ladies in mass" when passing from one room to another. When the Merrys received this document on January 12, 1804, Anthony Merry replied that he certainly should have been presented with these rules when he arrived to take up his post.[91]

After its flamboyant beginning in December 1803 and January 1804, the Merry affair did not proceed to a dramatic climax but in fact fizzled out. Etiquette *à la pêle-mêle* disappeared, and the Merrys stayed in the United States until 1806. The Foreign Office never responded directly to Anthony Merry's complaints about his treatment, and he did not lodge a formal protest. The Merrys began to socialize, although they refused to dine at Jefferson's table because they had never received an apology from the president. For her part, Elizabeth Merry persisted in fulfilling social duties, even as she was publicly abused by Jefferson's fellow democrats at parties outside her home. Until the end, the Merrys gave lavish parties and dinners, which they saw as necessary to their mission.[92]

As often happens with affairs involving women, etiquette, or sexual scandal, most historians either have dismissed the Merry affair as inconsequential or have not deigned to notice it. But the ramifications of the Merry affair were both obvious and important at the time. Contemporaries clearly thought the etiquette war significant, if only because Americans plotting against their new government went first to the British minister with their schemes. In the winter after the etiquette controversy, Anthony Merry was approached by New England Federalists Timothy Pickering, Roger Griswold, and others about a plan to separate New England from the rest of the Union. In 1805 Aaron Burr tried to involve the minister in his failed coup d'état.[93] In refusing to become embroiled in either attempt, Anthony Merry showed a great deal more political savvy (and restraint) than he has been credited with having. His competence shows, as well, in the uses he advised the British government to make of his knowledge of these plots.

However, their treatment at Jefferson's hands did make Anthony and Elizabeth Merry angry. This may seem a rather trivial effect, but ordinarily governments devote much diplomatic effort to preventing such an occurrence. It was not a good time for Jefferson to have embittered this couple, as the years 1803–6 were crucial ones for Anglo-American relations. A Jeffersonian newspaper, the *Aurora*, heralded the Merrys' arrival, declaring that the minister came at an opportune time. The usually Anglophobic Jefferson, in a letter to Robert Livingston, minister to France, even wondered if the United States might "eventually marry ourselves to the British fleet and nation" to protect New Orleans.[94]

The Merrys arrived in this atmosphere of optimism and uncertainty. Within a few days they felt themselves the victims of a plot. They thought Thomas Jefferson had lied about American protocol and that he meant to insult them—not for their personal qualities but rather as representatives of their government. Unfortunately for Anglo-American relations, these opinions informed all of Anthony Merry's official advice, his semiofficial conversations, and his private opinions (expressed by letter and in conversations) on a variety of issues.

The suspicions with which Anthony Merry approached official dealings over the impressment issue and the escalating tensions between the two countries may be directly traced to the Merry affair and to the Merrys' suspicions that a plot to humble them and their country lay behind their social treatment. On the issue of impressment, for example, Anthony Merry saw the "absolute hostile tendency" of the bills introduced into the House and Senate as proof not of "popular clamor" but only of "the unfriendly disposition of the executive." It is difficult not to hear echoes of the Merrys' reactions to their early treatment at American hands when the minister urged his government in May 1806 to adopt a sterner stand toward the United States in order to "gain respect" and to stand firm against American "pretensions" concerning neutral rights.[95]

One particular aspect of the affair left an indelible impression on Merry, one which influenced all of his reports to his country. Although in interviews and official discourse, Jefferson assured him of the United States' respect for Britain, Jefferson's actions convinced the minister that the president and his government were irrevocably pro-French. The favoritism shown Pichon (especially in inviting the French diplomat to that first dinner) may have had a significant role in forming that impression. During the crucial Louisiana Purchase negotiations, the Spanish ambassador, the chevalier de Casa Yrujo, found a more sympathetic listener in Anthony

Merry than he might have before they joined forces against Jefferson. Though Anthony Merry had not trusted the don when they first met in Spain, Merry recommended to his government that it try to stop the purchase and thereby strengthen British commercial and political influence in the strategic Mississippi Valley area.[96]

The most serious effects of the Merry affair lay primarily in the exacerbation of party rancor and, in consequence, the weight Merry placed on the increasingly rancorous Federalist and Republican party division in his advice to the British government. The Federalists had seized upon the affair from the first slipper toss and had used it, championing the Merrys in order to distinguish themselves from the rude Republicans. The Federalist newspaper rhetoric grew so vociferous that Jefferson was forced to depart from his pre-presidential print reticence and write anonymous editorials defending himself.

The hostility that Anthony Merry observed and reported was even more important than any rancor stirred up by the affair. At the center of a fierce partisan struggle, Merry logically saw issues of Jefferson's influence and popularity, the Louisiana Purchase, the Kings-Hawkesbury Convention, the variety of plots afoot, the nonimportation act, and the Essex decision as taking place in the context of American domestic conflict. Over and over again, he urged the British government to stand firm in its attitude and not give in to any pressure. The United States would ultimately collapse, Merry believed, because of its government's instability.[97]

If the plots for disunion had only limited impact in England, the more general reports of party rancor may have had effects more serious in the long run. Scholars of the War of 1812 have theorized that the war lasted so long because England overestimated the degree of division in the United States and waited for the Republic to fall apart on its own. The British believed they would be welcomed back to New England by the Federalists. Even though the Merry affair did not cause the War of 1812, as Augustus Foster claimed, the impression of vicious division that Anthony Merry imparted to the British government may have lengthened it.

THE DISORDER OF WOMAN

At different points in the unfolding events of the Merry affair, Jefferson bemoaned the trouble caused by this trivial matter; James Madison called it a "farce." In spite of all assertions to the contrary, it had the potential of an exploding bomb in the days of the early Republic, a potential recognized quickly by Jefferson's administration as they scrambled to make amends without actually apologizing. The quick retreat on the part of the White House and the quiet elimination of pell-mell indicate that Jefferson had deliberately set out to make a statement to Anthony Merry. Well practiced in the use of social events and clothing to exert control over situations, Jefferson also had considerable experience as a diplomat and had dealt with the previous representatives from Britain, George Hammond and Edward Thornton. Neither man had mentioned any insulting or odd behavior, making any contemporary or historical claims for Jefferson's naïveté seem, well, naive.

Jefferson risked political fallout because his principle of preserving the Republic from the infection of European practices was paramount. From his Anglophobic point of view, there was much to hate and fear from the Merry mission. One aspect in particular drew presidential wrath. In a letter to James Monroe in England, after pages of social and political news, Jefferson updated his minister on the happenings at his own court. At first he was decidedly generous in his treatment of the British minister: "Mr. Merry is with us, and we believe him to be personally as desirable a character as could have been sent to us." "But," Jefferson added ominously, "he is unluckily associated with one of an opposite character in every point. She has already disturbed our harmony extremely." He then followed with a list of Anthony Merry's crimes of pomposity and precedence. He mentioned Mrs. Merry only when telling Monroe of "the offense that Mr. Merry took" at Jefferson giving other ladies precedence over the minister's wife, "the consequence is that Mr. and Mrs. Merry will put themselves into Coventry."

This was a disastrous development, as Jefferson recognized, because "he will lose half of his usefulness to the nation, that derived from a perfectly familiar and private intercourse with the secretaries and myself." Though Jefferson had listed only the sins of Mr. Merry, the president then called Elizabeth Merry a "virago" and added that "in the short course of a few weeks [she] had established a degree of dislike among all classes which one would have thought impossible in so short a time."[98]

But even Margaret Bayard Smith, a devoted Jeffersonian, gave a rather different picture of the lady in question. She described the British minister's wife as a "large, tall, well-made woman, rather masculine, very free and affable in her manners, but easy without being graceful." Bayard Smith continued with an assessment of Elizabeth Merry's effect on others: "She is said to be a woman of fine understanding, and she is so entirely the talker and actor in all companies, that her good husband passes quite unnoticed; he is plain in his appearance and called rather inferior in understanding."[99]

Eleanor Parke Custis Lewis, another woman of "fine understanding" and the granddaughter of Martha Custis Washington, deemed Mrs. Merry's manners "extremely affable and friendly," adding, "I should be very much pleased to cultivate her acquaintance." When married to her first husband, Elizabeth Leathes had enjoyed the reputation of a good hostess with a gift for conversation. She also had a scholarly interest in botany. Both Thomas Moore and Augustus John Foster thought her a "fine woman." In Washington she captivated Aaron Burr, a man whom historian Malcolm Lester has characterized as "no mean judge of womanflesh." He found her most attractive and wished her to make the acquaintance of his intelligent and educated daughter, Theodosia.[100]

By her dress and presence, Elizabeth Merry ensured that the British mission would not go unnoticed. The ladies of Washington pronounced themselves impressed with her official wardrobe, and Bayard Smith included detailed descriptions in letters to her sister. On one occasion Mrs. Merry's dress was "brilliant and fantastic, attracting great attention," made of "white satin" with "a dark blue crape" overskirt, "so thickly covered with silver spangles that it appeared to be a brilliant silver tissue." Elizabeth Merry also wore a shawl, not on her shoulders but around her head, "a breadth of blue crape about four yards long hanging to the floor" and "bound to her head with a band like her drapery, with a diamond crescent before and diamond comb behind." Diamond earrings and necklace completed the ensemble.[101]

Little wonder Jefferson reacted so violently. It was bad enough that the Merrys were English; Mrs. Merry proved "more English" than even her husband. Satirists and cartoonists of the era used showy women and effeminate men as symbols of the ills of court life, and here the leader of the Country Party of the United States came face-to-face with the court personified. Elizabeth Merry exemplified exactly the kind of woman Thomas Jefferson feared and despised. No republican wife she, submissive, frugal, and devoted to her domestic labors. Elizabeth Merry's charm lay not in the quiet, wifely self-effacement Jefferson tried to instill in his daughters, but rather her allure was of the court kind, designed to command attention. Elizabeth Merry talked in public, perhaps even taking the lead in conversation. She was educated, a scholar of sorts, and her "fine understanding" possibly engendered in her an agility of mind and discernment that a man such as Jefferson would have found disconcerting, if not disgusting. Her greatest sin may have lain in overshadowing her husband, assuming the dominant role in public over the "plain" little man, "inferior in understanding."[102]

In short, this was an elite European woman—cultivated, charming, astute, and public—and thus everything Jefferson hated. Raised to fulfill a particular role in society, Elizabeth Merry wielded the weapons of aristocratic politicking: elaborate dress, public presence, personal appeal, and lavish dinners. This woman, with her ideas of hierarchical ranking, embodied everything Jefferson knew would threaten his Republic and his city. She was the first of her kind, the first European diplomatic wife, to enter the world he had created, and he may have meant to make an example of her. Without a doubt, her premier status (both temporal and hierarchical) earned her the brunt of his untempered dislike.[103]

For Thomas Jefferson and his followers, Elizabeth Merry, like Martha Washington earlier, quickly became a lightning rod for her husband, drawing hostility toward herself because of her unofficial position. Jeffersonian Washington knew its political responsibility and harassed Mrs. Merry forthwith. Augustus John Foster noted that the Republicans "took their cue from the style adopted at the Great House." This style included insulting Elizabeth Merry, "remarking upon her dress or diamonds or treading on her gown," vexing her so much that Foster had seen her burst into tears. At a party in Georgetown given to celebrate the acquisition of Louisiana, Mrs. Merry, dressed in her best to give honor to the company on this auspicious occasion, was told at the door that her "undemocratic diamonds" must be removed. Dinner guests could also be cutting, if not as personally hostile, to Anthony Merry, from the Kentucky gentleman who spit out his champagne on the floor in distaste to the congressman who commented acidly, after a mention of crayfish, that at least Americans were not reduced to eating vermin.[104] In spite of these personal insults, Elizabeth Merry knew her job and carried on.

The Merry affair enlarges, deepens, complicates, and clarifies our perspectives on several important historical issues: the extent of party rancor in the early Republic; Thomas Jefferson's political character; his fears of aristocracy and federalism; and the investment he had in Washington City as the last, best hope of republicanism. The contretemps over etiquette also casts light on Jefferson's Prospero-like political style, which combined a "minimalist" appearance with a need for total control, whether it was over dinner guests or diplomatic wives. We can also see the role that social events and private matters played in maintaining that control.

In spite of Jefferson's own pose of distance and detachment from the dirty business of politicking, the Merry affair reminds us that Jefferson was indeed a politician, and that the political culture of the early Republic differed from later party machines and delineations of official business. The seemingly personal events of the Merry affair (precedence at meals, clothing choices) assumed great importance in a culture in which politics was a more individual and personal business than it was barely thirty years later or is in modern times. The individual politician could not hide behind the anonymity provided by a party, and the lack of political machines rendered politics more uncertain and unstable than later, more institutionalized versions. If we rely only on official documents and official events, we cannot see the "grammar of political combat."[105]

In this etiquette war of the early Republic, Thomas Jefferson lost. Pell-mell faded out, and Jefferson never directly addressed the issue again. Social custom in Washington in the early years remained casual by European court standards but retained enough sense of its Continental roots so that no other foreigner ever felt as lost as the Merrys did when everyone at Jefferson's table lunged for seats.

Jefferson had run into trouble trying to manage both politics and society, assigning himself the twin tasks of translating a political theory of republicanism into a workaday government and turning a liberal political theory of society into a reality. In the latter attempt, he certainly failed. Though Jefferson proved a master in some social arenas, he overstepped his bounds when it came to the Merrys. He let his own deep-seated dislikes and anxieties rule his judgment; he paid no heed to the genteel, whispered warnings from Dolley Madison and Sally McKean Yrujo. But Jefferson was certainly right on the underlying principle: political style and social style are intimately connected, and they are the responsibility of political leaders. Ironically, if social events were necessary for courts and monarchies, they proved even more essential in republican Washington, taking on burdens usually shared with the interlocking extraofficial structures of government.

Thomas Jefferson also lost on another important issue: he could not keep women out of either Washington City or the circles of power. When they came (as they did, increasingly, over the decades), they brought the known forms of politicking with them, forms based on family and kin connections and social events; in other words, on aristocratic models. Elite American women had been trained to the fine and subtle vibrations of society and human relations, and under their stewardship after Jefferson, nothing comparable to the Merry affair occurred in early Washington City.

Instead, the Madison administration would bring new layers to the cultural discussion about the dangers and attractions of aristocratic and democratic ideas, made concrete in efforts to create a political and social style for a new America. This discussion would be led by the Queen of Washington City, the last of the founders, Dolley Payne Todd Madison.

2

Dolley Madison Takes Command

"A lass unparallel'd"

—WILLIAM SHAKESPEARE, *Antony and Cleopatra* 5.2.316

WHEN DOLLEY PAYNE TODD and James Madison took possession of the President's House after his inauguration in 1809, the official residence was a mess. Seeing it unfinished in both structure and decor, young Frances Few, Hannah Nicholson Gallatin's niece, compared its grim exterior that of a "State Prison." The roof proved too heavy for the walls, and they had to be reinforced with bands of steel. Lack of funds blocked the completion of the steps, gates, porter's lodge, and landscaping. Congressional reluctance to authorize money for the "Palace" frustrated architect Benjamin Henry Latrobe to the point of resignation. Having discovered dry rot in the timbers of the Capitol, Latrobe gloomily reported to his patron, Thomas Jefferson, "I have every reason to believe the President's House is in the same shape."[1]

If the outside suggested a prison, the interior of the official residence resembled a poorhouse. During his first years President Jefferson had responded to scant funds and an urgent need for basic furnishings by borrowing heavily from his own personal possessions at Monticello. Later, he neglected the house, perhaps because other matters occupied him, or perhaps as a deliberate antimonarchical statement. In March 1809 Jefferson and his furniture were on their way back home to Virginia, while Dolley and James faced bleak, barren rooms; the twenty-year-old crimson damask furniture left in the ladies' drawing room, for years the subject of disparaging comments from guests, only accented the general shabbiness.[2] We may wonder if it occurred to Dolley and James Madison, as they wandered through echoing rooms, that the condition of the President's

48

House might be a fitting metaphor for the political situation Jefferson had bequeathed to them.

Without question Jefferson left his protégé a daunting political legacy, but just as Jefferson deserved only some reproach for the state of the President's House, so he could take only some of the blame for the sorry state of the government. In both cases a recalcitrant Congress exacerbated the circumstances. For Thomas Jefferson to saddle James Madison with a spectacularly failed piece of legislation—the embargo—was bad enough. Congress made it worse by replacing the measure with the Non-Intercourse Act three days before the inauguration, forcing President Madison to begin his administration with a law that combined the insecurity of a new policy with the worst excesses of the old. As the passage of the act indicated, Jefferson also left the new president a rapidly deteriorating relationship with Great Britain, aggravated by a Congress divided into factions, quarreling about foreign and domestic questions.

And the leaky ship Thomas Jefferson left his successor would continue to fill with water. Except for the ultimate failure—disunion—all the potential weaknesses of the new government emerged in bold relief during James Madison's tenure. These included the widening gap between the government and the citizenry, the obstacles to unity presented by sectionalism, the ambivalent attitudes toward power held by both citizens and legislators, and, most notably, the weakness of the presidency.[3] Given only limited official power by the Constitution, each president had to re-create the office to some extent. Jefferson's charisma and personal popularity, as well as his position as leader of the ruling party, had endowed the presidency with some effectiveness, but James Madison was no Thomas Jefferson, either in personal gifts or public regard. As a result, in 1812, partly through fault and partly through circumstance, Madison launched a shockingly unprepared United States into a war which led the new nation to the brink of disunion.

The Madison presidency, however, enjoyed particular success in another arena. During the years 1808–16, the executive and legislative branches made great strides toward creating a working national political framework. Under Jefferson the federal government had been a disconnected, unstructured body, ruled by a single charismatic leader. By the time the Madisons retired to Montpelier in 1817, the Senate, the House, the cabi-

James Madison, by Gilbert Stuart, 1804. (Courtesy of Colonial Williamsburg Foundation, Williamsburg, Virginia)

net, and the president had begun to build an organizational structure that would allow both branches to expedite the business of government and make policy.

In a larger sense, the great victory of the Madison administration lay in the development of a political and social style appropriate for a republican government and its citizenry, taking a giant step toward achieving national unity and respect for national authority, two major goals (and obstacles) of the early Union. Remember that Jefferson left his successor a troublesome social situation as well as the above-mentioned political wreckage. He had begun his term with a vision of political power and the goal of setting the forms and style of America's social life. Quick to tear down aristocratic protocol, he failed to build up a substitute. As a leader in the Revolution and later as president, Jefferson's strength lay in defining the opposition, and in this way Jefferson embodied the dilemma of the United States after the Revolution. Once the colonists had taken a stand against the colonizer's political system, they were left with the problem of what came next. In this democratic Republic everything from global policy to everyday life offered itself for re-visioning, a situation both exhilarating and frightening.[4]

Jefferson's disastrous attempt at pell-mell died a quiet death after the Merry debacle, and he abandoned the task of reforming American style, leaving a social vacuum. Modified versions of European forms coexisted uneasily with the feeling among citizens that something had to be done to render such forms American. Ironically, Jefferson's success at expanding the power of the presidency—his unprecedented control over the legislative process, the Congress, and cabinet—lay in his ability at statecraft, which depended on his judicious use of social occasions. However, though his geniality and charisma eased the way, Jefferson's social style focused more on personal power and political expediency than on setting a model for the nation.[5]

Not only did the Madison presidency succeed far more than Jefferson's in this task, but its role in establishing a social and political style defined as American remains perhaps its greatest triumph. This style embodied the political theories that had informed the creation of the United States in tangible, active ways. Unlike the reign of Thomas Jefferson, the Madison tenure gave white American women and men of the upper, middle, and working classes a positive sense of what the United States could be, not just what it was not. Understanding how this was accomplished and the full impact of the Madison presidency requires looking beyond the words of political men and official documents to concentrate on the words and actions of political women.

STYLE AND SUBSTANCE

Some say that the demand of particular historical circumstances creates the characters to meet them. Some say talented individuals shape themselves to meet circumstances. Probably, of course, both processes work simultaneously, as is clear in the relationship between the new capital, Washington City, and the woman who would rule it, Dolley Payne Todd Madison. The city needed her, and by answering that need, Dolley Madison fulfilled her astonishing political potential.

Dolley faced several formidable tasks upon her arrival in Washington City. William Cabell Rives, Madison biographer and acolyte, characterized James Madison's situation in his administration as one when "everything was to be created anew, and upon him . . . mainly devolved the task of originating, preparing, and defending the measures necessary for organizing and launching the new government."[6] This assessment could as easily have described the circumstances of both Madisons as they entered the executive mansion in 1809 and then guided the nation through war. In addition to "organizing and launching," Dolley's list of assignments also included legitimizing her husband's administration and the national capital (for both Americans and outsiders) and imparting to the citizenry a sense of Americanness.

Style comprised both the product and the process of Dolley's innovations in nation building. Blending regional traditions, European practices, and the innovations of the presidents' wives before her, she created a national etiquette and social style suitable for a seat of government, one that could display power, enhance the status of the rulers, and facilitate the process of building a capital, a governmental structure, and a nation. The term *style* describes not only what she did but also how she accomplished her goals, a process that took her project beyond the federal district's boundaries.

In present usage, style includes only the frivolous and shallow, while substance concerns the meat of the matter; yet reuniting these artificially separated categories results in a more fruitful reading of the past. Such a consideration does not necessarily preclude the existence of some events or occasions that are solely social or stylish. However, in any discussion of Washington City—a town built on, by, and for politics—any such differ-

Mrs. James Madison, by Gilbert Stuart, 1804. (White House Collection, courtesy of White House Historical Association, Washington, D.C.)

entiation seems bootless.[7] Indeed, separation of substance and style is a fairly recent innovation and may not be at all pertinent to a study of early nineteenth-century political life.[8]

Far from being superficial, style—as one scholar defines it, "the different ways that people perceive, speak, and act politically"—profoundly shapes the lives of individuals and society. Style dictates the presentation of political substance, thus influencing what the electorate perceives to be the real issues. The issues themselves may contain no inherent importance; rather politicians, political organizations, and mass media shape them and create their urgency. Style, whether referred to as political or social, acts as a lens that colors and shapes some objects, while filtering out others. Even as historians or political analysts dismiss or deplore frivolous demonstrations of style, they still implicitly acknowledge style's "mediating power," if only its ability to deceive the foolish and warp their political decisions.[9]

Style not only dictates what comprises substance, it is substance. The forms that politics take and the styles in which they are presented affect and reflect degrees of social freedom and equality. How rulers implement political power and resolve conflict—that is, their political style—profoundly affects the way citizens perceive their government and themselves as a nation among nations. Style (and here the line between social and political blurs beyond all recovery) creates symbols and institutions that bind people to the political system and to a government they may or may not consider theirs. In this capacity style can facilitate or restrict the ability of men and women to act on their political impulses. For American history, then, style is crucial to evaluating the processes of democracy.

By inventing her unique style, Dolley made republicanism, with its particularly ideological and abstract ideals of manners, into a working reality.[10] She provided social solutions to a central problem of republican politics, namely, how to make the federal government cohere without threatening the underlying values of republicanism as Thomas Jefferson and James Madison defined them. She tied the government, symbolized by the national capital and the President's House, more closely to the lives of ordinary Americans than any other politician before her. Dolley's combination of a glamorous focus on the executive with a self-consciously democratic flair that social leaders and more middling folk admired and emulated proved just right for the fledgling nation. Americans saw the roles created by their social leaders as important parts of life, connecting the deepest currents of American character, the moral and intellectual impulses, with the practices of everyday life. Located in the most visible, most influential position in American society and culture, Dolley fully exploited her position as social leader, creator of style.

The lingering paradox of persistent aristocracy in American national etiquette presented Dolley with her most complex problem. Her situation placed two obstacles before her: she was a woman, and she lived in the new capital. In the highly gendered world of nineteenth-century America, women had long been the focus of anxiety regarding aristocratic practices. "Creeping monarchy" tempted and endangered both men and women, but women nourished an inherent weakness for the luxurious consumer goods that often opened the door to dissipation, corruption, and eventually rule by despotic kings. Popular writers and illustrators depicted both women and men under the spell of aristocratic and monarchical longings as excessively feminine in their dress and manner, thus strengthening the natural tie between women and practices that would sap the young Republic's masculine vigor. Though these links had been identified in Western culture long before the nineteenth century, they acquired a particular urgency in the fragile Union.[11]

Much as they might have wished to purge republican politics of the contaminating influence of women, some political theorists, especially the influential Scottish Enlightenment school, recognized the power of women and the inextricable linkage of society and government. They attempted to acknowledge these facts by a new formulation of social life, one suited for the republican woman and focused on the role of manners as the way to regulate human society and government. In this sense, manners meant moral character, the way individuals treated each other and behaved in groups, different from the empty shows of etiquette in a court. Manners emerged as a way of discussing power; in the absence of strong external controls, such as a centralized government or army, a republic's peace and prosperity depended on internal controls. When Scottish theorist James Wilson queried, "What are laws without manners?" he echoed the *American Museum*'s 1789 assertion that manners "are the basis of government." Laws might regulate behavior, but manners formed the heart and mind. They played the crucial role in civilizing a culture, a particular concern for the insecure Americans, always defensive in the face of European remarks about wilderness conditions.[12]

Historians have dubbed the American version of this phenomenon "Republican Motherhood," but recent scholarship has demonstrated that the historical change, partially rooted in the civil jurisprudential school of the Scottish Enlightenment, represented a "broad, long-term transatlantic reformation of the role and status of women." The presence of women in political theory has a tendency to confuse, confound, and upend neat political models, and formulations meant for republican mothers and wives contained a deep contradiction. Though on the surface they were meant to convey a greater sense of female political participation—showing how in the domestic circle, social events, women, and manners could civilize men, soften them, and instill republican virtue—the Scottish Enlightenment theories most definitely restricted women to the domestic realm. Lacking political equality, women nonetheless were promised extensive influence through social dominance.[13] As a political wife and in her new role as social leader, Dolley had to tread a fine line that was potentially contradictory and conflictual.

In the republican lexicon even the existence of a national capital set off alarm bells. The early Anti-Federalists, anxiously viewing the president as a rising monarch, feared a capital would encourage the rise of an aristocracy around him, becoming a "dazzling center, the mistress of fashion." Everyone recognized that centralization supplied the key to monarchy and empire. Mercy Otis Warren also worried about the corruption that a capital would engender. Such a concentration of political power in a single city, she believed, would bring mobs, the introduction of monarchical ideas, courts, and the dreaded etiquette. Washington City had barely broken ground before it stood as a symbol of decadence and monarchy. In 1808 James Sloan, representative from New Jersey, proposed a resolution to relocate the capital because "whatever the motives or the principle upon which the ten-mile square was founded, it is today utterly repugnant to republicanism and to the liberties of a free and independent nation. Its essence and effect is monarchical, spreading its baleful influence from Georgia to Maine."[14]

Aristocratic society, luxury, and distinction do carry concrete attractions for many folks, and the government had barely settled in Washington City before observers noted aristocracy's infectious quality, even in a republican stronghold. "Dissipation increases here daily," reported Margaret Bayard Smith to her sisters with some dismay. Rosalie Stier Calvert, Belgian-born member of the local gentry, concurred, weighing in often with "aristocracy sightings" suggesting that "luxury is increasing greatly here," in the form of more restaurants, confectioners, and pastry shops. As an elite foreigner, Stier Calvert often found herself, her house, and her belongings the object of envious regard: "People always admire anything done by Europeans." Even her husband, a Baltimore native, basked in the reflection of his wife's Continental glow: "You will find Mr. Calvert has become completely European. They give him all sorts of names, such as 'My Lord' and 'Aristocrat.'"[15]

The flood of luxury items and corresponding infusion of European ideas was a more serious problem for Washington City than for any of the country's more established cities, no doubt because of the presence of the diplomatic corps and foreign visitors. Though the foreign population was never numerically significant, it was always highly visible and influential, a source of glamour and dash. With the Tunisian ambassador presenting gifts of horses to the president, and the French ambassador importing "shocking customs" (including "naked dancing"), Washington residents were guaranteed sizable doses of Continental ways.[16] Awareness of this influence may have been the prime motivation behind Thomas Jefferson's desire to eliminate all foreign embassies, a wish he never carried out.

Given this horror of aristocracy, especially in the context of a capital, one might suppose that Dolley should have simply banished all aristocratic forms and ideals. This would have been no easy task, as Jefferson's experiment in creating a social vacuum had demonstrated. No forms existed that were not some version of an aristocratic practice, and some, such as rules of precedence, were extremely useful in keeping order. American people also craved honors and dignities and thrilled at displays of pomp and luxury. The adoption of republican ideals at the time of the American Revolution did not wipe out an earlier commitment to rank. Indeed, far from eliminating the attraction of these hierarchical forms, the American Revolution and its resulting cultural chaos created a need for the stability and dignity that status symbols carried. Revolution can destroy aristocracy or appropriate it. The American middle class was making it clear, even in this early stage of its development, that certain perquisites of aristocracy—such as owning beautiful things and acknowledging social differences—were to be retained.[17]

Aristocratic practices also played a large role in establishing authority. Americans felt the need to confirm their new nation's legitimacy by reference to institutions and roles sanctioned and valued in both England and colonial America. Federalist and Jeffersonian Republican views reflected ambivalence toward "Mother England," for both coupled a rejection of all things British in favor of a separate, American identity with a deep admiration for British culture and values, as signifiers of a superior civilization. The very lack of a well-defined class structure, not to mention a mature political structure, made Americans doubly conscious of status and symbols.[18]

Dolley's awareness of these conflicting currents in America appeared in the first task she set herself. In her efforts to renovate and re-create the President's House, Dolley acted as a political woman, designing a tangible and concrete place for the expression of republican ideals and the political power used to extend them but also making room for aristocratic longings in the new Republic.

THE MADISONS GO TO HOUSEKEEPING

The Madisons had been residents in Washington City since 1801 and had even lived in the "President's Palace" for a short time when they first came to town. When they took possession of the official residence themselves, however, the Madisons went from being house guests and followers of Jefferson to leaders of the Republic and the capital. Participants in, and observers of, the new federal city's growth read a great deal of meaning into the physical environment, seeing development as everything from a telling metaphor for the misplaced pretensions of the new nation to an actual manifestation of the United States' prospects. Washington City's founders intended it to be both a city, with all the cultural, social, and commercial opportunities offered by an urban area, and a national capital, not merely a host to the federal government but also a physical embodiment of republican ideas. The location and the plan for the city contained the hope for a grand future for the Union, not a mere republic but a nation, the "permanent seat of empire."[19]

These two roles, with their high expectations, proved a heavy burden for the infant city, and its development did not match the planners' hopes. Americans saw Washington City as a symbol of nationality, and some became suspicious that its physical shape confirmed that the nation, like the federal city, was only "a magnificent scheme." The half-built structures led the more charitable observer to compare the Americans to dreaming children, attempting a task beyond their capabilities. To the cynical the crude architectural landscape bespoke danger and corruption.[20]

Much of the general disappointment focused on the executive mansion.[21] Whether as a result of bad planning, poor publicity, an indifferent citizenry, or the power makers' own ambivalence about constructing a power center, the White House languished. The symbol of executive power played no part in the ordinary American's life, and Congress only sporadically authorized funding for its upkeep. By locating it a mile and a half away from the legislative buildings, the planners no doubt meant to suggest lofty distance and high rank. In 1808 the effect came closer to suggesting isolation. Few made the trip to the White House, save on New Year's Day, the Fourth of July, or for one of Jefferson's intimate dinner parties. Because of the small numbers invited to these dinners, most members of Congress saw the president in his house only once or twice a term.[22]

Even before the Madisons had completely moved into their new home in March 1809, Dolley made it clear that the situation was about to change, as she launched her first renovation and decorating project in the executive mansion. The order in which rooms were completed, what she bought, and how she used objects reveal clearly that she did not design a comfortable fireside for a weary husband, a private haven in a heartless public world, like a Liberal Mother or a True Woman. Rather, Dolley set out to create a national symbol, a focus for the local Washington communities and the people of the United States, and a space for the day-to-day business of politics. Dolley worked in a milieu that recognized the importance of architecture in nation building. Euro-Americans invented and used many emblems—images with mottoes—and allegorical figures as expressions of political opinions, that is, as propaganda. Architectural metaphors in political discourse abounded, as the "Grand Federal Edifice" stood for the newly crafted Constitution. In 1787 and 1788, during the ratification process, the newspapers slowly constructed a "Temple of Liberty."[23] Dolley made these metaphors and this turn of mind tangible in the panels and decorations, the furnishings and style of the national home.

From the beginning of the process, James Madison turned the whole project over to Dolley. This was an unusual move, for men of that time, knowing the importance of "power houses" as representations of status and importance, often oversaw such activities themselves, picking out fabrics, paints, and eating utensils.[24] To apprehend this facet of upper-class life, we must abandon our culture's idea that decorating a house is a private activity, one overseen by women, and for both of those reasons an act with no public power. In early nineteenth-century America, among white Americans of the upper classes, issues of ruling privilege and public-social power manifested themselves in the manipulation of owned space. When James entrusted Dolley with the re-creation of the White House, he assigned her a public duty, one crucial to establishing his status and his right to rule.

After enlisting the surveyor of public buildings, Benjamin Henry Latrobe (Jefferson's architect and the husband of a childhood friend), Dolley took members of Congress on a tour of the mansion to demonstrate her need for a congressional appropriation. Initially granted $5,000, Dolley and Latrobe spent it so fast "it made heads spin." Eventually, Dolley and Latrobe would spend $12,669.31 of the $20,000 Congress appropriated to the Presidential Furniture Fund.[25]

These two creative people treated this project as a joint venture; their correspondence indicates that they understood their mission as more specific than rendering the shabby mansion habitable. Their initial plans focused on fashioning large public rooms, suitable both for entertaining and for establishing an image of material sophistication. Dolley and Latrobe began with two rooms: the small sitting room (now the Red Room, then called "Mrs. Madison's parlor") and the large oval drawing room. They completed the sitting room, chiefly intended for the reception of ladies during the intricate Washington calling rounds, in time for Dolley's first reception on May 31, 1809. The drawing room, designed for large-scale entertaining, debuted on New Year's Day, 1810. Latrobe was obviously in tune with Dolley's larger visions. Six days after the inauguration and before the Madisons had actually moved into the house, he spent $3,150 on "the most necessary articles of furniture": four pairs of mirrors.[26]

Latrobe's purchase of these mirrors and Dolley's subsequent approval indicate their concern with light in creating an impressive atmosphere—bright in the day, dramatic at night. Dolley's purchases of fine candles and lamps, much ornamental silver, and more mirrors demonstrate that she knew how to use reflective surfaces to make the most of the available light. Her plans for the sitting room illustrate how well she succeeded. A vision of sunniness in yellow (her favorite color), Mrs. Madison's parlor stunned visitors. One described the curtains as "sunflower yellow damask," with "a valance of swags and draperies" not only "topping each window" but continuing "all around the top of the room." These draperies were trimmed "with long and short drops [fringe], silk over bits of wood." This "same yellow damask" appeared on the fireboard "in a fluted pattern known as a 'rising sun.'" Not for a homey, middle-class parlor, the furniture upholstered in yellow satin appeared "elegant with no pretense of comfort." A new carpet, some pier tables and card tables, a pianoforte, and a guitar completed the room's furnishings.[27]

The oval drawing room, site of Mrs. Madison's Wednesday evenings (also known as "drawing rooms"), constituted one of the most elaborate interiors in early nineteenth-century America. Here Dolley's nationalist mission asserted itself most aggressively. With Jefferson's English-style furniture discarded, the Greek style of English furniture maker Thomas Hope prevailed. The whole room echoed a Greek theme, as befitted the new Republic. At a later address before the Society of Artists in Philadelphia, Latrobe explained the choice: "Greece was free; in Greece every citizen felt himself an important part of his republic."[28]

The Greek-style furniture—thirty-six chairs with the insignia of the United States on their backs, two sofas, and four settees at a total cost of $1,111—would have sufficed to carry the theme, but Dolley and Latrobe also added appropriate architectural flourishes, including the anthemion and husks over a looking-glass frame. Latrobe and Dolley disagreed over the curtains; Dolley wanted red damask and, when that proved unavailable, red velvet. With cream paper on the walls and woodwork shadowed in blue and gray, Latrobe fretted that crimson velvet would be too heavy and vibrant for the room: "The curtains! Oh the terrible velvet curtains! Their effect will ruin me entirely, so brilliant they will be."[29]

In the event, Dolley's choice for the curtains proved correct. They reflected and supplemented the light cast by the dozen patent bronze Argand lamps with spiral burners and double lights. Some guests noted an insufficiency of light sources, but many commented on the impression of "blazing splendor" of the drawing room, an effect no doubt achieved by the "brilliant" draperies.[30] Numerous awed and enthusiastic descriptions of these two rooms exist, and Dolley and Latrobe no doubt felt gratified by the reactions their efforts evoked.

Buoyed by success, the pair turned their attention to creating a state dining room out of a former cabinet room. Thomas Jefferson had used a small room for his dinners, but Dolley intended Madison dinners to be truly stately events. Deciding to make do with furniture already in the house, Dolley and Latrobe chose instead to spend their money on the architectural rearrangement of space, which included boarding up windows and installing a heating system.[31] Silverware and china comprised another major expenditure, along with a set of "scarlet japanned waiters," or serving trays ("the largest ever seen"), which Dolley would also use during her levees. Dolley originally wanted the Stuart portrait of George Washington for her drawing room, but Latrobe suggested making the dining room a picture gallery of presidents. James seconded this suggestion, and from eyewitness accounts, the two men prevailed, creating the theme of "the nation's dining room." Deprived of this iconic status symbol for her own space, Dolley substituted a portrait of herself.[32]

Befitting the theme of the nation, the art chosen to adorn the White House walls reflected patriotic rather than personal tastes. Though the paintings and engravings the Madisons displayed at their home, Montpelier, portrayed a variety of subjects, the theme of the White House art was definitely nationalistic, including portraits of heroes and statesmen and historic scenes. American manufacturers quickly discerned the display and marketing possibilities of association with the home of the First Family, so glassware and china manufacturers sent their wares to the house for presidential use.[33]

The documents contradict the long-held notion that Dolley and Latrobe filled the house with French furniture and designs. Though some of the most expensive china may have been French, the state dining service was almost certainly English Staffordshire, while American manufacturers supplied the bulk of the furniture and accessories, no doubt a conscious decision by the woman who arranged for her husband to wear (as the press noted approvingly) an American-manufactured suit at his inauguration. The erroneous impression of Francophilia stemmed no doubt from the Madisons' ideological and aesthetic commitments to French furniture and French taste. They began collecting pieces during their early years in Philadelphia, decorating their first Washington homes and later Montpelier with their acquisitions. But White House rooms had to present a public image for all Americans, one that could not embrace France too closely, no matter how republican (and anti-British) it would seem.[34]

The Madisons and Benjamin Latrobe knew that their audience would be composed of European diplomats, accustomed to refinement and convention; Federalists, for whom formality and elegance signaled a proper attitude toward tradition and power; and more democratically minded Americans from across the country. Dolley's genius lay not in her taste but in her ability to combine Republican simplicity with Federalist high style. With the objects she chose, she created a public space for the executive that reassured both Federalists and Republicans alike, while impressing European visitors and officials with the sophistication of the new nation.[35]

And the result of all this effort? The White House became a focus for visitors of all nationalities and all classes. This period marks the beginning of the American people's identification with "their" house.[36] "The President's House is a perfect palace," enthused one visitor, and descriptions dating from this time are many and favorable. It is hard to measure the influence of architecture on the public mind or the degrees of attachment, legitimacy, or reassurance it provides. But perhaps Henry Dearborn's conflation of the government with its built environment can give some indication. Dearborn, who had been secretary of war under Jefferson, assured his correspondent regarding the new president and his new heads of departments: "The materials of which the white house and other large houses are composed are pretty well known and many of our best friends are more uneasy than I think they have any good grounds for." Nation building requires that the people see themselves as properly ruled, and successful governors accomplish this through persuasion, rather than force. Such efforts require the use of symbols and other visual statements, of precisely the kind Dolley provided.[37]

In addition to being a national symbol, this public space in which Dolley would fashion a public image was also a stage set. In her first appearances in her new rooms, she often dressed in buff or yellow satin while entertaining in her parlor and in contrasting crimson at her drawing rooms.[38] Her visitors became not only her audience but players in their own right. Quite aside from its symbolic function, Dolley intended the White House for practical use. As the next step in her goal to make the executive mansion the focal point of Washington City, Dolley reached out to the various communities that comprised the elite citizens of the capital.

THE POLITICS OF COMMUNITY

Washington City in 1809 had changed somewhat from the primitive facility that first greeted the government community in 1801. The streets remained swamps in the spring, but newly arrived travelers and congressional families discovered a new turnpike and a bridge connecting the city to the more civilized charms of Alexandria, Virginia. Foreign observers, even the difficult British minister George Jackson, still commented on the "great beauty of the neighborhood" and the "beautiful prospect." Optimistic Frances Few found advantage in necessity: "The main river, the distant hills, and the surrounding woods make the view charming and houses are such a distance from each other as not at all to impede the view." The slow progress of civic improvements and development reflected Washington City's unique situation. Rather than beginning with a concentrated population center from which the urban landscape slowly grew, Washington City resembled "a loose collection of urban landmarks lightly laid on an established rural landscape," a big empty canvas waiting to be filled in.[39]

But some urban changes could not wait for the completed picture. The white population of all classes continued to grow, with almost all of the new arrivals connected to politics or the government. Thus, before the buildings were complete, Washington City realized its essential nature as a one-company town. Whether because of the general instability of the economic climate of the early nineteenth century or to the specific caution of investors toward this speculative city, no large-scale business or economic diversity developed. Without the commercial or manufacturing bases dreamed of by George Washington and other early promoters, the city grew unnaturally dependent on the government, a development most problematic in the area of civic improvements.[40]

With little industry and a single function as a government center, the city soon developed a highly stratified social structure. The top level consisted of the extremely wealthy local planters and investors, the former often families of long residence in the area, the latter newcomers. The vast majority occupied the bottom sections and consisted of African-American and other dark-skinned slaves, free blacks, white and black laborers, and artisans. The middle section of this pyramid—the white middling folk, skilled artisans, and low-ranking professionals who provided the adhesive for most American communities—barely existed.[41] This wildly unequal social structure produced many consequences, not the least of which was a local community with little sense of community. Perhaps if left to their own devices, the local elites could have come to some kind of accommodation. However, the seasonal influx of people from every state in the Union and all over the world confused the situation and retarded the process of community identification.

The existence of two social elites signaled another unique feature of Washington City. The glamorous, frantic pace of the official elites in the short but politically charged congressional season far overshadowed the social efforts of the underdeveloped local elites. The language used by a nineteenth-century historian to describe James Madison's inferior cabinet corresponds closely with what modern sociologists recognize as the usual pattern of city elite formation: that an upper class is drawn together by "established fashions," "sympath[ies] of tastes and habits," and "bond[s] of union growing out of previous acquaintance." An urban elite, whether it controls all aspects of city life (as it did in Boston) or divides the urban structure into controlled sections (as was true in New York and Philadelphia), consists of long-established families who share common origins and ties. These elites live beside each other in neighborhoods, send their children to the same schools and dancing academies, belong to the same clubs and churches, and lie side-by-side in cemetery plots. Their children remain in the area; intertwined in their families' wealth and influence structures, they intermarry and thus perpetuate family power. Cohesion, solidarity, continuity, and hegemony over their social environment comprise commonalties shared by all elite groups.[42]

The two Washington elites shared none of these characteristics. If "geographical diversity and high rates of turnover" are two aspects deleterious to forming an elite, they perfectly fit the official elite, with their seasonal migration. The local elite fared little better. Until a city plan was laid on top of the rural landscape, the planters and landowners did not consider themselves as living in connection with each other. Even when Washington City became a reality, they still did not share the urban neighborhoods that would create elite cohesion. Though it did enjoy the geographical stability the official elite lacked, the local community could never achieve the economic and political dominance expected of an elite class. Any attempt to do so met with formidable obstacles, for no industry provided rapidly expanding independent wealth. After 1802 local government rested in the "hands of a capricious Congress," and district residents had no representation. But they tried. Margaret Bayard Smith noted that "city boosters tried all sorts of schemes, all largely unsuccessful to lure wealthy families to the new capital city." Such as they were, these permanent residents formed a social matrix, albeit a fragile one, that held together a city composed largely of transients.[43]

Margaret Bayard and Samuel Harrison Smith must be included in this category of leading families, though they occupied an anomalous position. The couple moved to Washington to take up a political, though not a government, job, but their forty-four-year tenure in the city differentiated them from the mostly transient official population. As a newspaper editor, Samuel Harrison Smith was a local businessman as well as a "semiofficial," acting as recorder of congressional proceedings. The prominent couple cemented their position in the community in 1810, when Samuel sold his newspaper, and they became local landowners. For a few years they entertained solely at their home, Sydney (near the present-day campus of Catholic University), but they soon began taking a house in town for the congressional season because Margaret Bayard Smith missed society. Bayard Smith involved herself in female charity networks, and Harrison Smith invested in local projects. These investments were risky; when the Washington Theater burned down in 1820, the Smiths, along with richer families, lost a great deal of money. Local families—the wealthy Van Nesses, the aristocratic and eccentric Thorntons, the staunchly Republican Smiths, and others like them—literally constructed the Washington City community, in both tangible and intangible ways.

Though later the two elites would grow more compartmentalized, in the early days of the city the local gentry socialized freely with the upper-class elements of the official elite. The two groups needed each other to create a circle big enough to be interesting. Certainly, any visitor of interest—whether a female political economist or a sham European nobleman—attended functions hosted by and including members of both groups. Nineteenth-century historian Samuel Busey noted that during this time the social life in the capital "became more representative of the American spirit and character, and distinctly known as 'Washington society.'" Dolley Madison was not the sole author of this accomplishment; Margaret Bayard Smith and Marcia Burnes Van Ness also tried to bridge the gaps between groups. But because of her high visibility and position, Dolley's efforts to create solidarity among the governmental and local families had more dramatic effect. Later First Ladies and official social leaders would welcome or merely tolerate locals in their social circle, but Dolley and James actively cultivated relations with these families.[44]

Personal interactions aside, James and Dolley also participated in and supported their friends' local projects, making appearances at many of the fledgling society's efforts. They attended the annual three-day horse races, along with the members of Congress, which adjourned especially for the occasion. Though Dolley did not dance herself, she presided over the Dancing Assembly, combining her own sparkling personal presence with her official sanction. Intersocial activities may have seemed only reasonable developments, blending personal friendship with smart politics, but subsequent events would reveal the crucial value of these efforts.

If cementing the shallow-rooted and heterogeneous local community seemed like a tough job, bringing together the official elite must have seemed akin to cleaning the Augean stables. By the time Dolley took her place as official society's leader, patterns had been set, the most influential being the uneasy mixing of diverse men and families with politics as their only common tie. "I have given you every information of a political nature which this city affords," wrote Albert Gallatin to Hannah Nicholson Gallatin. "As to politics, you may suppose that being all thrown together in a few boardinghouses, without hardly any other society than ourselves, we are not likely to be either very moderate politicians or to think of anything but politics." In this isolated outpost, "a few indeed drink and some gamble but the majority drink naught but politics and by mixing with men of different or more moderate sentiments, they inflame one another."[45]

The fragmented nature of the political community might be traced to the spatial separation of the living and working quarters of the members of the various governmental branches, a separation built into the landscape and based on constitutional roles. In addition, the republican horror of powerful government discouraged cooperation among legislators (lest it seem like collusion), so to soothe their constituents, the representatives and senators adopted the pose of outsiders and loners. These antipower attitudes, coupled with the generally dreary state of boardinghouse life, ensured that "political society [was] the antithesis of desirable human relations."[46]

Certainly the members of the legislative and executive branches found considerable obstacles to solidarity. Washington City contained the most regional- and class-diverse group of Americans to be found in one place. Lacking common ties of almost any kind, the Washington community operated without any of the usual qualifications or rules of community building. An official society forced these very different folks into close contact with each other. Urban societies familiar to the new Washingtonians used standards of money, breeding, family background, or personal character in determining who was to be included or shunned. In Washington City, merely official status entitled the holder of a particular office to the place in society assigned to that office.[47] It seemed that political power might come to replace social standing.

Personal observations and stories reveal the reality of pronounced sectional differences among the official population and the attendant dismay, shock, distaste, and anxiety.[48] In addition, American men were beginning to elect representatives from other than the ruling classes, another arena of otherness that did not pass unnoticed. Humorous anecdotes abound concerning the consequences of this influx of unfamiliar types of men, women, and children into settings (official and unofficial) once exclusively dominated by families of the elite class. These stories play on incongruity and often feature butchers as the symbol of comic extremity. In one tale a new congressman, upon observing the miserably lean piece of mutton on the White House table, so forgot his new standing as to exclaim "that at his stall no such leg of mutton should have ever found a place."[49]

According to another yarn, at a dinner given for an American cabinet member and his wife, the hostess, Mary Bagot, the British minister's wife and self-described "Exile in Yankeeland," caught sight of a woman with her arm up to the elbow in a salad bowl. Unable to restrain herself, Mrs. Bagot blurted out, "My dear Mrs. S——, what can you be doing?" The American guest replied promptly: "Only rollicking for an onion, my lady!" In 1807 Margaret Bayard Smith in high amusement regaled her niece with a story of two senators who had never before seen a piano. Though these two visitors were "venerable," and one was a judge, they "suppos[ed] all Susan's sweet melody was drawn by chance or random from this strange thing."[50]

Regional and class differences might have existed as charming oddities if not for the fierce party rivalry that rendered them dangerous for the Union and the business of government.[51] Awareness of the precarious nature of the Republic's situation infuses letters and diaries from the time. European-born Federalist and local landowner Rosalie Stier Calvert often predicted that disunion would be the result of continued democratic rule, resulting in a king in the South. Threats of and hopes for disunion flourished when the constitutional convention had barely finished; South Carolina threatened to secede in the 1790s. Conflicts in Congress erupted not only between parties but even within them. Republican New York congressman Samuel Mitchill explained, in answer to his wife's query, that the Republicans "quarrel[ed] so" among themselves because "the majority is too great. The minority is too inconsiderable to keep them in order." With no one on the other side to contend with, men "(who are disputing animals) . . . rather than be easy . . . quarrel among themselves."[52]

The years of the embargo and war were especially disruptive. The congressional overturn of 1810, in which half the older members of the House (most of whom were against the war) lost their seats to the "War Hawks" led by Henry Clay and John C. Calhoun, indicates the unstable nature of this population. The embargo brought a flood of visitors, merchants, and others "formerly immersed in business . . . [who] now find it convenient to indulge their curiosity in visiting the seat of government."[53]

From her earliest days as a cabinet wife, Dolley strove to bring the various constituencies of Washington City, if not exactly together, at least into some sort of harmonious whole. In the early nineteenth century, the rest of America was engaged in the construction of a middle class, a task that carried its own concerns. What can class mean in an increasingly democratic culture? Who from the lower orders would be allowed into this middle class? What elite niceties and values should be part of their class consciousness? Which upper-class standards should be rejected as dangerously aristocratic and corrupting in a republic?

Dolley and the other political players in Washington City had quite a different job: they had to create a ruling class. Society in other big cities could decide if birth or wealth or pianos in the parlor determined class standing; in Washington City, a town built on politics, the parameters were much clearer. Society had to include butchers and their wives, country folk with no education, southerners whose only claim to distinction was money made off the backs of slave labor, because these were the people that the voters had sent to the capital. In a strict Marxian formulation, class status is determined by relationship to (and control of) the means of production. In Washington City the means of production was the government itself. Government had many products, but a ruling class had to create and build the machine.

If the 1790s were an "Age of Passion," the 1810s were an age of anxiety and passion, with the capital as its nervous center. The official and cultural unease with power, coupled with the pose of mere sojourner adopted by individual members of Congress, boded ill for the state of the Union generally and proved disastrous for the process of constructing a working governmental structure. The growth of the nation-state depends on the existence of a modern political system run by interchangeable functionaries. To achieve this, the participants in the bureaucracy and legislature must share a language of state.[54] If the work environment precludes this kind of community formation, cohesion can occur within a social context, and precisely here Dolley Payne Todd Madison found the greatest scope for her abilities.

HIGH SOCIETY AND HIGH POLITICS

Having lived alongside Thomas Jefferson for eight years, in a southern culture that prized hospitality, Dolley and James understood the importance of social events. Early in the Madisons' partnership, Dolley took charge of this element of their personal and political lives. In 1807 Samuel Latham Mitchill focused on the centrality of society in evaluating

ed these dinners as official by a conscious invocation of Americanness. Though the Madisons served Continental food on occasion and French wine frequently, she actively sought recipes from all over the country to feature on her table. Some guests expressed surprise that though "the dinner was certainly very fine," it was not as fancy as they had expected, "not surpass[ing] some I have eaten in Carolina." The exchange of recipes between women of that time, especially southern women, served as an invitation to and a reinforcement of intimacy. In her quest for regional dishes, Dolley built bridges with elite families all through the infant United States. She offered her "receipts" as part of the transaction, including the exotic ice cream wrapped in warm pastry, a forerunner to baked Alaska. Perhaps this small part Dolley played in introducing ice cream to families across the country explains why popular lore ascribes the invention of this most American of desserts to her.[60]

However adept Dolley proved herself at adapting time-honored social customs, the most important social institution of the early Republic was one of her own invention, one that most directly contrasts with Jefferson's dinner parties. Mrs. Madison's Wednesday night drawing rooms began on March 30, 1809, and lasted through both terms.[61] At some points before and during the War of 1812, they provided the only place where political enemies met and talked civilly. Dolley accomplished and extended many of her goals and projects with these soirees, for they integrated official and local elites; provided an event for visitors, distinguished and ordinary, that allowed them to feel a part of the national scene; and established her White House as the focal center of Washington. Above all, Dolley's drawing rooms created a new kind of political space, one that afforded access to men in power and, like European court events, allowed for the participation of women and other political family members. The style of Dolley's entertaining reflected and created the substance, as she made her contributions to reconciling the tensions between aristocracy and democracy in an American political and social style.

In creating her own style, Dolley had precedents to choose from, pioneered by Martha Custis Washington and Abigail Smith Adams. The tensions between aristocratic-monarchical impulses and republican-democratic energies in American culture manifested themselves immediately in the establishment of a ruling style for a republic. The paradoxical title bestowed on Martha and Abigail's collective efforts, the "Republican Court," accurately reflects the tension between two elements that seem mutually exclusive and yet must be accommodated. Americans, especially the increasingly important middling classes, made clear their unwillingness to abandon the positive courtly qualities of gracious ease and dignity, preferring instead to marry them to the high ideals of republican simplicity. As they invented a role for the president's wife, the first First Ladies took on this task to stabilize their respective husbands' governments. Though possessing very different personalities, Martha and Abigail both strove to create personae that contrasted with a queenly one, using a dignified, formal style that could command respect without a crown or a throne.[62]

By assuming the role of innovator, Martha also acted as a lightning rod for criticism of her husband and cultural anxieties about aristocratic impulses. In a pattern Dolley and later First Ladies would recognize, Martha, and Abigail after her, garnered quite conflicting opinions about their Republican Court. As official wives often deflected and absorbed criticism, they (and other elite women in the culture) also served as repositories for the "courtly dignities" Americans secretly cherished.[63] Later in the nineteenth century, True Woman rhetoric portrayed middle-class women as guarding the ideals of disinterestedness and charity in a culture that prized these qualities, even as it found them increasingly incompatible with a competitive marketplace. In the early years of the nineteenth century, elite and upper-class women began serving both as the vessels of inappropriate longings for aristocratic forms and targets for opprobrium.

Much controversy surrounded the question of titles in the early Republic, but official discussions made clear that the president would not be addressed as "Your Majesty." Not part of the official discourse, titles for women thus remained possible, though the use of them would arouse all the ambivalence Americans felt about royalty. John Fenno, a strong Federalist, meant to honor Martha Washington with "Lady Washington," but instead he ignited a storm of controversy. Nevertheless, he continued to use the term and even dubbed other society women with the same honorific, a practice that became widespread in the culture, even among ordinary Americans.[64] Martha never used the title, but she never publicly repudiated it.[65] Americans from all classes would go further in Dolley

Madison's case, repeatedly proclaiming her the "Queen of Washington City." Like Martha, Dolley never commented publicly on this practice; unlike Martha, she affirmed the appellation constantly.

Dolley was far from alone in using material culture in social and political ways; indeed, modern scholars note the development of what they designate "vernacular gentility" in precisely this period. The rising middle class largely invented this force in American life, one as important to its development as Christianity or capitalism. Vernacular gentility provided a hands-on way of weaving democracy into the fabric of American culture. More strongly informed by democratic ideals of accessibility than by the elite styles of women like Dolley, the new gentility nonetheless incorporated some of the finer points of upper-class ways as an American social milieu was created. The evolution of middle-class gentility carefully blended aristocratic and democratic elements to form a palette of tasteful and subdued neutrals. Dolley's personal solution, which preceded that of the middle class, involved no tertiary shades. Her palette consisted of rich, vibrant hues laid out side by side.[66] Aristocracy, embracing both graciousness and fussy precision, blazed next to democracy, including both social equality and dirty boots on the carpet.

POLITICAL PARTIES

Presidential ceremonies, even today, must always be considered in the larger context of the battle between aristocratic and democratic impulses. Nowhere is this more true than in examining Dolley's social events. Truly an innovator, she also built successfully on the work of her predecessors, and subsequent executive and legislative social events only played variations on her themes.[67] She created public ceremonies suitable for a new Republic, and she did it in her own public spaces.[68] The Madisons dubbed their entertainments "drawing rooms," a more democratic appellation than "levées," though the functions were based on the same notion of accessibility to the president that had fueled the Washington and Adams events. Differentiated from every other party in town, they also went by the nicknames "Wednesday Night" and "Mrs. Madison's crush" or "squeeze." It is notable that in an era so patriarchal that a husband could refer to "*my* child" even in communicating with his wife, people identified these parties as "Mrs. Madison's."

In the beginning Dolley placed announcements of the drawing rooms in the newspapers as a general invitation. No one could attend the drawing room without having been introduced to James and Dolley, but some visitors came bearing written introductions. This restriction was not onerous, no more than that "prevailing in private drawing rooms."[69] However, even this rudimentary rule may have fallen by the wayside. Later sources indicate that the drawing rooms were open to Americans from many classes.

Precursors to the modern cocktail party, these soirees required that the majority of guests stand throughout the event. A few chairs were scattered about for ladies who needed a respite. Martha Washington's (and later Abigail Adams's) levees had been held in fairly informal settings but were characterized by courtly procedures and postures. In contrast, Dolley's events combined the most formal of settings with extensive freedom of movement. During the evening groups of guests formed, broke up, and reformed as people moved through the three large public rooms Dolley had created. In her political novel *What Is Gentility?* Margaret Bayard Smith described the crowd following Mrs. Madison, who, unlike the regally seated Martha Washington, was also on the move.[70] Sometimes there would be music, instrumental and vocal, while black slaves and possibly white servants carried the huge japanned waiters through the crowd, serving coffee, tea, wines, punch, and light foods.

Washington Irving, newly arrived in the capital, worried about his lack of introduction but upon receiving one at the last moment, "swore by the gods I would be there. . . . I mounted with a stout heart to my room, resolved to put on my pease-blossoms and silk stockings, gird up my loins, and sally forth on my expedition." Irving approached the drawing room, "like a vagabond knight-errant," "trust[ing] to Providence for his success." He describes emerging "from dirt and darkness into the blazing splendor of Mrs. Madison's drawing room. Here I was most graciously received." Mrs. Madison, Irving noted approvingly, "is a fine, portly, buxom dame, who has a smile and a pleasant word for everybody." James Madison, on the other hand, cut a poor figure: "Ah! poor Jemmy!—he is but a withered little apple-John." Catharine Akerly Mitchill attended many of these "genteel squeeze[s]" during her years in Washington. She described to her sister the "dainties" served, including ice cream, complaining that when they came round, one was "obliged to keep a sharp look out . . . it was almost impossible for the servants to get near everyone, and if they attempted it, the good things would all slip away before they succeeded."[71]

Dolley created a social milieu peculiar to Washington City, one which Frances Trollope would later describe as having "so little attention to ceremony . . . [that] it is possible that many things may be permitted there, which would be objected to elsewhere." This power of possibility did very nicely for a political environment of bureaucrats, legislators, and other officials trying to create a working structure. By inventing these soirees Dolley constructed a political space unlike any other in Washington. In contrast to Jefferson's rigidly controlled dinner tables, which accommodated no private conversations, Dolley's soirees allowed for a fluid, freewheeling atmosphere of political activity, one that could take in all numbers and combinations of people, encouraging display and offering ample opportunity for private conversation. By regularly providing a large space everyone could count on, a place "to see and be seen," as Catharine Akerly Mitchill proclaimed, Dolley ensured that political business of all kinds could take place.[72]

Unlike Jefferson's dinners, the Wednesday nights included Republicans and Federalists, cabinet secretaries, and members of Congress. In addition to accommodating partisan government officials, the open-house nature of the events allowed for visitors, "gentlemen from New York" and other parts of the country in Washington on "visits of business or pleasure"; wives, daughters, and other female members of political families; and kin from across the country. Dolley created the political space, and then she invited everyone to participate. Margaret Bayard Smith observed that "the drawing room—that center of attraction—affords opportunity of seeing all those whom fashion, fame, beauty, wealth or talent have rendered celebrated." She estimated that "seldom . . . less than two or three hundred, and generally more" people attended the Wednesday nights during the winter after the 1812 war.[73] Little wonder attendees dubbed them "squeezes"!

Not everyone loved Dolley's drawing rooms, and though many described the events with enthusiasm, many negative accounts exist as well. Some hated the crush, the noise, the refreshments, or the kinds of people one met. In 1810 a newcomer to the city, Abijah Bigelow, representative from Massachusetts, attended "Mrs. Madison's levée" for the first time and left declaring, "Once more will suffice for me." He elaborated on his dissatisfaction, beginning with the refreshments: "Wine and Punch, neither very good, is carried round, and ice creams, which I did not taste of, and which those who did said were poor." Bigelow was aghast at the company (he spied "that infamous scoundrel Turreau," the French minister), disappointed by the appearance of the president, and unaffected by the physical presence of the charismatic Dolley, whom he described as "a large, stately woman, not handsome, but decent and her cheeks red, undoubtedly with paint. So much for this levée." Mary Bagot was even more critical and cursory: "The men—many of whom come in boots and perfectly undone and with dirty hands and dirty linen—stand mostly talking with each other in the middle of the rooms. Tea and coffee and afterwards cold punch with glasses of Madeira and cakes are handed round, and by ten o'clock everyone is dispersed." Given so many complaints (some politicians complained repeatedly), one might wonder why everyone continued to go. The answer is quite simple: they could not afford not to go, as the drawing room offered rare political opportunities.[74]

The chief commodity supplied by these weekly gatherings was access—the building block of interest groups, the first step toward fashioning a working political culture. Access begins the process of communication and then nurtures the personal relationships that keep the political machine running. Formal structural relations are "rarely neutral . . . handicap[ping] some efforts and favor[ing] others." Unequal distribution of this advantage leads to much extraofficial maneuvering. Though they are useful in "marking some . . . limits," describing the "official channels" cannot delineate "all the meanderings of the stream of politics"; power often flows from one point to another in a subterranean process. In the American federal system, the separation of powers, especially between the executive and legislative branches, and the system of checks and balances make it likely that access to one branch of the government is not access to all. Neither does membership in one area automatically ensure a tie or obligation to another.[75]

In such a governmental system, access to officeholders in all branches is central to all of the activities undertaken by politicians to get things done.

These activities could include, but are not limited to, obtaining, giving, or disseminating information; proposing future legislation or political projects; office seeking and patronage; mediating conflicts and compromises; and horse-trading of all kinds. Dolley was very successful in facilitating all of these activities.[76]

Obviously, attending "Mrs. Madison's crush" provided access to the president. James attended these drawing rooms as faithfully as he performed his other duties, shaking hands with everybody. Governmental players from all regions of the country and branches of the government had the chance, once a week, for a personal discussion with him during the course of the evening. Sarah Gales Seaton observed that "Mr. Madison had no leisure for the ladies; every moment of his time is engrossed by the crowd of male visitors who court his notice, and after passing the first complimentary salutations, his attention is unavoidably withdrawn to more important objects."[77]

Diplomatic dispatches most explicitly discuss the political opportunities the drawing rooms offered, especially as war loomed. The secretary of state drew aside French minister Sérurier to assure him that the U.S. government intended to adopt a tougher stance with Great Britain. Augustus John Foster learned that the president "really wishes for war now," becoming "desperate," at a Wednesday evening shortly before the official declaration. In another instance Dolley invited the minister of Spain to her drawing room especially to reconcile a diplomatic conflict.[78]

Plenty of Americans also did their politicking surrounded by the music, refreshments, and noisy chat of the "squeeze." Congressman James Milnor warily avoided the pressing inquiries of the chairman of the Foreign Relations Committee, fobbing him off with "*suitable* answers." Frustrated by Milnor's reticence, the chairman walked away, commenting, "Ah, I am afraid we shan't at this rate go to war with much spirit." The atmosphere and access Dolley created quickly became crucial to the everyday workings of the government, so that when she canceled the drawing rooms for a time in 1813, she closed down an important "avenue of influence."[79]

Even the death of Vice President George Clinton in 1812 did not distract from this crucial activity. Two days later Sophia May, a visitor to the city, observed, "It was generally thought upon the Hill there would not be any levées altogether, but they would not pay even that poor compliment to his memory." It was too important, for according to Dolley, even as Clinton lay dying, "electioneering for his office goes on beyond description."[80]

Contemporary observers also were quite aware of the political uses of the drawing room. "Mr. Madison and Mr. Foster were in very familiar chit-chat at the levée tonight," noted the *New York Evening Post,* in support of its contention that "the whole war fire" would soon "evaporate in smoke." Sometimes the words of enemies provide the most convincing evidence of all. Federalists, and even some Republicans, viewed the political possibilities with which Dolley presented her guests as sinister. The *Alexandria Gazette* believed that James Madison wanted war and had convinced Congress to vote for it by use of Dolley's weekly entertainments, what it termed "his extravagant imitations of a royal court, levées . . . at which so many congressional attendants bow and cringe, and dangle and play the parasite."[81]

While Dolley's political parties offered the opportunity to participate in politics to a wide group of citizens and partisans, she had her own particular mission: to deal with and guide a fractious Congress, which Madison described as "unhinged."[82] No president had a worse Congress. Part of the problem lay in the growing institutionalization of what had been in Jefferson's time a motley crew of individuals. Congress, like a rebellious adolescent, was discovering its own power, its members fighting against the president and among themselves over the declaration of war. Once James Madison declared war, the legislators' hostility escalated. Several times the infighting threatened to split the Union, culminating in the Hartford Convention's unsuccessful bid for secession in 1815.

In an effort to curb executive power, the framers of the Constitution had deliberately provided no legislative representation for the president. Hence, ordinary citizens had a far better chance of influencing legislators, by their votes and their formal and informal petitions, than did the president. The living and social spaces of Washington City mirrored the constitutional separation of powers; until Dolley's tenure in the White House, the congressional community had conducted a separate social life.[83]

When official channels fail or do not exist, however, social settings assume a greater importance. Dolley's soirees contributed mightily to the formation of the alliances and structures that moved Congress into pre-eminence immediately following the war. The emergence of stars, such as Webster, Calhoun, and Clay, testifies to the body's growing importance in the 1810s, but the less celebrated members' ability to build their own power structures also demonstrates the increasing influence of the legislature. This was a pivotal time in the development of that institution, and Dolley no doubt played a part, both intended and unintended. Her primary motivation in establishing good relations with the members undoubtedly stemmed from her desire to help her husband.

During the election of 1812, the Federalists decided to boycott Dolley's parties en masse, as a show of solidarity against James. Republicans responded in kind, using attendance to make their statement, flooding the President's Palace with their social presence. Dolley saw the Federalists' act, and another similar attempt by the Republican faction that supported DeWitt Clinton for president, as efforts "to break us." However, the social machinery Dolley set in place did its job, and only a short while later, she reported smugly that "such a rallying of our party had alarmed [the Federalists] into a return." Congressman Harper noted that nothing in the entire session had distressed and mortified the Federalists more than "finding that the Republicans, in consequence of their conduct, paid their respects to Mrs. Madison almost to a man."[84]

Like Thomas Jefferson, Dolley attracted the members, cajoling, charming, and bullying them, in a gracious way, of course. Her letters to her family and friends reveal that she knew the conflicts her husband faced and her importance to him. When reassuring her "adopted" daughter, Phoebe Morris, that James Madison was doing all he could to obtain an appointment for Phoebe's father, Dolley exclaimed in exasperation: "There is nothing to be done in such times as these! Mr. Madison is anxious to employ your Papa in some good place, entirely within his own gift, when we should not be subject to the political or personal objections of a capricious Senate (almost treason, my dear) but it is really true that M. has but a small voice, at present, in appointments that go into the House."[85] Through James, Dolley eventually secured the appointment for Anthony Morris (as minister to Spain). More often, she obtained posts not by involving the president but by relying on her own congressional and bureaucratic contacts. During her social events Dolley gathered and gave information, made connections between people, and secured offices for her friends and family. But her primary goal was to bind people to her and her husband, which she did by sheer force of personality and willingness to play politics.

Contemporary observers agree that the "Lady Presidentess" secured a second term for her husband with her social lobby.[86] James Madison was elected under the old system, before congressional reforms, when the president was nominated or renominated by a party caucus in Congress.[87] In this system cultivation of individual members made the difference, and that was Dolley's job. Among the members of the 1810 Congress, it was no coincidence that her closest new friend was the rising power, Henry Clay, and she counted John C. Calhoun among her intimates as well. When Dolley and Henry Clay began sharing a snuffbox, they signaled their new political intimacy to insiders.[88]

Dolley's friendships with individual congressmen allowed her access to arenas that blurred the line between the political and the personal. Dueling and other affairs of honor, rampant at the time, operated not as expressions of uncontrolled anger but as part of the dominant political language. Dolley interceded between two congressmen from Virginia, the brilliant but erratic John Randolph and Jefferson's son-in-law John Eppes, who planned to duel as part of their official debate over the Non-Intercourse Act. The fiery Randolph's published apology astonished everybody as "so contrary to custom"; Washingtonians decreed that "all the honor of the affair remains with Mrs. Madison." Her willingness to take so public a role to save John Randolph is significant, given his often violent diatribes against her husband.

Her detached ability to rise above Randolph's rhetoric indicated her own political gifts. In that age politics was so personal that participants saw policy disagreements as attacks on personal honor, and murder, in the form of dueling, comprised part of the political language. Yet Dolley could sit comfortably in the House gallery and listen to Randolph's vituperative attack on her husband's politics and personality, offering as her only public reply: "It was as good as a play."[89] This seemingly neutral comment actually constitutes an adroit put-down that acknowledges the fictive quality of political attack not widely apparent to everyone.

Many "Dolley stories," cited to demonstrate her generous, inclusive nature, show that she foreshadowed a modern attitude toward politics, one that anticipated the need to negotiate within a two-party system. In an age characterized by passion, by heated all-or-nothing rhetoric, Dolley's assumption that compromise would be the salvation of the system marks her as one of the most sophisticated politicians of her time. Power sharing and compromise—the requisites for an effective political culture—seemed inconceivable to the men who held office, but not to Dolley, who built coalitions and connections every week in her drawing rooms. Dolley's techniques, in some ways reminiscent of old-fashioned court styles, did not encompass violent expression. Instead, she accepted the inevitability of partisanship and used it to her husband's advantage. How well she succeeded in her goals may be judged by Daniel Webster's assessment of her at the end of her long career: "The only permanent power in Washington, all others are transient."[90]

Dolley has long been lauded for her welcome and tolerance of families and men of both parties at her social events. Representative from Pennsylvania Jonathan Roberts commented: "Mrs. Madison has acted with singular discreetness during a very embarrassing season. By her deportment in her own house you cannot discover who is her husband's friends or foes." Historians and biographers have viewed this tolerance as a personal quality, as evidence of her good nature and good heart. To them, her ability to welcome men of the rival party into her home, ignoring their public vilification of the president, was natural and certainly not political. Yet for a wife who deeply loved her husband, a woman whose actions demonstrated her fierce loyalty and protective devotion, surely the natural response would have been to forbid those men her door. Her ability to suppress anger and express warmth lay not in her "good heart," though her personality provided a beguiling mask. She disguised her emotions, providing enemies with access to herself, her husband, and other officials, because she was a master politician. Her ability to create a bipartisan milieu of cooperation marks her as the member of the founding generation most like present-day politicians.[91]

Upon entering a room, Dolley drew focus, and her character pervaded all occasions she attended, a quality that would last all of her long life. Because her persona was one of modest, gentle charm, few found her domination obnoxious. Indeed, her physical presence was often observed to have the effect of soothing contentiousness. Catharine Akerly Mitchill, who witnessed the development of social life on the Potomac under Dolley Madison's skillful hand, noted that in those disputatious days, when officials would physically assault each other on the floors of Congress, everyone maintained social decorum and the conventions of polite behavior in Dolley's presence. Far from being generically nice, Dolley put her charisma to specific uses. Bayard Smith wrote that her "uniform good nature, kindness of disposition, frank, gay, cordial manners . . . had softened the asperity of party feeling, disarmed prejudice, consolidated general good will, and won a popularity for her husband which his cold and reserved manners never could have done."[92]

Dolley won adherents for her husband and controlled his enemies not only by making friends but also by manipulating kinship ties. One of the secrets of her influence on Congress lay in her many kin at all levels of government, people she bound closely to herself and her husband. Dolley especially depended on her brothers-in-law. She did not hesitate to call Representative Richard Cutts, husband of her beloved sister Anna, from his home in Massachusetts to Washington to cast his vote for war. Even after his wife Mary Payne Jackson's death, Congressman John G. Jackson still called Dolley, Mary's sister, his closest confidant "in all things."[93] Another sister, Lucy Payne, linked her clan with the Washingtons through her first marriage, and in 1812, as a young widow, she married Thomas Todd, a U.S. Supreme Court justice. Edward Coles, Dolley's cousin, succeeded his brother Isaac Coles as private secretary to both Jefferson and Madison. When Edward fell ill, Dolley stepped into his place and served as her husband's secretary.

One of the chief purposes of society lies in its ability to link families to political and economic institutions. This connection-creating function appears especially valuable to "social groups seeking legitimacy" in geographies with "increased population, urban growth and political realignment," an apt description for Washington City's conditions. By using kinship networks, Dolley ensured ties between elite families and the federal government that benefited her own family, the growing governmental structure, and the new capital.[94] Dolley recognized the function of kinship and the power to create kin from tenuous ties. Almost anyone could be claimed as kin, so deeply and closely woven were the marriage and blood links among the southern gentry families. When she could not find a link, she invented one. Dolley bound an old friend, Anthony Morris, more closely to her family's interests by becoming "Mama" to the widowed Morris's daughter Phoebe, performing many of the services a mother rendered a daughter of marriageable age. Indeed, strong evidence exists that Dolley wanted Phoebe to marry her son, Payne Todd.[95]

Not surprisingly, the family members on whom Dolley focused most attention were wives and daughters. Whenever her husband's cabinet met, she held "dove parties" for the cabinet wives to discuss current events and philanthropic projects. Dolley often brought the wealthy Washington gentrywoman Marcia Burnes Van Ness into this official company to implement projects of benefit and interest to local society and the entire Washington community. To further her contacts with the congressmen who would, among other tasks, renominate her husband in the caucus, she visited every congressional family in Washington, a "physically daunting act" that may have "signaled humility in the president's attitude to legislators." Dolley made it all seem easy. To be sure, the goodwill and energy many biographers attribute to her existed in good measure, but so did conscious choice and dogged determination. After the great election turnover of 1810, with "new members in abundance," she confessed, "I have never felt the entertainment of company oppressive until now."[96] Oppressive it may have been, but she still visited every one of them, as well as Washington visitors, a feat unrivaled by any other First Lady before or since.

If Washington women, both resident and newly arrived, praised and admired Dolley, helping her in any way they could, it may have been because Dolley's presence in Washington as the leading lady of both the Jefferson and the Madison administrations opened up new worlds for them. Her soirees allowed women more freedom than they had ever known in small New England towns or even cities like Philadelphia. Like French salons, the drawing rooms offered aristocratic permissions of conduct and speech for women, freedoms that would fade with the growth of vernacular gentility. As architecture and interior design reflect and reinforce gender difference, so the social space Dolley provided in the White House literally allowed women more scope and movement. By Dolley's constant attendance at congressional debates and Supreme Court deliberations, she not only implicitly suggested that other women partake as freely, but she also openly encouraged them to do so by organizing parties of ladies. Men privately grumbled or, like John Randolph of Roanoke, publicly railed about women in the galleries, but Dolley's popularity and position protected her sisters' newly won privilege.[97]

The unprecedented access to public spaces extended to nonpolitical matters and places, including attendance at horse races, exhibitions, and public restaurants. A Greek visitor to the Tayloes' horse races told his correspondent: "You must not be astonished at hearing that a number of beautiful females were present, sitting exposed on the tops and boxes of carriages, and in other conspicuous seats." To his eyes it appeared that "every line of separation is so entirely obliterated that where there are men you may be sure to meet women. . . . For my part, I have no doubt that the women in the end will ride uppermost."[98]

The picture of women in Washington at this time—women in female or mixed groups, walking and talking freely, engaging in conversations with politicians, at luncheons, orations, public events, and in daily attendance at the President's House—stands in contrast to the Washington City of Jefferson's day. The difference between the new capital and other places did not pass unnoticed by the women themselves. Margaret Bayard Smith remarked: "The women here are taking a station in society which is not known elsewhere. . . . I think the manners here are different from those in other places. At the drawing room, at our parties, few ladies ever sit. . . . The consequence is that ladies and gentleman stand and walk about the rooms in mingled groups, which certainly produces more ease, freedom, and equality than in those rooms where the ladies sit and wait for the gentlemen to approach and converse."[99] Dolley allowed women a presence in Washington in more ways than one. They would make use of their freedom and play a part in creating the next power base in Washington: Congress of the 1810s and 1820s.

In some ways Dolley Madison created a third sphere between public and private, echoing both the eighteenth-century notion of society and the theories of a public sphere of letters that flourished in European coffeehouses. Dolley's social world, however, differed from these models in its complexity and flexibility. Unlike the coffeehouse culture, the social space in Washington City made room for both women and men, acting and interacting in a variety of ways. Here both women and men could appropriate male and female gender prescriptions for their own uses. This kind of society functioned in many settings, from the houses of Congress to private parlors, and accommodated many kinds of goals.

The biggest difference, however, lay in society's political purposes. Eighteenth-century society was supposed to be set off from the realm of politics, and the public sphere served a critical gadfly function in relation to the state. The public society created by political women and their families in Washington was all about politics, in every sense of the word. The public sphere model and the liberal theories of society, filled with contradictions as they are, may be seen as direct precursors of the formation of the middle class in the early nineteenth century, but the class task in Washington City was somewhat different. Rather than seeking to give the middle class a voice and an identity, the work of women such as Dolley was to create a ruling class.

But rather than continuing the process of demarcation and delineation (especially since early nineteenth-century American culture had not yet created a fully coherent private realm with which to contrast the public one), perhaps the most fruitful approach is to see public and private as making up a continuum.[100] A politician or member of a political family could move along the continuum as he or she saw fit. Public and private spheres do exist, not as concrete or distinct categories but as constructs of context. When politics provides the context, the spheres often blend and blur. Seeing houses and rooms not merely as shelters or private expressions of wealth and taste enables us to analyze them as part of an unofficial sphere that makes official interactions possible.

The unofficial space, outside the legitimate public forum, allows more room to maneuver than official space. Its inherent liminality permits the flexibility necessary for the successful transaction of business. At Dolley Madison's drawing room, male politicians used the atmosphere of sociability to propose, to probe, to negotiate, and to compromise. Food, drink, music, conversation in a dramatic setting enabled the release necessary to risk. In a crowded room one may propose matters that would seem too chancy if made in an office. The myriad distractions of the event could be used by both parties to deflect or withdraw if the situation warranted it.

The role of the unofficial space, peopled by unofficial and official actors, remains a mystery in most political history. Part of the reason for this lies in sexism. Whether because a patriarchal society considers that women do trivial things or that things become trivial when women do them, women's very presence signals unimportance. Another explanation exists, however. The very usefulness of the unofficial sphere lies in its unconsidered nature. Exposed to the same objective study and criteria as official documents, it would cease to function advantageously. To make unofficial space useful, its participants must present it as merely the site of a social occasion, a place for relaxation.

As the social center of Washington City, Dolley's drawing room also served as part of the federal government's public sphere. It was indubitably her space, and the interactions there could be classified as emotional or personal. Musicians played, slaves passed food, women in bright, alluring clothing chatted and laughed. At the same time the sources reveal the significant political business that went on in this private, social space. Nineteenth-century historians often mention Dolley's "heart," a convention of the time, in discussions of her social behavior in the drawing room. The leitmotif of heart could apply just as well to the room as to the woman. The heart of the White House, of the federal government's executive branch, lay in the drawing room of the White House. This metaphor should not be read as an argument for the female space as an emotional center, to stand in contrast with an intellectual male space, but instead allows us to view the drawing room as serving the same function as an actual heart, renewing the lifeblood of the city. Dolley's space was a center of activity and life in Washington, circulating the elements that made up the body politic. Emotion and personality thrived in such an environment, to be sure, but that only reminds us that the driest political negotiations can be occasions for personal passion.[101]

Spaces and material culture play other important roles as well, serving as concrete symbols of comfort, security, and stability. Impressions of legitimacy and tradition become especially valuable on a frontier, where the overwhelming wildness of the physical landscape dominates. In an uncultivated environment architecture can take the place of ritual in cementing a culture and a ruling class. Building an expensive house or displaying lavish clothing and jewelry are "acts of faith in a fragile city."[102] Identity symbols provide faith and reassurance in uncertain times, and they were commodities that Washington City needed in abundance during the War of 1812.

THE REPUBLICAN QUEEN

Beyond merely creating the space and ceremonies, Dolley presided as an identity symbol. Descriptions of her physical person dominate discussions of life in Washington City during the Madison administration. At first glance this seems to be nothing but the usual fate of women in a patriarchal culture, to be defined and limited by their physical appearance. However, these descriptions reveal two facts that hint at another interpretation. Dolley was no beauty, no supermodel of the early nineteenth century. Elizabeth Jackson, the Prussian ex-baroness married to an unpopular British minister, described her as "fat, forty, and not fair."[103] More important, the descriptions dwell only partly on the physical; observers tended to project comfort, reassurance, stability, power, and other abstract emotional qualities onto the figure they described. Dolley's ability to personify positive emotional attributes emerged as a legitimating function from the start of the administration, and it escalated during the War of 1812. Both the physical and the emotional descriptions indicate the First Lady's position as the charismatic figure in her husband's administration.

Political scientists consider the charismatic figure a crucial political actor, but political historians study the phenomenon only if the subject is male and an official leader. The charismatic figure was especially important in the days of personal, face-to-face politics. The lack of organized political machinery in early Republican America ensured the prominence of the individual and a focus on questions of personality and character, which often played out as concerns about virtue and honor. Of all the central figures, the president most needed charisma, saddled as he was with a constitutionally mandated powerlessness.[104] Indeed, for the presidency, "the power of the office cannot be divorced from the personal qualities of the man in the office."[105] Whatever charisma is, or could accomplish, it is clear that James Madison did not have it. Jefferson had charisma, a quality he downplayed in his quest to be the republican anticharismatic figure (while, of course, exploiting it when the occasion demanded). Virtue came not from display but from modest retirement. To contemporaries, James Madison's lack of presence demonstrated his visible republican virtue, even while it hampered him as a leader.

Contemporaries and historians have nothing but praise for James's sterling character; observers and friends insisted that in small groups and in unofficial moments, he could be quite witty and even captivating. But they also concede that when it came to large groups, to "presiding," he was at a complete loss.[106] At his inauguration, his first public appearance as the chief executive, Washington Irving's "withered little apple-John" looked "embarrassed." Years later a sympathetic Margaret Bayard Smith described his performance at the event for Sarah Hale's magazine: "When he rose to speak, or rather read his address, he was extremely pale—he seemed scarcely able to stand; with a tremulous and inaudible voice he read what none except a few nearest to him could hear." As James went on, "he gained more composure," though his voice was still "too low and feeble" to carry through the room.[107] And these assessments come from his admirers!

Others were less charitable. One chronicler compared Madison to a "country schoolmaster in mourning for one of his pupils who he had whipped to death." In these descriptions physical attributes and character overlap, leading to the conclusion that though James Madison's republican style reassured those who feared the rise of a monarchy or a demagogue, it did not inspire public confidence. At his own gatherings his insignificance sometimes led guests not to recognize him: "Being so low of stature, he was in imminent danger of being confounded with the plebeian crowds, and was pushed and jostled about like a common citizen." On the other hand, Dolley (who was exactly the same height) seemed to tower over her husband at such gatherings and dominate the crowd. Descriptions note both her physical presence and her commanding personality. Commentators also note admiringly the way she worked the room, with the "skills of a candidate running for office," never forgetting a name or making an inappropriate comment. The contrast between Dolley's and James's respective talents inspired some interesting political humor. Federalist senator John Pope from Kentucky remarked in 1812 that Dolley made "a very good president and must not be turned out." Despite having no official mandate, Dolley displayed a rare talent for sociability, "build[ing] on a role to create a position."[108]

When observers search for the presence or the absence of charisma, physical characteristics (bodily endowments), physical presence (carriage and bearing), and physical appearance (use of adornment and clothing) often serve as indicators of inner gifts. Dolley created herself in part through clothing. As Martha Washington and Abigail Adams combined informal settings with formal movement, the two former presidential wives also preferred to contrast their formal manners with simple dress: plain white muslins and snowy kerchiefs. Dolley chose differently. She reserved white for state occasions, while at her own drawing rooms she wore richly colored satins, silks, and velvets, trimmed with ermine, lace, and other lush accents. In her atmosphere of informal talk and movement, she dressed as a queen, a sartorial choice that did not pass unnoticed: "She really in manner and appearance answered all my ideas of royalty."[109]

Descriptions of her clothing by men and women frequently dwell on her turbans, including one "with a crescent in front and crowned with nodding ostrich plumes"; accessories such as "gold chains and clasps about her waist and wrists"; bonnets, one "of purple velvet and white satin with white satin plumes"; gorgeous gowns, one of "rose-colored satin with a white velvet train"; and other extravagant items. Observers noted, with a range of emotions from amusement to adoration to horror, the regal themes of Dolley's ensembles. No one could imagine Martha Washington in a "robe of pink satin trimmed in ermine," and more than one visitor noted a "silver headdress in the form of a crown." In her last appearance as First Lady, she wore a "white velvet turban trimmed with white ostrich tips and a gold-embroidered crown." Harriet Otis, a lively minded young woman from a Boston Federalist family, noted with New England disapproval "a *sparkling diadem* on her head." Harriet sermonized that "if this people were as jealous of all approaches to royalty as the ancient Romans what would they say[?]"[110]

Modern political sensibility considers clothing and jewelry to belong to the private, frivolous world of women and fashion, but in centuries past they served as rank markers for both women and men, consciously chosen to the purpose by their wearers and as consciously read by observers. The sumptuous apparel displayed by women of the gentry and ruling classes could in every sense be called "power suits." While that modern term usually conveys the image of a woman donning masculine garb to partake in a world of male privilege, the attire worn by women in the late eighteenth and early nineteenth centuries was intensely and utterly differentiated from male clothes.[111] Colorful, luxurious, and alluring, the cut and fabric of these clothes bespoke an ideal of feminine desirability. The grand costumes played on contrasts for effect, in some ways breathtakingly minimal and revealing of female attributes, especially breasts. At the same time skirts, trains, cloaks, and headgear took up considerable space and commanded attention. Such literal intrusion was easier in the days of wigs and crinolines; Dolley's ability to achieve the same domination of space and focus in the more tailored cut of her French clothes and turbans testifies to her personal allure.

Jewelry, too, must be seen as a language, a formal grammar of power, not merely as a decorative expression of personal taste or sexual attractiveness. Women wore elaborate designs and large stones to denote wealth, power, and status, as men wore badges and medals to mark their standing and to signal that they, as individuals, expected deferential treatment. "Hard, glittering, full of mystique," women's stones carried intangible qualities of privilege and place that they transferred to their wearers. Jewelry often passed down through the female line, and individual pieces became recognized as pedigrees.[112]

Dolley clearly understood the power of her jewels, even after she left the Washington bustle. Judith Walker Rives, a young Virginia aristocrat, and her husband William Cabell Rives visited the Madisons in their retirement at Montpelier. The young people were on their way to Washington, where William would take up his first political post and begin a long career as part of America's ruling elite, a position he acquired through his marriage to Judith. Dolley took Judith aside and gave her certain pieces of her own jewelry, advising her to wear them in society in Washington. She indicated that these pieces would be recognized by her friends and signal to Washington society that Judith Walker Rives moved under Dolley's blessings and should be treated accordingly.[113]

Clothing, however, represented only one element in establishing a charismatic presence; bearing or mien also solidified a leader's claim to rule. While praising Dolley's ensembles, many observers hastened to add that her appeal was not merely as a conveyer of clothes. As Sarah Gales

Seaton proclaimed, "'Tis not her form, 'tis not her face, it is the woman altogether, whom I should wish you to see." Dolley, though always a dignified presence, adopted or adapted an even more formal persona before entering on her new station of First Lady. Both Catharine Akerly Mitchill and Margaret Bayard Smith made a note of her modified demeanor. "On the eve of becoming Lady Presidentess," Akerly Mitchill observed approvingly, "she was more than usually dignified in her deportment." Seeing Dolley at the Inaugural Ball, making one of her first public appearances after her husband's installation, Bayard Smith, who had seen her in more playful moments in the preceding nine years, pronounced: "It would be *absolutely impossible* for any one to behave with more perfect propriety than she did. Unassuming dignity, sweetness, and grace."[114]

Dolley lived in a culture that quite self-consciously associated personal bearing with the right to rule. The notion that a leader should look the part had long roots in court behavior. The American Revolution and the dawning of the new Republic shifted, not abandoned, this point of view. Virtue was essential to republicanism, a confluence of personality and public behavior that showed itself in externals; exterior conduct mirrored inner virtue.[115] Dolley was an American, and a republican, but it is also clear that she demonstrated an awareness of the function of charisma worthy of a court lady.

In the milieu of the court, speech and gesture are not what they are in everyday life; instead, they focus on the two goals of courtly government, policy and action. In premodern times valor on the battlefield supplied the criteria for leadership; in an emerging modern capital or court, behavior and words take the place of war. To the best politicians, "conduct becomes so highly structured that life approaches art; the courtier is himself a work of art, his appearance a portrait, his experience a narrative."[116] The minute examinations to which Washington visitors and residents subjected Dolley and their subsequent approval testify to the durability and longevity of courtly ideals.

Though Dolley was not widely traveled—she had never been to Europe, much less to a court—her social appearances demonstrated the posture and ease of motion characteristic of a leader. Not only did simple country folk and Federalist young ladies discern Dolley's consciously evoked royal message, so did people who had spent time with real queens. No officials know better the importance of charismatic performance than diplomats and their spouses, and most of the diplomats who came to the U.S. capital heaped extravagant praise upon Mrs. Madison. A Danish minister who attended many Madison drawing rooms exclaimed, "What need you manners more captivating, more winning, more polished, than those of that amiable woman?" Though he had "resided in all the courts of Europe," he could positively state, "I never have seen any duchess, princess or queen whose manners, with equal dignity, blended equal sweetness." More than clothes, Dolley's bearing carried the message of dignity and political legitimacy. "Her stately person, her lofty carriage, her affable and gracious manner" would make her stand out in "any court in the world." In his praise he admired the democrat in Dolley, who "mov[ed] through admiring crowds, pleasing all, by making all pleased with themselves, yet looking superior to all." He concluded: "She moves like a goddess, and she looks a queen."[117]

Dolley's role as the charismatic figure, her efforts to build political and local communities, to provide the space politicians needed to form parties and coalitions, to privilege political families, and, above all, to give a sense of legitimacy to the whole enterprise—all would be severely tested in August 1814, when the British invaded Washington City. In triumph, the conquerors destroyed the White House and, by doing so, came near to destroying the capital and the Union.

LAST OF THE FOUNDERS

With the declaration of war in 1812, Dolley intensified her efforts to create compromise, community, and unified national sentiment by enlarging the scope of her parties. Her entertaining efforts became more purposeful in the months leading up to the invasion, as James Madison had to cope with enormous pressure from Congress and the country. These parties gave the increasingly divided members of Congress a place to work out their troubles and presented a reassuring face to the American public. Her job was to keep the capital of the nation calm and hopeful, and she rallied her troops to the cause. Sarah Gales Seaton reported that Dolley had called on her to ensure her presence at the next drawing room, urging Gales Seaton, with a military metaphor, "not to desert the standard altogether."[118]

In August 1814, on the eve of invasion, James Madison left the White House to join his troops in defending the city. Dolley ensured her husband's place in history by saving his cabinet papers and her own by rescuing the portrait of George Washington that hung in the state dining room. With her usual perspicacity about people, Dolley knew what it would mean to Americans if the portrait was burned, or worse became a prize of war. She sent it off with two New York gentlemen, instructing them, "Save that picture! Save that picture, if possible; if not possible, destroy it."[119]

Dolley's flight, which captured Americans' imagination almost immediately, only completed her identification with the national cause in the public's mind. Always the more conspicuous of the Madison team, Dolley gained visibility during the war as she consciously assumed an iconic position. The American forces enjoyed few victories, but Dolley made much of military heroes, such as Oliver Hazard Perry and William Henry Harrison, highlighting their achievements and honoring them personally when they came to town. Dolley, not James, spoke to the troops—"presenting them with an elegant standard, accompanied by a patriotic address"—and christened ships. When the Americans captured the British warship *Macedonian*, the crew presented the ship's flag to her during her drawing room. As they spread the British standard at her feet, a rare glimpse of the emotions behind Dolley's public persona emerged; one observer reported, "I saw her color come and go."[120] To the American audience, and especially to Washingtonians, Dolley was the public personification of the war effort.

This identification of the war with Dolley, the charismatic figure of the Madison couple, would continue after the British burned Washington City. After days of wandering around the countryside, James and Dolley reunited and returned to view the desolate ruins of the republican dream-city that had been under their care. Dolley angrily railed against the English, wishing aloud as she observed American soldiers marching by her window that "we had ten thousand such men as were passing *to sink our enemy to the bottomless pit.*" Then depression set in. William Wirt described the president as "miserably shattered and woebegone. In short, he looks heartbroken." Dolley, too, seemed "much depressed, she could scarcely speak without tears." However, her discouragement did not last long. The woman who had declared earlier in the war that "though a Quaker," she kept "the old Tunisian saber within reach," was a woman of action.[121]

Even before the last fires died down, Washington City faced an even greater threat to its existence: the issue of relocating the capital. The temptation to move was great, especially since, on August 27, the "select and common councils of the city of Philadelphia" issued a generous invitation, offering ample buildings for the public offices and departments, as well as housing for all members of the government. Logistically, such a move would have delayed by many months the reactivation of the federal government. But the greater danger was psychological. The growth or even survival of the federal government, and to a very real extent the Union, depended on the existence of a stable capital. No doubt the New England Federalists would have seized upon the confusion, disorder, and psychological image of retreat to press a case for secession or worse.

To resolve this pressing issue, President Madison insisted that Congress meet early in the term, and on September 19, 1814, less than a month after the disastrous British invasion, debates began with members crowded in temporary lodgings. Expected to last several days, the discussion in the House went on for four weeks and took three and a half additional months to be acted upon officially by both Senate and House. Some legislators argued for removal in an attempt to gain the capital for their home region. Others as vociferously contended that any removal would show the British that they had won. Pro–Washington City forces quickly booed down a compromise motion for temporary removal; as Nathaniel Macon, representative from North Carolina, stated, "If the seat of government was once set on wheels, there was no saying where it would stop." After a prolonged battle the Congress decided by a small margin that the capital should stay in the ten miles square chosen by General Washington.[122]

Though personal attachment and/or self-interest did not appear as an official argument, it is hard to imagine that it played no role in individual legislators' pro–Washington City positions in the debate. The city's lack of development meant that any attraction or advantage it had lay in large part in the vigorous official society Dolley had initiated. Under her direction a power structure—woven of kinships, friendships, and other personal contacts—had begun to develop, a configuration that many congressmen used for political and financial advantage. These structures would be hard to replicate in another city, especially an older, established one, with its own social elites and governing organizations already in place. Perhaps surprisingly, region and party did not always dictate where a legislator would fall on the issue. Northern legislators did have regional advantage in mind when they argued for Philadelphia or New York as a new home "for the political ark," but even some New Englanders championed Washington City.[123]

Dolley's strongest allies in the fight to keep the capital in Washington City proved to be the local families she had so assiduously cultivated and the resulting connections and channels of communication between the official and local elite communities. Fearing financial ruin if the capital moved, the local gentry eagerly offered money and services. The initial funding for rebuilding came not from the government but from local banks. Thomas Law, a British aristocrat who emigrated and married into the Custis-Washington clan, used diplomacy, influence, his talented pen, and his deep purse to retain the Congress in Washington. He, Daniel Carroll of Duddington, and others subscribed to funds and erected a building—the "Brick Capitol"—which they offered to Congress. John Van Ness and Richard Lee, as part of the city association, proposed to erect other public buildings. The members of the government accepted help from the local men with whom they and their families socialized at Dolley's soirees and dinners. The Van Nesses also provided the kind of psychological boost Dolley could appreciate when they built their new mansion in the city only months after the invasion. Never ones to do anything in a small way, the couple built one of the finest private residences in America.[124]

While the men involved themselves in building projects, Dolley rallied the female gentry to establish another tie between the government and the city, one that demonstrated official society's good faith to the ordinary citizens of the town. Poverty had been a problem in Washington City since its beginning. For a new city it had a disproportionate share of poor, probably because of the mass of laborers attracted by rumors of a building boom that never quite materialized. The destruction of the public buildings during the war, especially the Navy Yard, left many lower-class white and free black adults unemployed and their children impoverished, abandoned, or orphaned.[125]

Though Dolley had always been a part of local, private charitable works, she chose this moment to involve herself quite publicly when Marcia Burnes Van Ness founded the Washington Female Orphan Asylum in 1815. Burnes Van Ness conducted the day-to-day business of the asylum, with Dolley as the "First Directress," who also contributed twenty dollars, a cow, and her services as a seamstress. Extensive publicity, not usually associated with female activities, surrounded the effort from the start. The local and official ladies met in civic space, occupying the House chamber in the Brick Capitol, and engaged in extensive public fundraising. The press continued to follow the career of the asylum, reporting on its progress in raising money and its opening ceremonies.[126]

As soon as she could, Dolley resumed her work of entertaining. With the beautiful Octagon House as her setting (and later at the temporary official residence in the "Seven Buildings" at the junction of Pennsylvania Avenue and Nineteenth Street, N.W.), Dolley determined that the administration must always take center stage. The new executive mansion in the Seven Buildings possessed none of the architectural features and material opulence that she had earlier used to such good effect. Instead, the "little White House" had only one room for entertaining and that one inadequate in size. Washington visitors who had seen Dolley as the queen of the beautifully decorated President's Palace noted with dismay the lack of carpet, the scanty curtains of mere embossed cambric, and the pitiful furniture. Instead of sunflower-yellow damask and massive mirrors, "a small sideboard, two little couches covered with blue patch," "two pier tables," and some small secondhand mirrors comprised the room's decor.[127] But she made do and, like a road company, got her effects from portables.

Even with no linen and only oddments of china and silver, Dolley presided like a queen. She supplied grandeur with her imagination and her own person. At one such occasion she made up for her lost mirrors and chandeliers by illuminating the whole building with pine torches held by slaves. She had never been as glamorously gowned as she was in the months following the invasion of Washington. With Dolley in rose-colored satin and white velvet, a train lined with lavender satin, a gold girdle, gold bracelets, and a necklace, everyone could be oblivious to the setting. The new British minister, Charles Bagot, enthused, "She looked every inch a queen."[128] Once again, Dolley's person provided the image of stability, reassurance, legitimacy, and prosperity.

As she had done with the American cause in the war, Dolley personified the effort to restore and revitalize the capital, symbolized in Washington City's reception of the Treaty of Peace.[129] President Madison received the draft document on February 14, 1815, and the cabinet and others "deeply interested in the event" gathered at the Octagon House. With the officials closeted away, Dolley, "doing the honors of the occasion," welcomed out-of-town visitors, congressmen, and the curious to the substitute executive mansion. The room quickly filled, a "happy scene," with former political enemies now "cordially felicitating one another." "But the most conspicuous object" dominated the space, "the observed of all observers," Mrs. Madison, in the "meridian of life and queenly beauty." Her power lay in her ability to personify: "*She* was, in her person, for the moment, the representative of the feelings of him who was, at this moment, in grave consultation with his official advisors." Indeed, "no one could doubt, who beheld the radiance of joy which lighted up her countenance and diffused its beams around that all uncertainty was at an end and that the government of the country had, in very truth . . . 'passed from gloom to glory.'"[130]

Dolley had succeeded in making the President's House and the capital a presence in many Americans' minds. Her flight from the White House and her preservation of the icon of America set the tone of renewed patriotism. For many she was identified with the nation's crisis; her story "that day was the story of Washington in its first hour of trial." When the news of peace spread, observers said that she was the most popular person in the United States. Soldiers passing the Seven Buildings cheered for her as they demobilized. The decisive victory at the Battle of New Orleans added to the country's optimism and aided public acceptance of a treaty that was barely honorable and settled no practical issue.[131] The decision to stay in Washington and rebuild, the reestablishment of the executive, the timing of both the news of peace and the outcome of the Battle of New Orleans—all enabled the federal government to hang on long enough to reassert itself as the power center of the nation. If hyperbole were still the style in history, one might say that in its darkest days two people held the Republic together—Andrew Jackson, the Hero of New Orleans, and Dolley Madison, the Queen of Washington City.

Fittingly, the concept of Republican Queen contains as deep a paradox as Republican Court, because the role encompasses a variety of mutually conflicting tasks. The ideology of republicanism precluded the assertion of authority and legitimacy, as well as the structure and coalition building that the embryonic federal government required to grow and thrive. The role of Republican Queen, as invented by Dolley, transmuted the abstractions and ideals of republicanism through selective borrowing from court culture, adapting republicanism for political needs. Ironically, the Republican Queen also preserved republicanism in its purest form. By taking on the pragmatic work of politics, Dolley and her set allowed their husbands and male kin—the official, public figures—to remain virtuous, allowing them the struggle to maintain pure republicanism in an increasingly political system.[132]

It is important to note that Dolley Madison succeeded not in spite of her gender, a female achiever in a male world, but precisely because she was a woman, and therefore politically innocuous, a mere wife and mother. Her solution to a political (and therefore publicly male) problem—adapting the ideological abstraction republicanism to real life—was a feminine one, focusing on society. Dolley visibly, even flamboyantly, embodied the traditional roles of wife and helpmeet, mother, hostess, lady, and physically attractive woman from which she derived her authority. Her power came not from being like James Madison or trying to do what he did, but from playing to the hilt the role her culture had given her. Her intellectual and political prowess was legitimate precisely because it was laundered through traditionally female roles and virtues. Covered by culturally sanctioned behavior and expectations, Dolley became the centerpiece of the Washington court and oversaw the creation of the essential formation of executive and congressional power.

And the way she did it, the style she used, so ladylike, so queenlike, cloaked her and shielded James Madison and his administration from criticism and accusations of abuse of executive power. Dolley acted consciously to help James, the administration, and the country and to reach her own political goals. This does not mean she calculated the nature and persona that helped her to succeed. She was conscious, but not calculating; it was a role but not an act.

As the Republican Queen of Washington City, Dolley used the covering function of her role to become a visible symbol, an ideological representation of Columbia. Women further down the political food chain—

allied to congressional figures or cabinet members—used the camouflage of gendered prescriptions and interpretations to accomplish similarly pragmatic functions. Though these women harbored more modest goals than Dolley's aim of legitimating a new nation, nonetheless by striving for coalition and cooperation, they built channels for power that proved as necessary to the federal structure as more ideological symbols.

❧ 3 ❧

Washington Women in Public

"Prisoners to her womanly persuasion"
—WILLIAM SHAKESPEARE, *The Taming of the Shrew* 5.2.120

IN NOVEMBER 1817 Thomas H. Hubbard journeyed from Hamilton, New York, to join the Fifteenth Congress in Washington City, the first full session since the declaration of peace. After sampling the urban delights of Albany, New York City, and Philadelphia, which included attending dinners, church services, and the theater and admiring "splendid buildings and public squares," Hubbard made his way into unfamiliar territory. He saw Baltimore by moonlight and noted with emotion the landmarks of the recent war. He passed through the "barren waste" of Bladensburg, Maryland, where the British had routed the American forces before "plundering and burning" Washington City. "The reflections which naturally occur in passing this section of the country, and the solitary character of the surrounding fields, render the approach to the capital of America dreary in the extreme," noted Representative Hubbard. From a distance "Capitol Hill resembles the picture of the ruins of Palmyra, more than the heart of the great city." Once in the city, however, he discovered that "the prospect is more pleasing," that the city was "laid out upon a grand scale" and "more compact and in general better built than I had supposed."[1]

A few months later Charles Bulfinch, traveling from Massachusetts, also observed upon approaching the city that "nothing announces a metropolis." But from "Capitol Hill, the ground suddenly falls and expands into an extensive vale, beautifully surrounded by high grounds" and bounded on one side by a "majestic river." From among the ruins of "Congress hall," he pronounced the view "beautiful" and declared that "a

Mrs. Samuel Harrison Smith, by Charles Bird King, 1829. (Courtesy of Redwood Library and Athenaeum, Newport, Rhode Island)

great city must here grow up." The architect who would rebuild Washington's buildings on a scale he called "vast" and calculated to "produce grandeur in the execution," Bulfinch would play a prominent role in the rise of the phoenix city.[2]

The capital had passed through its darkest hour, greeting the dawn with the sounds of both private and government construction and expansion. In the postwar prosperity citizens and government officials built more houses in the first twenty months of peace than in the preceding five years, and by the end of 1817, real estate sales had increased 500 percent over 1813. Eliza Parke Custis Law, local gentrywoman and eldest grand-daughter of Martha Washington, estimated a population of "around 12,000" and reported to David Baillie Warden that "houses are rising in every direction; Pennsylvania Avenue is built up ... and [there are] as many good houses on that avenue as in Boston or Philadelphia."[3]

Though the roads remained lamentable, new gravel paths connected the principal congressional hotels and boardinghouses. This "forward-ness," as Catharine Ackerly Mitchill dubbed the development process, also appeared in the rapidly multiplying shops and churches. Rebuilt bridges, new steamboats, and increased stagecoach service facilitated travel be-tween the capital, its neighbors, and distant points north and south. Thomas Law, Eliza Parke Custis's former husband, versified:

> *By perseverance we'll have all complete*
> *Worthy this chosen spot this capital seat*
> *Which now forever fix'd, with vigor grows*
> *As Phoenix from her ashes brighter rose.*[4]

All of this civic improvement stemmed from a boom in Washington City's sole business: government. Not only had the outcome of the war fixed the capital permanently in the Potomac city, but the federal govern-ment had emerged from its time of trial as the definitive center of power for the United States, an important player in international politics, and a focus for American nationalism. The concentration of political power in Washington acted like a magnet, drawing foreign dignitaries and visitors, entertainers, preachers, anyone with a product or an idea to sell, as well as politicians and would-be politicians.

The city's popularity had risen during the war; the 1814 invasion barely stemmed the tide of visitors, which increased through the postwar era. Margaret Bayard Smith, Washington City's most astute observer, acknowl-edged that "Washington possesses a peculiar interest and to an active, re-flective, and ambitious mind has more attractions than any other place in America. The interest is daily increasing, and with the importance and ex-pansion of our nation ... it is every year, more and more, the resort of strangers from every part of the Union."[5] In addition to houses and buildings, the postwar era brought the growing city a new public, a public that included large numbers of women.

Washington City embodied an architecture of ideas. The street plan, the building designs, the landscaping, each element concretized republican ideals and emphasized the new nation's classical roots and its utopian potential. This was not a city created for people, not even for men and certainly not for women. As Thomas Law proclaimed:

> The Map, if examined, exhibits a plan
> More suited to Giants than poor dwindl'd man.

The galleries of government spaces provided the only clue to the public's function in the built environment. Galleries had been a part of legislative spaces throughout the United States' short history. The temporary legislative halls in Philadelphia had them, as did the short-lived structure on Capitol Hill.[6] While construction continued on the Hill, Congress met in the Brick Capitol, and even this temporary structure had galleries. Though the city's planners may have reduced members of the public to mere spectators in the government process and the life of the city, the large numbers of Americans who flooded to Washington City during and after the war peopled the space in ways its creators could not have imagined.

Planned for or not, women were everywhere in Washington and had been from the beginning. "Females of all classes" attended the inaugurations of Presidents Jefferson, Madison, and Monroe; even earlier, they had been part of a "brilliant crowd of spectators of both sexes" when George Washington laid the cornerstone for the Capitol in 1793 and when President John Adams made his first speech to both Houses of Congress in 1800. By 1815 James Kirke Pauling commented, "You cannot conceive of what consequence a bachelor like myself is in this odd city where there are at least one thousand women."[7] Pauling was not including working-class black and white or enslaved women in his estimation. He was astonished by the large number of white women of the elite and newly emerging middle class at public sites and social events.

Most of these women had come to Washington City as members of political families, as the relatives and friends of government officials. The increased female presence in Washington was intimately connected to the postwar development of the federal government, one symbolized by the rising edifice on Capitol Hill. Since the declaration of war in 1812 and under Dolley Madison's skillful hand, Congress had evolved from a loose group of fractious individuals into a coherent, semistructured body. Individual senators and representatives remained quarrelsome and even violent, but as a branch of the government, Congress was becoming as solid an institution on the political landscape as its grand new home was on the cityscape.

The White House was substantially reconstructed by the time James and Elizabeth Kortright Monroe took possession in 1817, but the Capitol was being restored to a degree of grandeur far surpassing its previous incarnation. Though Congress began meeting there in 1819, the building would not be completed until 1825. The British minister Stanford Canning, who had seen his share of plush settings, reported, "Instead of . . . venerable simplicity . . . the H. of Representatives, besides being stoved, carpeted, desked, and sofaed in the most luxurious style, rivals, and indeed surpasses, the Legislature of Paris in decoration and drapery."[8] Located on a hill high above the city, the Capitol in the early years of the government might have seemed a bit forlorn and desolate. Now, in the revitalized city, it appeared elevated rather than isolated, a proper home for an increasingly powerful and important group of men.

The office of the presidency, constructed as weak by the Constitution, lost even more power over Congress during the Monroe administration. Thomas Jefferson had created his own avenues of influence by force of personality (and dinner parties), and James and Dolley Payne Todd Madison dealt with their combative congresses by creating an extensive social lobby. James and Elizabeth Kortright Monroe, however, showed no inclination to avail themselves of the networks and procedures Dolley and James had established. James Monroe, wishing to proclaim the United States' legitimacy to the world, determined to set the White House on a "European footing of form and ceremony," thus severely limiting access for everyone. Elizabeth announced that, unlike Dolley, she would neither pay nor receive visits, and social events at the White House became somewhat fewer and more formal.[9] Socializing in the city increased during these years, continuing the pace set by Dolley Payne Madison, but with a shift of focus from the president's family to congressional and cabinet families.

James Monroe upheld a weak presidency as a safeguard against executive misuse of power. As soundly republican as his ideals were, Monroe's attitudes only increased conflict in Congress, as members of House and Senate struggled for preeminence.[10] Faced with a relative political void, congressmen did not wait for Monroe to take the lead in any matter and showed no hesitation in opposing him on any issue.[11]

Even if James Monroe had wished to replicate the charismatic control of Congress achieved by Thomas Jefferson or Dolley Payne Todd Madison, he would have been defeated by sheer numbers. The admission of new states and reapportionment almost doubled the number of legislators arriving in Washington City in the decade after the war. Increased numbers made the kind of majorities Jefferson cultivated through personal relations impossible for James Monroe to achieve. Few other avenues remained for President Monroe. A president who wishes to lead a Congress that he cannot command must be prepared to persuade members to follow him by offering rewards and making clear the penalties for noncooperation. Using either carrots or sticks, the president must convince the legislators that their own best interests lie in following the executive agenda.[12]

President Monroe possessed but few carrots and proved reluctant to use them, as in the case of patronage. Neither did he exercise his veto power with the panache that Andrew Jackson would later exhibit. Many of the institutional weapons of the powerful modern president did not exist in the first decades of the U.S. government. The president could not influence Congress through congressional allies or exert pressure via interest groups or party discipline. In the days before open campaigning and public elections, the chief executive could not offer congressmen help in reelection efforts with presidential endorsements, money, publicity, or personnel. The president himself did not campaign publicly and thus could not provide a legislator with coattails or a motive for building a legislative record that would enhance the party, the president, and himself in the next election.[13]

Neither could a president "go to the country" over the heads of a troublesome Congress and claim constituent support or popular mandate for his policies. Legislators were the ones elected by the people, and they claimed the role of citizen spokesmen for their own. With limited mass communication to the citizens of the country, the early presidents could not reach and guide public opinion, appeal directly to the people, or easily command national attention. Little wonder that these have been characterized as years when the "presidency slept," its power dormant, to be awakened only later.[14] But as nature abhors a vacuum, so does politics, and the federal structure allowed both the Congress and part of the president's own branch—the cabinet—to fill any gap in the political power structure.

Congressional power coalesced with the rise of two important institutions: the committee systems and the congressional caucus. The committees began during the War of 1812 as ad hoc advisory groups, but they quickly became permanent "little legislatures," powerful enough to kill any chance for Monroe or his immediate successors to take a leadership role. No wonder foreign visitors concluded that the "real business of the country" took place in the committees, with their powers of initiative, amendment, and quasi-veto in legislative matters: "No bill connected with any branch of public affairs could be brought into Congress with the smallest prospect of success, which had not previously received the initiative approbation of these committees."[15]

Not only did Congress, virtually free from presidential influence, have almost total command over its own legislation, but it also controlled the president himself. Congress elected presidents through congressional caucuses, a Republican innovation that began in secret in 1804. By the mid-1810s the congressional caucus operated openly, choosing presidential and vice-presidential candidates and making their recommendations public. After the caucus made the decisions, the caucus members would then instruct their respective states' legislators as to which would-be candidates to advance. In a culture which eschewed personal campaigning, these proxies legitimated and promoted candidates throughout the campaign season. From 1804 to 1820 the choice of the Republican caucus became president.

As Congress rose in power, the section of the executive branch that dealt directly with it benefited. Like the congressional committees, the cabinet also evolved from a rather weak advisory body into an independent and powerful minibranch of the federal government. In the years 1817–28 cabinet members, like "little presidents," did not hesitate to avail themselves of bargaining chips that the presidency either lacked or that the presidents refused to use. Cabinet members protected their interests in Congress by the use of congressional agents, influenced votes and built congressional support through social events, used newspapers and other media for propaganda, and dispensed departmental patronage to pay off and create congressional debts. During this era, then, the significant political spaces shifted from the White House to the Capitol and all the places where congressmen, cabinet members, and their families met, worked, and socialized.

Increased numbers played only one part in the story of the rise of Congress. As more men came to serve their country in Congress, they stayed longer, a phenomenon that can be seen as both cause and effect of Congress's increased power. Building coalitions and alliances requires and encourages stability in personnel; as Congress's power to effect change grew, more and more of its members were inclined to stay around to reap the benefits—whether from a need for personal power or a feeling that their work made a difference to their country, or perhaps both. In this atmosphere possibilities for advancement grew. The career paths of congressmen of this period indicate that a significant number of members moved from the House to the Senate and then to positions in the cabinet, the diplomatic corps, the Supreme Court, or even the presidency. These men, and others who returned term after term to represent their states, mark the beginning of the professionalization of politics in the United States.[16]

Individual careers aside, the congressional body itself struggled toward institutionalization. With books bought from Thomas Jefferson, Congress reestablished its own library. It also formed a permanent staff of clerks and other functionaries, including stenographers, who recorded debates. As procedures became codified and committees developed internal and external working channels, something like a national politics began.[17] Thus, the emergence of a political machine recognizable to modern politicians began not in the highest office in the land—the presidency—but in the imposing structure on Capitol Hill. Though numbers brought power, they also brought problems. Ironically, the gangling, growing Congress needed the stabilizing influence of a strong presidency more than ever before, but its exploding numbers and responsibilities precluded this development. Congress looked to its own community for stability.

Congressmen still felt the obligation to adopt a pose of outsider while onstage on the floors of the House and Senate. But the growth of the institution and the needs of the burgeoning federal government demanded internal cooperation. The Washington political community solved this dilemma by developing coalitions of cooperation extrainstitutionally. Newly arrived Washington congressmen almost immediately formed "boardinghouse messes," which engendered and encouraged much fraternity. The extent to which these "boardinghouse blocs" represented early party activity has been debated, but it seems reasonably certain that the men consciously formed their messes by inclination, using region and political agreement as criteria, and that living together in messes provided members with an identity. These boardinghouses were hives of political activity, and discussion and coalition (or, to enemies, "cabal") took place over the dinner tables, in the parlors, and even in the members' sleeping quarters. Politics was not only these men's bedfellow but also shared their meals, leisure, and every waking minute.[18]

Women played significant roles in creating congressional and government stability. The intimate connection between increased female presence and the rise of Congress did not go only one way; as the Congress grew in stability and strength, more women came. In addition, the presence of women aided the rise of congressional and cabinet power. Adding women to the story of postwar Washington adds subtlety to the usual models of cause and effect. Congress evolved into a structured body, men came to public service in increasing numbers and stayed longer, the cabinet and Congress developed mutually beneficial relationships, socializing and the social lobby increased: the influx of women into official Washington was both cause and consequence of all these developments.

HONORED WITH THE ATTENDANCE OF LADIES

By 1818, as Thomas Hubbard wrote to his spouse, Phebe Guernsey Hubbard, gentlemen who came without wives appeared "like the odd half of a pair of scissors," not only out of the ordinary but useless. "Indeed," Hubbard recounted during the 1818–19 session, "I have often been obliged to excuse myself for coming here without my better half."[19] Congressional female family members lived in the boardinghouses with their husbands and other male relatives, freed from domestic duties, especially the time-consuming tasks of food acquisition and preparation. Because they often left small children at home, bringing to Washington only teenaged daughters and sons they wished to see launched, congressional women found themselves freed from child care as well. These circumstances, more than any others, allowed the freedom of movement women experienced in the capital.

"You know, sister, I came here for the express purpose of seeing and being seen," declared Catharine Akerly Mitchill to her sister, Margaretta Akerly Miller, in 1806. "I am therefore ready to receive all invitations and visits the Ladies think proper to favor me with." Akerly Mitchill came to Washington as the wife of Samuel Latham Mitchill, representative from New York and one of the nation's leading intellectuals; his congressional colleagues nicknamed him the "Stalking Library." Intellectually gifted and superbly educated herself, Akerly Mitchill painted a compelling picture of the capital during the congressional seasons of 1806–12, depicting Washington as an international center, populated with exotic visitors, celebrated authors, and, increasingly, with female family members of government officials, who had come to see the sights and participate in city life.[20]

Participants in American small-town life complained of its dullness, and often the more privileged of them traveled to nearby urban centers to gain a little polish. Washington City, however, offered the female members of congressional and executive families sights and diversions unlike those of any other American city. Women who came to Washington participated in the delights of urban existence, and the town's intimate involvement with power and issues of political significance imparted a sense of excitement and importance to all activities. Everyone talked politics in Washington, and women who would have refrained from such an unfeminine activity in Boston or Philadelphia stayed up late talking politics to men and to each other. When they discussed current events at a dinner or around a fireside, they might find themselves doing so with some of the most illustrious and learned politicians of the day.[21] For the white elite and middle class, everyday life in Washington possessed an edge of excitement not present in more established towns.

In addition to glamorous scenes and prominent politicians, Washington City also offered its female residents more freedom of movement than they could enjoy in any other city setting or rural retreat. Unlike European cities, most American urban centers lacked polite walks and places for ladies to show themselves. Only men could move about in public spaces freely and safely.[22] In contrast, Washington was not developed enough to support major areas of urban crime, and women in Washington showed themselves in all public spaces. In Washington City the major activities of female visitors and the families of government officials took place outside the home. Whereas a lady in Boston or New York might spend most of her time behind her own front door, Washington City's political women, living in boardinghouses, passed their days in the galleries of Congress and the Supreme Court and in calling on one another.

With the formation and rise of vernacular gentility among the middle classes in the first decades of the nineteenth century, American white women became increasingly restricted by tenets of proper public behavior, just as they grew bolder in their demands on the public sphere. For instance, nineteenth-century etiquette books and city guides increasingly enjoined women not to travel the streets without male escort. A proper lady had to depend on the goodwill of a man—her host or a relative—if she wanted to go out. While in public, these advisers cautioned, women should strive never to call attention to their persons, most especially if, by some extremity, they should find themselves unescorted.[23] Though in Washington City a woman could travel alone without encountering rudeness or gossip, most of the white women on Washington's streets obeyed the rules that required male escort. Far from being restricted by propriety, however, these public women interpreted the rule in a variety of liberating ways.

They often depended on each other, traveling to the sites of public business and private commerce in groups. No male escort was apparent during Catharine Akerly Mitchill's visit to a Georgetown shop as part of such a group, and the raucous crowd she described exhibited none of the self-effacing restraint required of well-bred ladies. In some cases, a group of women traveling to an evening party or to observe the congressional debates were escorted by one man, a token nod to decorum. These ladies seem almost imperious in commandeering men for their pleasure, even on a last-minute whim. When Akerly Mitchill heard that the House would be sitting late one day, she "swallowed her meal in haste" and "took a beau" to find out what was happening. The married or single congressmen with whom the women shared lodgings emerged as particular targets for escort duty, especially married men without their wives. Thomas Hubbard ended many letters to Phebe Guernsey Hubbard with statements such as: "The Ladies below have just sent up a black girl to ask me to gallant them out this evening."[24] So though female arrivals to Washington City retained the conservative rule of their hometowns, they stretched it to accommodate a freedom of movement unknown in other eastern seaboard cities.

In Washington City the sexes mixed freely, primarily because female freedom took women into public places that in other cities remained the sole province of men. The government was the business of the city and the focus of male activity. Women would never have thronged a counting-house in Philadelphia, laughing, chatting with the men, and airing their views, as they did in the congressional galleries. Frances Trollope, traveling through America in the late 1820s and early 1830s, noted the strict separation of the sexes among good society in major cities. In not the first such instance, Washington City proved an exception to the prevailing social direction of the rest of the United States.[25] If vernacular gentility dictated that women withdraw more into the private sphere, Washington City's peculiar needs allowed women more freedom to roam.

In addition, this female freedom had originated as a by-product of Washington City's unique situation as a frontier town. The capital was not like those in the West; frontiers usually occupy edges, far from the centers of power, and the capital was as centrally located geographically as it was politically. Washington City's frontier existed internally, in the psyches of the men and women who traveled to this sparsely settled, raw city, where important issues pervaded the atmosphere and a sense of political and social invention abounded.

In the traditional model of the frontier, women bring civilization to new settlements. In contrast, women came to Washington, a frontier with a European veneer, to be civilized, to learn taste, fashion, and etiquette, and to avail themselves of aristocratic permissions of speech and movement. In a milieu of invention, women often enjoy greater freedom and responsibilities. At the same time frontier culture often depends on women to act as the conservators of old values in a place and time of change, and men can perceive female freedoms as threatening. The freedom to move in mixed company that women enjoyed in Washington City did not go unnoticed among Washington men, and their anxiety and dismay appear in their letters home. Concerns centering around female bodies provided a way for men to voice their uneasiness.

The new dress styles brought over from Europe took their lines from classical Grecian shapes, which emphasized female freedom. The voluminous petticoats and body-shaping devices (corsets and panniers) of the late eighteenth century gave way to a high-waisted Empire garment, often made of diaphanous materials that clung to the body and revealed its shape. In the early days of Washington, the progressive Betsy Patterson Bonaparte scandalized society with her filmy draperies; but by 1817 many women had adopted some form of this fashion. The male observers' frequent use of the word *nude* signals the extremity of their reactions to the sight of mothers and daughters clad in thin, clinging garments. And they reacted volubly: it was a rare congressman who did not write home with a full, appalled report. Job Durfee, representative from Rhode Island, compared the women he saw at Washington parties to actresses and Indian savages. Louis McLane called women in the scanty dresses "nudities" and would not even describe "certain parts" of their dress, "or rather want of dress," to his wife for fear of "offending your delicacy."[26]

Male concerns with female nudity included both the lack of clothing sported by women during evening parties—"their bosoms and their backs half bare"—and their own masculine proximity to the unclad creatures. Washington people had dubbed the evening parties at the Madison White House and the houses of the foreign ministers "squeezes," and with good reason. At one of these packed affairs in the Monroes' time, Duncan McArthur, representative from Ohio, discovered that "the dresses [are] so constructed as to enable a person who is near and above them to see more than halfway down the back or front of the lady, from the upper part of her dress." No wonder Akerly Mitchill reported to her sister that she saw several gentlemen, while conversing with Betsy Patterson Bonaparte, "take a look at her bubbies." Willie Mangum fumed to his wife, Charity: "Really, you would think all modesty was gone and lost, if you could see the best bred ladies here, squeezing their way through the crowd." More than one congressman fervently hoped that his wife or daughter should never find herself pressing through a Washington crowd in such a condition of undress.[27]

Historians of social practices have traced a "rising threshold of embarrassment" about bodily functions, which culminated in a desire to isolate one body from another. In the ideals of vernacular gentility, even contact with body heat evoked fastidious horror as being too familiar and offensive.[28] Little wonder that congressmen who came from social worlds that dictated discreet separations between persons were overcome by the press of female flesh, the feel of silks and satins, and the sensations of smell and heat in overcrowded drawing rooms.

The theme of female nudity indicates one way Washington men criticized the freedom of women in the public sphere. Of course, a more direct genre of criticism exists. David Baillie Warden, a foreign observer who wrote fairly positively about America, labeled the "women of Columbia" ambitious and independent. Novelist George Watterston, in his send-up of Washington life, *The L——— Family in Washington*, rendered all the women in the congressional galleries prostitutes. By ignoring the crowds of elite females who sat in the galleries and making his prostitutes indistinguishable from respectable women, Watterston deliberately conflated "public women" with women in public. Political cartoons expressed their concern about the corrupting effect of capitals by depicting them as places where women could be "public," again, as prostitutes.[29]

Perhaps critics felt threatened by the proximity of women to political power; certainly this unusual freedom of movement gave women almost unprecedented access to public business. The lack of public amusements in Washington City and the burgeoning population of women made even the most staid government buildings places of public entertainment. Far from being hushed portals of power, the floors of the House and Senate, the legislative antechambers, and the Supreme Court became the resorts of Washington residents and visitors. "The House of Representatives is a lounging place for both sexes," began Bayard Smith's description to her sister Jane, "where acquaintance is as easily made as at public amusements." Bayard Smith depicted an almost carnival atmosphere, where men performed onstage, and ladies and men acted as the appreciative audience.

However, the interactions were not always one-sided. The members played and responded to the galleries, and the spectators chatted and laughed among themselves. With famous men deciding affairs of state on the floor below and the audience above discussing the action, "it was as good as going to a play, but here all the characters are real instead of fictitious."[30]

By the postwar era, the gentlemen had "grown very gallant and attentive" to the ladies. In 1814 one member had just finished his speech and had resumed his seat when a party of ladies entered, led by Dolley Madison. According to Bayard Smith, "He recommenced, went over the same ground, using fewer arguments, but scattering more flowers." Observing a lawyer arguing a case before the Supreme Court, Bayard Smith was sure "he thought more of the female part of his audience than of the court," cutting his argument short so as not to weary them. To refresh the ladies in the galleries above, members in the House tied oranges and other comestibles in handkerchiefs, with notes identifying the recipients, and extended them up on a long pole. During one speech by Henry Clay, the presence of "near a hundred ladies there" ensured that such "presentations were frequent." They were also "quite amusing," as legislators proffered these delicacies "even in the midst of Mr. C.'s speech." The ladies in the gallery divided the food among themselves and "were as social as if acquainted."[31]

With the completion of the Capitol in 1825, the activities in the rotunda contributed to the carnival atmosphere. Crowded with men and women from all classes, newspaper correspondents from across the country, and vendors hawking popcorn and candy, the rotunda became the place to lobby a congressman, to sniff out a news story, to make a sale, or "to see and be seen." In these ostensibly male, official settings, women and men acted and interacted. They did not take the same roles, but the presence of females blurred all the dichotomous distinctions.[32]

During the official day Washington women moved freely between venues, leaving one if they found the proceedings tiresome; and by their freedom of movement, dress, and participation, they asserted their presence and took a position in the public proceedings unimaginable anywhere else. Everyone noticed them; from the descriptions of both men and women, one might assume that only ladies populated the galleries. Women new to the milieu, even women of fashion from urban areas, found this unprecedented conspicuousness a bit daunting.[33] Senators often escorted ladies onto the Senate floor, and members of both houses joined them in the gallery. Margaret Bayard Smith seated herself on "some steps, quite out of sight of the House," to hear one of Henry Clay's speeches. Afterwards, he spied her and "sat a few minutes on the steps by me, throwing himself most gracefully into a recumbent posture" to discuss the speech.[34]

When the galleries filled to overflowing, ladies came onto the floor of the Senate and sat in the members' seats, as did one lady who sat in Robert Y. Hayne's chair as he stood to debate Daniel Webster. During the well-attended Missouri debates, Vice President Daniel Tompkins offered seats on the Senate floor to the ladies. To his dismay the galleries emptied, as observers crowded the sofas and footstools. To avoid such an unseemly repetition, according to Sarah Gales Seaton, the vice president placed a notice on the chamber's door the next day, "excluding ladies not introduced by one of the senators." When crowded galleries, construction, or secret proceedings prevented parties of ladies from entering the halls, they expressed their disappointment, quite as though they had been deprived of a right.[35]

SOCIAL STRATEGIES

Along with rhetoric that welcomed the presence of women—"We have been honored several days with the attendance of Ladies in the Gallery"—frequent comments disparaged and belittled the female members of the audience. During a closed session John Randolph of Virginia publicly took advantage of the empty galleries to abuse women who attended congressional proceedings, denigrating them in comparison with the "rabble black and white" who also watched from above. A German nobleman wryly dubbed the Senate the "finest drawing-room in Washington," comparing it to a European opera house in its capacity to entice young ladies who wished to "exhibit their attractions." Even gallery regulars like Margaret Bayard Smith worried that too much attention was being paid to the ladies in the audience.[36]

No doubt displays of fashion and flirting were part of the social atmosphere of Washington City's only regular public amusement, but many women attended to the governmental proceedings quite seriously. Some

ladies, such as Akerly Mitchill, listened with great care to the debates, taking notes and relating in great detail both the legislative processes and the
business enacted in the new capital as well as their own opinions. Upon
observing her first filibuster, Akerly Mitchill wryly commented, "You
have no idea of the difficulty of getting along with the public business, in
this land of liberty, where everyone has the right to talk as long as he
pleases, and whenever he thinks proper."[37]

Often such accounts kept female correspondents elsewhere abreast of
the latest news from Washington, as when Akerly Mitchill wrote her sister
explaining the committee system and including a list of the resolutions
and votes. The business of the House and Senate also occupied a good
deal of dinner-table conversation in some boardinghouses, as on the occasion when John Randolph made the "most boisterous, indecent, and inflammatory speech" the members had ever witnessed. Catharine Akerly
Mitchill did not hear it: the House had been debating with closed doors.
Yet she knew it well, for Randolph's speech had been the "theme of conversation at our house, ever since it was delivered, and I am willing to quit
[recite] it myself."[38]

During the rise of Congress in the postwar era, members achieved considerable national celebrity, and famous personalities ruled both House
and Senate. Public speaking by renowned orators such as Daniel Webster
and Henry Clay attracted spectators of both sexes. Ladies also responded
to the less spectacular, more important public affairs with faithful attendance and large numbers. Women packed the galleries during the counting of the votes in the 1808 presidential election and closely followed the
debates preceding the War of 1812. A single event, such as the Webster-
Hayne debate, could attract over three hundred ladies.[39] A more prolonged episode, like the extended deliberations over Missouri, commanded steady attendance of over a hundred ladies a day.

For women so inclined, life in Washington City proved energizing, exhilarating, and politicizing. In the capital they could feel involved in the
great issues and dilemmas facing the infant nation as they could nowhere
else. Boardinghouse life nurtured national politics, increased individual
male political sophistication, and encouraged the members to work together. The implications for the boardinghouses' female residents were the
same. Female family members also ate, drank, and slept politics, observ-

ing and participating in the process both as spectators in public and as in-
terlocutors on the inside. Boardinghouses with ladies proved an attraction
for men deprived of their families, and they flocked to the parlors to socialize with women and talk politics. At boardinghouse tables and parlors,
white women of the elite and middle classes became politically educated,
developed political identities, and learned to be better players in the game
by learning secrets, passing information, and facilitating the party-building processes of boardinghouse life.[40]

To recognize the female relations of male officials as a public is an important step toward discovering their relationship to politics and learning
what their experiences can tell us about the political process. Nineteenth-
century Americans and Europeans used the term *public man* to describe a
"gentleman-about-town," one active in the spheres of business, government, and the life of the city. No such term exists for women, for a public
woman was a prostitute. Redefining *public woman* will make it possible not
only to analyze the impact of a female or mixed-gender public but even to
recognize its existence.[41] Women in Washington, by their participation in
civic life—attending debates, discussing political issues among themselves
and with politicians in the boardinghouses and galleries, even serving as
an audience in shaping the national discourse—reformulated the composition of the bourgeois public sphere. Moving beyond the dichotomy
public/private and examining unofficial space make it clear that these
women had crucial roles to play in the very structure of the new government.

Though richer and more permanent government families built or
bought houses in Washington City, most official families lived in boardinghouses. Boardinghouse life proved ill-suited for certain kinds of socializing, such as drawing rooms and large parties. Government families
sometimes gave dinner parties in their "messes," but such projects entailed
a great deal of trouble. In 1818 and 1819 Harrison Gray Otis, that Boston
bon vivant, hosted two dinner parties at his mess; eight guests attended
the first one and six the second. Though he reported to his wife after the
second affair that the "dinner went off as you say very smartly," Otis had
to rearrange his rooms, bring in furniture, and tolerate mismatched place
settings as well as a casual level of cleanliness. On the day of his third and
last party of the season, Otis discovered to his dismay two other par-

ties—"large ones and from our kitchen"—scheduled for the same day. He solved the problem by bringing in his food and scouring the town for plates and silver.[42]

"Dinner parties are seldom given; intercourse is kept up by calls and evening parties," wrote Charles Bulfinch to Hannah, and calling did form the major social interaction for the government families. One might attend an evening party once or twice a week or a ball once a season, but calling happened every day. Catharine Akerly Mitchill explained to her sister: "There is so much visiting done in the morning that this is the most busy part of the day, and it is morning here until four o'clock."[43]

Washington calling practices evolved as a local variation on a growing urban custom. Calls were short, ritualized visits, lasting between fifteen minutes and half an hour, usually paid in the morning or in the afternoon and usually performed by women, with local custom dictating the particular conventions. These regular, ceremonial acts kept the social machinery of white upper-class (and, increasingly, middle-class) people well-oiled and running. Calling gave the upper class a way to exchange information, make connections between individuals in business and politics, plan the larger social events of the community, and provide the "unofficial spaces" that would later be supplied by men's organizations and country clubs.[44]

For families newly come to town, calling was the first step to entering the social world of their new home. Making the first call upon the established families in the area opened the door to further social interactions; the host families indicated their willingness to continue the exchange by returning the calls or issuing invitations to dinners, teas, or other events. Newcomers might even take the first step themselves by giving a party or ball, but only after they had called on their potential guests.[45] Calling allowed a family to situate themselves in the social network, enabling members to reap the economic, political, and status benefits of upper-class membership and power.

Calling assumed great importance as a screening process, providing the introduction to a social world where claims could be made on any member. The privilege of asserting such claims could not be granted lightly. The set structure of calling allowed established families an almost impersonal way to vet a newcomer. If they wished to further the acquaintance, the "called upon" simply returned the call or issued an invitation. If they did not desire further intimacy, the first call ended the relationship. Because the rules were part of a generally known code, the message was clear.[46] This weeding function grew increasingly important in the burgeoning modern middle-class world of the nineteenth century. As social and geographic mobility increased, the ability to detect and reject undesirable, vulgar people, social parvenus, and impostors became crucial, even as it grew more difficult to do so, especially in an urban environment. As one etiquette book cautioned, "Visits of form . . . [are] the basis on which that great structure, society mainly rests. . . . It is a kind of safeguard against any acquaintances which are thought to be undesirable."[47]

The increasing ritualization of calling resulted from its growing importance to the social process, and the calling card stands as a metaphorical image for this evolution. Originally a blank card, about three inches long and two inches wide, on which one wrote one's name, calling cards became more elaborate, sporting engraved names, mottoes, gilt edges, and pictures. Their function as well as their form amplified in sophistication; more than identifiers, calling cards acted as an intermediate step, another layer of buffer, in the screening function of calling. A lady who did not wish to meet a party, though required by etiquette to acknowledge a visit, sent a footman to the door with her card. A caller could open an interaction with an unfamiliar household by merely sending in a card, removing their person from the judging process, as the family decided whether to receive the overture. Using cards as proxies made the system more flexible and less personally hurtful.[48]

In calling customs, as in other aspects of life, Washington City proved both anomalous and typical in the extreme. Because politics ruled the town as its only business and only purpose, calling in the capital was not like calling in any other city. The context of power sought and power lost stripped away the facade that masked social practices in other cities, revealing that calling, everywhere, was about keeping and augmenting power. All through the early nineteenth century, calling occupied an enormous part of the life of Washington's official and local elite.

Margaret Bayard Smith, an inveterate player in the Washington social scene, once tallied the calls she received over three weeks' time. To her astonishment Bayard Smith discovered that she entertained 197 visitors, though, she explained, "not all different individuals, but the aggregate of each day's visitors, who are often the same persons." Still, Bayard Smith considered herself lucky, at one point owing a mere fifty calls in her effort to "keep up an interchange with only seventy or eighty persons." One of her friends, the wife of General Peter Porter, owed more than five hundred. The ladies knew these precise numbers because, like social participants in other cities, they kept lists of ceremonial visits paid and received.[49]

Extreme in almost everything else, capital life also exaggerated the card behavior just beginning to take hold in more sedate cities. The need to cover more ground (literally and figuratively), to network extensively, and to reinforce connections necessitated a good deal of calling, and card dropping quickly substituted for personal presence.

> *Cards are a labor saving machine*
> *Without your seeing or being seen*
> *You visit; and if sent, your walking*
> *Is sav'd as well as idle talking*

declared one satirist. In many situations there was no pretense of an actual meeting, as when Thomas Hubbard exchanged "visits" with the foreign ministers by merely dropping off cards, "without any inquiry" as to whether anyone was at home. Official families often acknowledged both the absurdity of these practices and their convenience, as Job Pierson did when he described these "pasteboard meetings" to his wife and daughter: "This heartless, formal way of making and returning calls is very convenient, and I like it accordingly."[50]

The topic of calls and calling abounds in diaries and letters from Washington City. Clearly these customs, which occupied so much time and attention, played a significant role in political life. It may seem too cynical to suggest that anything that so engaged the time and effort of politicians had to have political uses, but it is as true as the general observation that nothing in Washington City excluded politics. The complaints that pepper congressional and cabinet families' letters—"the most disagreeable circumstance of my situation," "this is the worst place for visiting I ever knew"—exist side by side with acknowledgments of the necessity for incessant "visiting and racketing." The beginning of a second session of Congress reminded even newcomers like Thomas Hubbard that the "expectations formed by the acquaintances" made during the preceding session and "court and civility calls . . . by the established custom of the place, demand [a congressman's] attentions."[51]

Like other kinds of socializing, calling was shaped around the official day. Congress did not meet until eleven in the morning or even noon, allowing government men to make visits after breakfast and before the start of official business. On Sundays, in other cities a day for home-centered family events, the "streets belong[ed] to the slaves and free people of color" and the members of Congress, who called more on Sundays than any other day of the week.[52] These established schedules accommodated the men's need to participate in the calling rounds, an indication of their political function.

Though a social activity does not become worthy of political consideration only because men do it, it is significant to note the extent of male participation in Washington City. Among the middle classes of other cities, women did the calling during the workday. Even among the non-working elite, men accompanied women during their calling rounds only occasionally. In contrast, Washington men spent part of each day in calling rounds and used their one day of leisure to complete their duties, as did Secretary of State John Quincy Adams, who startled Thomas Hubbard by calling on the Sabbath, while Hubbard was at church: "He probably called on Sunday for want of time on a weekday—the poor man."[53] Significantly, though Washington women of both official and residential elites proved frequent and conscientious callers, men of the residential elite, like their counterparts in other cities, did not call nearly as frequently as did the male government officials.

In this aspect as in many others, Washington's political context necessitated a flexibility in gender roles not needed in the larger culture. In Washington City calling customs disclose the official men's conviction that whether they liked it or not, calling was necessary. Even in a culture of complaint, some like Harrison Gray Otis and William Wirt occasionally even enjoyed what Otis called the "delectable drudgery." He knew that however enjoyable, "returning visits is a most important concern and . . . it is attended with no small trouble." Even when calling seemed an "unavoidable" chore, one must pay it great mind, for, as Harrison lamented to his wife, Sally, "blunders from persons in high stations are never forgiven," rendering the luckless perpetrator the object of "contempt" or, at best, "indifference." William Wirt found socializing and calling in particular "most congenial with my temper and habits!" though he also acknowledged that sheer volume made calling difficult to tolerate. He wondered to his wife, Catherine, "How do you think you will stand all this?"[54]

In a lovely metaphor for traversing unofficial channels, Harrison Otis indicated that by "perambulating avenues and circumventing hills," calling helped him do a "world of business." In January 1818 Thomas Hubbard provided more detail of how calling blurred the line between official and unofficial transactions. He and several gentlemen approached President Monroe with a petition on behalf of the New Stockbridge Indians, who had fought for the United States during the War of 1812. Hubbard and his colleagues presented their solicitation, and the president "promised to give the petition his instant attention." All of this took place during a morning visit: Hubbard's delegation arrived at the President's House at 10:30 A.M., the time of morning calls. They were received at the door, where a porter asked if they were members of Congress. Answering in the affirmative got them into the anteroom. The porter then announced them to the president merely as "visitors." Instead of the members being led into an office, President Monroe came into the anteroom to receive them.[55]

Though William Wirt spent many hours a day calling on a long list of officials, the concern he expressed about Catherine Gamble Wirt's capacity for similar duty reveals the primacy of women's labor in this political task. Indeed, he added, "You will have to go through it all; ay, and more too." The experiences of male officials provide important clues to the political uses of calling, but paying and receiving calls remained women's work and a female power strategy in Washington City, as in other urban cultures. The social and political stakes of calling may have been higher in Washington City than in other towns, but that did not exclude women from their own game; it only added men. In other settings the establishment of social reciprocity entitled families and individuals to make social claims; in Washington City, social claims were intimately connected to political ones.[56] Men used calling to do a "world of business." So did women, and they did so by taking the lead as practitioners of this social political strategy.

IN THEIR SOVEREIGN CAPACITY

For both established political families and those aspiring to political and social power, a move to Washington City definitely represented an elevation, if not in comfort then at least in proximity to power.[57] Those who came from outside the capital faced problems as old as courts themselves, the twin dilemmas of how to maintain the local power bases that propelled outsiders to the center of power while building powerful relationships in a new, national sphere. Calling provided an important way to retain and maintain the power bases at home. Taking care of local constituents in the absence of men had long been women's work among elite families in England.[58]

Correspondence between men in Washington and women at home reveals that in the United States constituent and kingmaker alike used women as proxies for their husbands (as targets of petitions and requests), as sources and mouthpieces (seeking and passing on information), and as campaign managers (proposing electoral plans and strategies for the absent husband's political future).[59]

Once in Washington, women continued to link the voters and the legislators. Constituents—consisting of male voters, usually men of some property, and their wives—loomed large in the political awareness of early Republican politicians. They topped the list of groups to whom congressmen thought themselves accountable. The second group that commanded their loyalty was their colleagues; the president of the United States came last. Congressmen depended on their constituents to tell them how to vote and expressed frustration when this information was not forthcoming. When constituents came to Washington, their demands and expectations often drove their representatives to distraction, but congressmen believed that the folks from home, like the ubiquitous visiting demands, were ignored at the politician's peril. Job Pierson's greatest complaint about his situation was that he spent half his time receiving constituent visits "or more properly . . . the infliction of their visitations."[60] Plague they may have been, but a plague that had to be accommodated, as William Rives acknowledged when, though he would rather have stayed at home, he felt obliged to accompany and present a visiting constituent at Senator Johnston's party.[61]

Constituents came to Washington to obtain a variety of benefits: to collect money owed them through pensions, to obtain jobs or government contracts, to encourage or advocate the passage of bills from which they would benefit. Washington women interceded for them in the capital, as they did at home, in quite active ways. Catharine Akerly Mitchill's account of one episode reveals the government's workings and the roles women played. In January 1812 Mrs. Benton, an acquaintance of Akerly Mitchill's and a good friend of her good friends the Fays, arrived in Washington. Selah Benton, wife of a Revolutionary War naval captain, came to the seat of the federal government in order to rescue her husband's military pension claim, which had died in committee. Akerly Mitchill "wish[ed] with all her heart" that Mrs. Benton might "accomplish the object of her visit," though privately Akerly Mitchill thought she had little hope. "Old Soldier" claims were not received sympathetically at this time, and moreover Captain Benton had not sustained any wounds in action; the captain based his claim on a disease contracted by exposure during his service. Samuel Latham Mitchill, who had met privately with Captain Benton in New York before he presented the now-moribund bill, turned the problem over to his wife, "saying he thinks a Lady will have more influence with congressional Gentlemen than one of their own sex."[62]

Akerly Mitchill accordingly "commenced my operations," writing notes introducing Mrs. Benton to the chairman of the claims committee, Thomas Gholson of Virginia, and several committee members. The gentlemen responded positively to the notes and Selah Benton's personal visits and agreed to revive the bill, but Akerly Mitchill expected it would meet with considerable opposition. The key now was to get as many members of Congress as possible to vote for it. She and Mrs. Fay, the female half of a fellow New York congressional couple, set to work. Akerly Mitchill first discussed the issue with the "gentlemen of our family"— the boardinghouse mess—and "they all said that Mrs. B. had better stayed at home, for that the law did not provide for her husband's case, and it was not probable that Congress would give him a pension." In spite of their discouraging attitude, Akerly Mitchill persuaded them to examine the claim documents, continuing to argue the "old Captain's" case. Her efforts paid off. As she reported, "All the Gentlemen who live in the house with me (except one) voted for the bill."[63]

With the bill moving to the upper house, Akerly Mitchill decided she needed reinforcements. Figuring that "one or two could be more useful than a dozen," she asked the assistance only of Mrs. Gholson, the wife of the committee head. The two used their "utmost exertions to prevent its rejection in the Senate." Finally, the bill passed, and "by a very good majority." Selah Benton exhibited "good spirits" as she called to take her leave. Akerly Mitchill assessed her own contribution astutely, though modestly: "Although Mrs. Benton on this occasion may feel disposed to ascribe to me more influence than I really possess, yet I am convinced that without a little female assistance she would not have succeeded in her undertaking."[64]

This episode provides several significant pieces of information about this largely uncharted activity. Though Selah Benton may have been accompanied on her travels, she arrived in Washington City without her husband, whose "scorbutic ulcers" prevented him from traveling. The couple may have decided Selah Benton would do better on her own, after Captain Benton's use of official channels, his meeting with Samuel Latham Mitchill, had produced only limited success. This does not mean that women were necessarily better than men at this kind of politicking or that official channels inevitably failed, but the Bentons' actions demonstrate the power of the practical. Gender proscriptions notwithstanding, the couple obviously decided to avail themselves of all possible strategies.

Another important theme runs through this account—that of family and its emotional context. Working for their family's interests allowed women a freedom to act in aggressive and public ways, offering a selfless construct in which they could frame and understand their actions. Selah Benton's devotion to her husband drove her to embark on this mission. Akerly Mitchill also explained her desire to help Benton as an issue of "heart," one which led her to closer discussion with her boardinghouse "family."

The most significant aspect of this account is the assumption of ordinariness that pervades it. Selah Benton's arrival in Washington as a petitioner, Latham Mitchill's suggestion that Akerly Mitchill take over the matter, her discussions with and letters to the legislators: nothing suggests that anyone greeted the idea of a woman acting as an influence peddler with shock or horror. Akerly Mitchill mentioned her decision not to engage many of her friends, suggesting both that a female network was already in place and that using it constituted a time-tested and reliable strategy.

And there is a hint that while Akerly Mitchill chose not to engage a female network, Mrs. Fay might have. The two women worked independently on the problem, and Akerly Mitchill credited Mrs. Fay's efforts for Benton's eventual success. Detailed accounts of such episodes are few; this is the problem of recording female activities and the unofficial sphere. However, so many assumptions underlie Akerly Mitchill's narration that it seems safe to conclude that her experience was not uncommon. Indeed, ample evidence exists of a related public business of Washington women, one which had even more serious, widespread political consequences.

THE PRIVILEGE OF OLD ACQUAINTANCE

In European cultures it had always made good political sense to award jobs, titles, lands, and sinecures as rewards for loyalty and/or to secure a regime, as well as to establish reciprocal power relations on both central and local levels. This association with aristocratic rule made patronage a major political challenge for early Republican politicians; patronage was both the lifeblood of politics and the symbol of its corruption. In the American Republic politicians and critics of every stripe scorned and reviled this base Old World system, with the opposition exercising vigilance lest those in power be contaminated by its use. However, when elections and new administrations brought these same watchdogs into power, the new officials discovered that surrounding themselves with appointed friends and like thinkers provided the surest way to effect political action and build coalitions.[65]

The federal structure of the era reflected this ambivalence. The presidency, deliberately constructed to restrict personal power, did not control many appointive jobs, and the early Republican presidents proved reluctant to exercise whatever powers of patronage they had. The cabinet departments and the legislators responded to this vacuum, soon exercising the considerable advantages of patronage in building alliances, securing elections, paying debts, and indebting powerful persons. The federal government was barely in place before senators and representatives demonstrated a sophisticated grasp of the implications of patronage, from the obvious and immediate—the exchange of jobs for votes—to the more subtle and farsighted—that having "particular friends" in "important offices" could secure a more certain personal economic future.[66]

The power to confer office was a considerable one in an era before "pork"; with no internal improvements, few peacetime government contracts, no reelection funds or endorsement power at their disposal, the members of Congress quickly learned that the path of patronage provided the surest way to secure loyalty back home and to build their own personal power in the capital. Early Republican politicians learned to juggle the desire to have one's allies in supportive official positions while avoiding the accusation of creating a spoils system. It proved a delicate balance, and even the virtuous Jefferson, who wrote more about patronage than any other issue, was accused of cronyism.[67]

Proponents of republicanism not only feared an autocratic executive who could impose his will by force, they also abhorred the power wielded by lesser members in the intricate court structures. In their nightmare designing ministers, courtiers, and other hangers-on also abused power through extraofficial networks of intrigue and influence. Elite European women had always been intimately connected with such patronage practices, serving both as actual participants and as rhetorical lightning rods, symbolizing all the dangers of aristocracy. Associated with lavish display and upper-class material culture, they embodied the decadence and luxury feared by republicans. Even more seriously, though unelected and unappointed, women had long exercised power over personnel and policies, answering to no official body. Kings justified their rule by mandates from God, but aristocratic women in the European courts claimed their ruling privileges through unregulated relations of marriage, kinship, and sexual relations.[68]

In early federal Washington City, women of the new ruling classes used the familiar aristocratic practices—especially patronage—to further their families' interests, as elite and gentry women in Europe and colonial America had long done.[69] However, their efforts assumed even greater importance in the contradictory condition of the infant capital. The new government badly needed structures to mediate cooperative relationships between branches and individuals. But the ruling rhetoric of republicanism espoused by public men prohibited the politicking practices that could build such a political machine. While virtuous republican men struggled to reconcile an unworkable ideology with political necessity, women in their own families used patronage and personal relations to pursue political power.

The law of supply and demand influenced the extent of this power considerably. Federal offices available for distribution included jobs outside Washington (such as postmaster appointments and judgeships), but the Washington-based government posts (clerks and bureaucrats of the various departments) generated the most competition. The professionalization of medicine and law has been traced to a need for employment and advancement for the sons of the growing middle class. Politics, long the domain of a leisured, elite class, also underwent this process, as middle-class parents and children of both sexes realized government's economic and prestige potential. An entry-level position as a clerk in a federal department could lead to a long, profitable career in national politics. The competition was brutal, not only from young men who wished to start a career but also from men of all ages who had failed in business or agriculture, a likely prospect in the volatile economic climate of the early nineteenth century. Moreover, a post in the federal government was a family acquisition, enabling a young man to support his natal family and an older one to establish his children with jobs and marital alliances.[70]

Not surprisingly, patronage issues and office seeking emerge as among the most-discussed topics in the correspondence of politicians and political families. Washington observers, official and unofficial, seemed dazed by the competition prompted by these posts. As Margaret Bayard Smith described the spectacle, "In fact, no sooner does a vacancy occur, than it is instantly supplied and for this plain reason, that hundreds of candidates for every place, from the highest to the lowest, are registered on the office books—waiting often for years for a vacancy to be made."[71] Many descriptions of the overwhelming crush of office seekers on the Washington scene appear as complaints from besieged legislators and cabinet members, but even they, along with outside observers, expressed deep sympathy for the applicants and their mostly futile efforts.

Stories of hopeless cases abound, tales of well-qualified applicants, with every reason to hope for success, defeated by sheer numbers. John Smith, representative from Virginia, sent home a report in 1808 designed to "prevent a repetition of such numerous applications" as he had experienced when the government granted military positions to his state. Though the call was for one troop, twenty thousand men applied. Smith concluded that the "chance of success is too small to countenance the application." In another incident, recounted by Harriet Otis in 1812, "poor Mr. Melville" had just left Washington "hopeless and penniless," after "four months dancing attendance on the members and having hopes of success that seemed justly grounded." By the time he left, Melville "said that he had been so long unfortunate that success would have seemed to him miraculous."[72] Many applicants waited so long that they ran out of money and could not get home.

In the face of such dismal prospects, many acknowledged that success did not lie in following official procedures. Customarily, to obtain a post one submitted a letter of application accompanied by as many recommendations from important personages as one could muster. Many a candidate was dismayed to discover that credentials and official recommendations that would garner respect and attention anywhere else in the Union were lost in a sea of similar applications. "Yesterday, I went over in the dusk of the evening to have a confidential chat with a young man, but an old friend of mine, Eugene Vale, about the best means of procuring employment in one of the departments," wrote Bayard Smith to her sister Jane. Her conversation with Vale revealed that "written applications or recommendations were worth nothing—seldom read but amid the multiplicity of letters loading the department table, overlooked and thrown aside." Vale, who had just enjoyed a promotion in the State Department, "gave [Bayard Smith] a great deal of information, but all concluding that personal favor conferred and personal presence was by far the best means of obtaining that favor." Another friend of Bayard Smith's confirmed this information: "As Judge Southard stated on a former occasion, an individual who has powerful friends within the government has a better chance of success than those long registered expectants."[73]

The successful applicant had to have a friend at court, and often that friend was a woman from a powerful political family. In 1821 Bayard Smith reported that "this Florida business," the acquisition of the territory, "has filled our city with strangers" seeking appointments: "I am told above a thousand persons are here seeking for some place." Only very few appointments that stimulated much public discussion were to be had. "No one seems yet to have the least idea who they are to be," Bayard Smith recounted. "I have seldom known such absolute silence observed. Not even a conjecture is formed, although it is known from good authority that there have been above a hundred applications from persons of great respectability." The capital elite was paying particularly close attention to the part played by Floride Calhoun, wife of South Carolina senator John C. Calhoun: "Mrs. Calhoun has done her very best to obtain the clerkship of the board for Mr. Tasslet. She went herself to the president and others, but I fear there is no chance for a poor man and a foreigner."[74] Even in a culture which forbade political talk in front of proper women, Washington City society's evaluation of Mrs. Calhoun's aggressive involvement and public efforts on her protégé's behalf centered not on her personal character but her chances for success.

By the late 1810s Bayard Smith had become a powerful person in Washington political circles, already well established in her long career as an influence peddler.[75] In this field of operations she displayed certain characteristics shared by other women who wielded similar influence. One- or two-term congressional wives might obtain a modest post here or there for a constituent, but it took women such as Dolley Payne Todd Madison, Hannah Nicholson Gallatin, and Bayard Smith to enjoy repeated successes. They had lived in the capital for years, had husbands or fathers who served in government for long periods of time and/or in high capacities, and had grown up in elite, politically connected families. In addition, Bayard Smith's expertise in working the unofficial channels may have been sharpened because her own fortunes depended on the patronage system. After selling his newspaper in 1810, Samuel Harrison Smith relied on government jobs to support his family.

Bayard Smith was able to find places for both male relatives (such as the sons of her sister Jane Bayard Kirkpatrick) and non-kin candidates who presented themselves to her. Many of her notable successes took place in the years 1815–24, though she would continue to participate at least until the 1830s. Despite Samuel Harrison Smith's unpopularity with the presidents (he had opposed both James Madison and James Monroe), Margaret Bayard Smith succeeded many times in placing a friend or relation in office. Part of her success lay in her close relationships with influential members of Congress, particularly William Crawford and his family and Henry and Lucretia Hart Clay. Another reason for her success during Samuel's eclipse may lie in the structure of the patronage system itself; because patronage was women's work, a family could retain its power to get jobs and favors even as the male family members suffered official isolation.[76]

Bayard Smith's earlier benevolence efforts no doubt eased her path into full-fledged influence peddling. As a young bride she visited poor families on the outskirts of Washington City, bringing food, fuel, and clothing. She knew, however, that her efforts were only stopgaps; the poor needed jobs. To that end, Bayard Smith acted as an informal employment agency, obtaining male laborers for local building projects and securing white male and female domestics for her friends' households.[77] Though she felt sorry for the poor she aided, she was horrified by the situation that befell another desperate group: middle-class families. In the days before insurance, the removal of the working male through death or desertion could reduce a family to destitution. The economic climate of the time could, in a sudden swoop, doom an intact family to poverty as well.

Bayard Smith housed and financed these middle-class families, sometimes taking a widow and her children into her home the very day their belongings went on the auction block. She endeavored to find employment for the mother or grown daughters of a family as teachers, housekeepers, or seamstresses. As long as Bayard Smith urged her friends to buy produce from the underprivileged and solicited jobs for newly poor women, her activities fell safely within the rubric of "women's work," "private sphere," or even "benevolence." Even when male civic leaders asked her to find a teacher to start a school for children of the residential and political elite, she could still be seen as performing within strictly female limits, much like the politically active women in other towns.

But Margaret Bayard Smith's letters reveal that in addition to finding places for the mothers and daughters of the genteel poor in middle-class households, she and her friends also found government jobs for the fathers and sons. Bayard Smith and her friends may have understood their efforts as extensions of female benevolence, but these practices clearly crossed the line into the powerful world of political patronage, challenging all assumptions about spheres and the separation of male public life and female domesticity.[78]

The clientele of a business often reflects the effectiveness and reputation of the enterprise. Similarly, one particularly illustrious mother's request demonstrates not only how capable Bayard Smith was, but also how highly her contemporaries regarded her skill. Martha Jefferson Randolph was a woman of impeccable pedigree. Thomas Jefferson's sole living daughter, she had been her father's favorite, his confidante, and occasional White House hostess. In addition, she married a Randolph cousin, scion of a politically powerful Virginia clan and an influential member of Congress during his father-in-law's administration. Occupying the highest pinnacle of the social ladder whenever she was in the capital, Mrs. Randolph became the head of whatever occasion she attended. No matter what the social skirmish, no one disputed her right of precedence.[79]

By 1828 Mrs. Randolph and her family were living on the edge of poverty at Monticello. Her father had left her nothing except a debt so large that it consumed several generations' and families' fortunes, including her husband's. Her only hope for support was to get a male relative into a government job which would provide the means and opportunity to leave Monticello and its expenses and live in Washington. Her daughters and sons would profit from a residence in the capital, with its opportunities for employment and good marriages. Martha Jefferson Randolph, of all people, should have had no trouble calling in a favor. Although she could have turned to any Washington lady or gentleman for help, she was out of the loop of everyday political activities, and so she turned to Margaret Bayard Smith, Washington insider.

It was a good choice. In 1828 Margaret Bayard Smith was at the peak of her political power. In October, Bayard Smith wrote to her sister Maria Bayard Boyd that she "had a most affecting letter . . . from Mrs. Randolph. She made no complaints and expressed no anxiety but the simple narrative . . . needed nothing to touch any heart." Martha Jefferson Randolph appealed to Bayard Smith for a clerkship for her son-in-law Nicholas Trist (who had married Virginia Jefferson Randolph in 1824), "without which it would be impossible to come to Washington."[80]

Bayard Smith's motive for helping Martha Jefferson Randolph may have sprung from a warm heart, but her assessments were coldly professional: "The moment I heard [of] Mr. Forest's [an officeholder] death—I went to Mr. Clay—showed him her letter and added to it every argument justice or benevolence could. If ever I was eloquent it was then." Speaker of the House Henry Clay sympathized but told her that the clerks in his department expected the vacancy to be filled by promotion. However, he ended the interview by assuring Bayard Smith that "his feelings were one with me, and he would do everything justice would allow." Bayard Smith did not work alone, enlisting Dolley Payne Todd Madison (and her kinswoman, Miss Cutts) to urge the same suit. Internal departmental pressure notwithstanding, Nicholas Trist got the job and went on to a long and distinguished career in public service.[81]

Four years later Mrs. Randolph again turned to Bayard Smith for help in placing a member of her large family in a position. This time Bayard Smith took her cause to the wife of Secretary of War General Peter Porter, Letitia B. Porter, with whom she often collaborated on these missions. Appealing to justice and feeling, Mrs. Porter obtained a place through her husband's connections. She wrote to Bayard Smith that if Mrs. Randolph had a son of suitable age, General Porter agreed to get him a cadet's commission and advance him so that the young man would have "almost all the advantages as if he had entered" military service at the proper time, some five months before.[82]

These particular missions proved unqualified successes, but Bayard Smith did sometimes fail. The significance of her work, however, should not be judged by the success or failure of a particular object or campaign. Rather, it lies in the reactions of those around her, the general assumption that she acted quite reasonably and rightly. A female network underlay Bayard Smith's patronage efforts, an important clue that far from being unique, her influence peddling constituted acceptable, desirable behavior for a group of influential women. On one occasion, when Bayard Smith hoped to succeed where her husband had failed, she reminisced, "Ah, when my good Mrs. Porter was here, with what freedom would I go to her on such occasions with a certainty of success, where circumstances admitted it."[83]

Another episode in Bayard Smith's career illustrates the female networks and the milieu in which they took place. On several occasions both Bayard Smith and her husband tried mightily to procure appointments (including a seat on the Supreme Court) for her brother-in-law Andrew Kirkpatrick, chief justice of New Jersey and husband of Jane Bayard Kirkpatrick. After failing several times, in 1826 Bayard Smith defended yet another attempt with a long account of her unsuccessful venture. In a letter filled with news of family health and activities, she interrupted herself, "And now, my dear sister, for the business mentioned in your last letter"; these transactions, though for the benefit of Judge Kirkpatrick, were conducted in personal correspondence between the sisters. "Being aware of the necessity of promptitude in such affairs," Bayard Smith and her adult daughter Susan went into the city the day after receiving Bayard Kirkpatrick's letter and called on "Mrs. ——," who "with her usual kindness, immediately asked me to stay to dinner, which invitation I accepted, having ever found gentlemen more good humored and accessible at the dinner table than when alone." One can scarcely imagine a more succinct summation of the assumptions behind the dinner-table strategy! The success of this tactic depended upon the cooperation of the lady of the house, who had issued the invitation upon learning of Bayard Smith's mission.

Over dinner Bayard Smith did her best to "dissipate the coldness and reserve common of late to Mr. —— and succeeded pretty well, he became as amicable and gracious as when I first knew him." Though Bayard Smith is not forthcoming on the reasons for the "coldness and reserve," her awareness and attempts to overcome them indicate a professional attitude, which does not let pride stand in the way of a goal.[84] After the servants had cleared and withdrawn, "Mrs. —— rose to leave the table," an indication that the other females in the room should retire with her. "I asked her if she could trust her husband tete-à-tete with me—she, (knowing my object) laughingly consented and withdrew with my Susan and her son." The presence of the two young people helped to make this official transaction looked like a friendly social dinner.

Alone with the gentleman, Bayard Smith, using her "very best manner . . . broached the subject," adding two interesting disclaimers. First, she would not be requesting a job if "not prompted by affection," and second, "Mr. Smith as he well knew had always declined such interposition." By invoking the pull of affection, Bayard Smith was indulging in the ritual denial many women of this era used before embarking on political actions or discussions. Ironically, in this situation her acknowledgment of her husband's reluctance could only imply that in an antipatronage culture, patronage was, and could only legitimately be, women's work. Bayard Smith's account continued: "After this preface, I said all I could think of to interest him in our friend." One might conclude that her host did not want to be involved, because he immediately suggested "a more proper person to apply to." Bayard Smith cannily told him that she hoped to have that man's influence, but "that I annexed much more importance to his influence, knowing it to be much more powerful than of any other individual."

No doubt flattered, but still reluctant, the gentleman "modestly disclaimed having any influence, or at least but little"; but Bayard Smith had not come so far to have him wiggle off the hook. "'Give us that *little* and I will be contented and indeed sure of success,' said I, adding some compliments." Relenting, he promised that though he made no guarantees, he would "certainly remember all I had said, would give due weight to the circumstance I had mentioned and to whatever misrepresentations might be made by others." He cautioned Bayard Smith that much had to pass before the matter was settled and advised that "our friend" should "obtain letters from the most influential characters in the state and throw into his scales so great a weight of public opinion as he could obtain." Bayard Smith stressed to her sister that in her report she had condensed the high points of a "long and desultory conversation," throughout which the man "evidently avoided committing himself," although she hastened to assure Jane, "It was obvious his feelings were kind and friendly."

Bayard Smith's concluding explanation of why Samuel Harrison Smith could not intercede for Jane's husband is equally instructive about the process of patronage. Noting that "what he will not do for himself, will not be deemed unfriendly not to do for another," Bayard Smith claimed that her husband "keeps himself wholly aloof from the present administration, and [would] feel it an indelicacy in him to ask any favor from those who he has opposed." Because of his political stance, "he never visits," demonstrating the close connection between calling and politics in the capital. In other words, Samuel could not call, because his actions would be interpreted politically. His wife, however, led a separate existence, and whatever intercourse existed between the Smiths and official society "arises from my personal friendships with the ladies." Bayard Smith then ended her letter: "I most sincerely and affectionately interest myself in everything that interests you and should rejoice in any or the best degree, to prove by something more than words the interest I feel."[85]

THE LANGUAGE OF HEART

This account not only confirms the centrality of women to the business of patronage but also establishes that such transactions took place in women's spaces, such as parlors and dining rooms, during social activities usually considered private, such as calling, visiting, and dining. In 1815, ten years before Bayard Smith's efforts on Andrew Kirkpatrick's behalf, Samuel Smith had brought up his name at the president's dinner table, only to have the strategy backfire. A man Samuel thought friendly proceeded to disparage Kirkpatrick in front of the president.[86] Perhaps this disastrous incident convinced Samuel to implement his policy of noninterference and leave these matters to his wife. He certainly made no time for a future brother-in-law of one of Jane's daughters, who arrived in Washington in 1814 with a letter of introduction from Margaret Bayard Smith's brother, Samuel Bayard. No matter that her husband would not involve himself; the young man's future Aunt Smith invited him to a round of parties, teas, and dinners where "I took pains to introduce him to all the members," among them "two dozen more of the most distinguished members" and seven men, including Henry Clay, she listed by name for her sister. Through Bayard Smith's intercession, this young man immediately found himself moving in high company indeed.

During her own party for her future kinsman, Bayard Smith improved the opportunity by "mention[ing] him particularly" to those with whom she was "very intimate." Though Samuel Harrison Smith had been too busy to initiate occasions to help this young aspirant to office, Bayard Smith's party allowed her husband the opportunity, without much effort, to "sp[eak] of his [the candidate's] business in a way that might turn their attention to it" and to introduce the young man to the chairman of the Ways and Means Committee. Margaret Bayard Smith followed up on her husband's efforts by inviting the chairman to dinner, along with other influential men.[87] In addition to her direct efforts to aid her young kinsman, Bayard Smith provided the social space that multiplied opportunities and efforts for and by others.

In politics, private spaces have often served public purposes. Diplomats have long recognized that the business of diplomacy is rendered most effective with trust and confidence between government officials.

This is not easy to establish, and the most efficient way lies in using homes and social settings to make the process seem natural and easy. A home setting shifts the focus from the official males to the unofficial women, which allows the official players room to maneuver and negotiate. Wives, daughters, and other female kin create an atmosphere that makes officials feel they are truly getting to know each other on terms of intimacy.[88] Like homes of foreign ambassadors in Washington City, the homes of politicians became places to establish trust. In a diplomatic context, Washington parlors constituted one more type of political space.

It may seem ironic, in view of the extent and prevalence of the Washington female public, to discover that their most profound political work took place in spaces entirely female and private. Women in Washington developed public lives of their own; why, then, did they resort to the same social techniques women used in other settings to transact public business? Numerous answers to this question exist, most notably that the culture may have supported a woman getting close to the action, even sitting in the debater's chair, but would not allow that woman to stand up and make a speech. But perhaps these women's social practices offer a more intriguing perspective, for such crucial politicking activities can be only done, by both men and women, in unofficial space.

Women, cut off from official channels, develop a keen sense of the nuances of the unofficial, such as the insistence on personal presence that emerges from women's correspondence on patronage. A large percentage of those unread applications, piled in department offices, came from men who placed too much confidence in the power of official documents. In contrast, Bayard Smith and other female patronage players insisted that the candidates present themselves personally. Though the $800-a-year post Dolley Payne Todd Madison obtained for her nephew Samuel Todd was not as lucrative as she had hoped, she explained that "the advantages of your being in this place will be considerable towards your obtaining something better." Bayard Smith offered the same advice to Jane Kirkpatrick on the various occasions she helped find employment for Jane's sons and other male kin: "So, let me repeat, let our friend come and make himself known. I intended using the privilege of old acquaintance." The reasons were obvious: "If he were here on the spot, that would be a great point gained—a very great one—he might make acquaintance and others might become acquainted with his qualifications and personal merit and would feel a much livelier interest for one whom they knew, than for one who they never saw."[89]

In addition to blurring the lines dividing public and private events and spaces, women's accounts of their patronage work also confuse the historical construct of the separate spheres, in which women supposedly retired to the home, leaving the corruption of the marketplace and smoke-filled rooms to men. In one way the business of patronage neatly reverses this paradigm; while women engaged in the nuts and bolts of politicking, men remained aloof and pure. When they did participate, men employed feminine wiles in social situations, as Samuel Smith did by introducing the topic of Andrew Kirkpatrick over the dinner table. In contrast, Bayard Smith discussed salaries, conditions of employment, and opportunities for advancement with her candidates and patrons at social occasions. She also approached non-kin males in their official capacities as employers and couched her requests not in the Esther-like style of war widow petitions but with open discussions of money and qualifications. Gendered behavior prescriptions blended with reality, as both sexes employed whatever strategy they needed to get what they wanted.

Perhaps most significantly, in these crucial matters women and men worked together.[90] Rather than presiding over sex-segregated areas, women and men approached each other, discussed, proposed, and negotiated. Men and women did not conduct business identically, but perhaps less differently than previously assumed. An official male always had to be the end point of a patronage process, because he had to make the official appointment, but males, of course, were also the supplicants. Men supplied the official documents, including not only the letters that confirmed appointments but also the letters of recommendation. Women helped make the system work on the ground.

Males as well as females were part of a patronage seeker's network. For Bayard Smith, they were colleagues, connections, and sources of information, as her visit to her young friend at the State Department, Eugene Vale, indicates. On one occasion, Bayard Smith, who often presented herself as a world-weary, home-loving domestic creature, railed at being housebound and thus prevented from gathering information and calling in some important chips. "Had it not been for her [daughter Susan's] increased indisposition, I should have seen and conversed with a gentleman in office who has always shown me much regard about the affair of an appointment and another gentleman, who is somewhat indebted to me for the place he holds and who is now in high favor and on the most confidential terms with the president." Far from the stereotype of the True Woman avoiding the public sphere, Bayard Smith knew that being out and about in public or inviting the male public home was crucial to her interests: "If I was not thus detained at home, I should have been going about seeking for information. Now we invite no company to the house, so I have no chance of seeing gentlemen who might aid in researches."[91]

Given early Republican American culture's oft-expressed horror of "petticoat politicians," these women's actions in political business may seem improper or even radical. On this point, Bayard Smith's documents prove most revealing, especially in their articulation of what may have remained unspoken in other women's lives. These elite white women certainly did not see themselves as lone feminists or radicals breaking barriers. Paradoxically, Bayard Smith, as well as Dolley Payne Todd Madison and others, saw their political activities as extensions of two of the most important and most womanly duties of their lives: caring for the family and charity toward others. The righteousness of her causes, such as aiding fatherless males with mothers and siblings to support, may have allowed Bayard Smith full rein to be aggressive and therefore effective. By the mid-1810s, when her own kin came of employment age, she had a system in place and the confidence to aid not just her relatives but any young man or family she deemed worthy.

By framing her efforts in the language of benevolence and emotion, Bayard Smith could assure herself (and her correspondents) that she was only doing what her heart deemed proper. People in nineteenth-century middle-class culture viewed women as creatures of the heart; as long as they followed its dictates (within the limits of male desires and anxieties, of course), they could do no wrong. A letter from Jane Bayard Kirkpatrick regarding her son Littleton reveals how women of the era contained their patronage dealings within psychologically and socially acceptable boundaries. After Bayard Smith succeeded in placing this nephew in a highly advantageous position, his mother wrote to her: "Seldom, my dear Margaret, in the course of my whole life have I from any circumstances been rendered so happy as by the intelligence contained in your last letter. By the blessings of providence and your kind exertions our plan for L. is completed."

Bayard Kirkpatrick continued by describing how her "heart is over-flowing with gratitude to my Heavenly Benefactor," crediting God not only with "providing" but even with actually placing her son in a situation "so favorable to exertion, so calculated to every generous sentiment of his nature." Her sister casts Bayard Smith as an angel of personal happiness (and divine assistance) and places employment in the realm of personal improvement, rather than the crass arena of the marketplace. The letter flows on in the same vein, full of the softest sentiments, lauding Bayard Smith's "generous heart" for obeying the "law of love" and predicting "ample recompense"—from the "hands of a just and beneficent providence."[92] Little would the uninformed reader know that the writer's sister had acted as an influence peddler, negotiating terms and salaries with an employer. Bayard Kirkpatrick's language preserved her own pride of place as eldest sister and presented Bayard Smith's efforts in terms acceptable to the two well-bred women and their world.

Bayard Smith and other women undertook this work in the context of overlapping families, which reminds us of the importance of seeing historical actors both male and female not as great or exceptional isolated individuals but as embedded in complex kinship networks. In later decades the ideal of the nuclear family in retreat from the world and pursuing self-sufficient privacy would dominate, but during this period the ideology and myth of individualism had not yet become an important part of elite and middle-class culture. Natal and marital connections told the upper and middle classes who a person was. Individual merit was not insignificant, but background controlled and indicated personality and capabilities.

On the simplest level Bayard Smith and her counterparts understood their efforts to obtain employment for male family members as an extension of their duties as loving, responsible mothers. However, they also justified obtaining jobs for non-kin men (as Bayard Smith did for Nicholas Trist) as benevolent aid to deserving families in need, using the "bonds of womanhood" to benefit anxious mothers or to protect innocent sisters.[93] They also worked within the institution of family in the process of carrying out their missions, appealing to wives and mothers, using family homes (their own and others') as their forum, making their requests during a social call or at a dinner table. Bayard Smith and other elite white women worked within the assumption that it was better to see a candidate personally than to read about him and that it was best of all to know a family, rather than just an individual. These assumptions may seem like common sense, but they have only rarely been taken seriously as factors in political analysis.[94]

Beyond all of this selfless rhetoric, Bayard Smith's letters make it clear that at least some women knew the significance of their work and that they took pleasure in their success. Before recounting a successful patronage foray, Bayard Smith exulted: "I write with more pleasure now, as I have more pleasing intelligence. I know of nothing more delightful than to succeed in plans in which we are much interested," adding playfully, "I have had this pleasure in so great a degree this morning, that I feel unusually exhilarated."[95] Though sometimes acting as men's voices, speaking when and where their husbands dared not, these women knew they were not tools or intermediaries or even "deputy husbands." They acted as independent agents, pursuing their goals in forthright and focused ways.

Possessing power imparts a sense of self-importance. Bayard Smith was not above boasting about her capability, as in an acerbic comment concerning a young man who, once a frequent and pleasant visitor, had become corrupted by the *usage du monde*, thus neglecting his old friends: "What trifles influence the destiny of men—Little does he suspect the influence I have had in his present condition." "Unknown to him," she revealed, she had obtained a place for this young Mr. Ward in a traveling party bound for the West, "consisting of western members [of the House], Governor Cass, Governor Clark and family, Mr. Lyon." The "intimate acquaintance" Ward formed with these "respectable and worthy people who are now among his best friends" thereafter ensured his success. Even before the young man left Washington City, Bayard Smith continued, "I likewise took an opportunity of interesting Mr. Clay for him." This she accomplished in the most traditional of social ploys: "I maneuvered to place him . . . alone on the sopha by Mr. Clay." The maneuvering worked, and "an interesting conversation took place. Mr. Clay, I hear, is his constant correspondent and a patron of his paper."[96] However, in a cultural climate that did not allow even men to express ambition openly, Bayard Smith did not indulge in too much preening. Note that she began with a disclaimer, presenting her influence as a trifle. For all of the obvious pride and pleasure Bayard Smith expressed on the occasions she discussed her efforts, she understood her work, or at least wrote of it, in ways very different from today's conceptions.

In considering the crucial role women's relationships and activities played in obtaining jobs and favors for men, it is worthwhile to stress that patronage provided the foundation for the structure of the early federal government. Placing supporters in highly desirable places ensured constituent satisfaction, thus securing a return to the center of power. As important, the process of making contacts and deals, of learning political systems, of indebting oneself to powerful people, of enmeshing oneself and one's family in the national power structures, also contributed to creating oneself as a personal political force.

Patronage's long history stems partly from its neat, reciprocal quality. Being a successful friend at court ensured that one's family would themselves gain a new friend in a position of power. Being in the debt of someone more powerful was a good thing; having someone powerful in your debt was even better. An effective influence peddler acquired both kinds of debts, the first while working for a candidate and the second from a grateful candidate who might, through one's efforts, leapfrog up the political ladder. The process of networking became richer and more complex when connections were being made not just between individuals but among whole families. In a time of unprecedented growth in Congress, with a relatively weak executive, these networks of kith and kin, of personal and professional favors, provided the federal government with the structure it needed to grow and thrive. With so much at stake, no wonder that disruptions of the social scene and violations of the social rules caused what Washington women called "heartburnings."

THE URBAN GARDEN

Margaret Bayard Smith's activities challenge the general assumption that politicking could only be the business of official men. On the contrary, in Euro-American political systems, elite men and women both politicked in unofficial spaces. This was especially true for democratic politics in an age before organized parties became the dominant political units. Transactions in the unofficial space privilege face-to-face, personal interactions over speeches to audiences, official procedures, and exchanges of documents. In a democracy, where successful legislation depends upon a majority and decisions are necessarily by consensus, personal relations prove crucial. These relations always provide the base of the political, in a democracy or a republic perhaps even more than in a monarchy. On the simplest level, a working democracy includes increasingly large groups of interested people, and the layers and levels of relations multiply. The failure to understand this aspect of democratic politics explains lawmakers' conflicted attitude toward politics during the early Republic. Having eschewed a system of monarchy based on corrupt personal power, the founding generation could not yet recognize that the alternative system they embraced also had to rely on personal relations.

And no wonder Jefferson and the other early Republicans were obsessed by patronage, a risky, unrepublican, and crucial practice. Politics and patronage provided the keys to making a government run. An absolute monarch can unapologetically display his or her power over these areas, while a republic, which also needs connections and self-interest in order to function, must dissemble. Ironically, the growth and stability of the first modern democracy depended heavily on these aristocratic practices and deployed the same personnel to implement them: women. As in the larger political and cultural context, women became the repository for aristocratic practices, desires, and longings, so here they facilitated politics as usual. The austere republican man could remain pure and uninvolved in patronage, as "Mr. Madison" did while "Lady Madison" employed patronage and networking to build congressional consensus and support for her husband's administration and policies. In an ironic twist on the separate spheres, women performed the dirty work of politics to ensure their husbands' political purity.

The experiences of women in Washington differed from those of women in other cities because of the unprecedented freedom of movement the city offered. In every American city and small town, wherever the family business was politics, elite and middle-class white women participated. But the knowledge Washington women gained from their public lives made them much better players. Though women in other cities participated in political discussions, their information and experience of politics came second- and third-hand. Most citizens, male or female, never saw national or state government in action; male political talk originated within a context of local affairs, government reports, newspaper accounts, or rumors. To add another filtering layer, many women outside Washington gleaned their political news from overhearing discussions based on these sources.

In contrast, women in Washington saw the process in action, both the public poses and the subterranean movements. They heard debate on the floors of Congress and at the tables of boardinghouses. They knew the participants, they felt political passion firsthand, and some grew active and involved. They approached the business of influencing legislation and patronage with a confidence gained from personal knowledge and from the respect accorded them by their fellow lodgers, their male friends, and their relatives.[97]

Flexibility was the key to success in Washington City. In their hometowns these women may have been local gentry or shopkeeping wives, part of the great movement to build a middle class, with their own activities relegated to a female private sphere. In Washington, where women and men functioned in the public sphere, women from all over the country and from many backgrounds shifted their class identities, adapting themselves to the tasks of politics, especially to the problem of creating a ruling class.

Postwar Washington City was an urban garden, with its streets and public sites populated by women. In their highly gender-specific costumes—colorful, bright, exotic—they re-created the landscape. Arm-in-arm, women and men both walked the streets of the new city. Men spoke from the floors of Congress under the watchful eyes of their female constituents. High-pitched and modulated female comments and judgments blended with the stentorian tones of male orators. Men and women populated the private spaces of the new capital, and in the unofficial spheres spectators became performers as they negotiated, struck, and closed deals. This was a system as old as aristocracy itself, and in the 1820s it would move to a new level in Washington City as the race for political prizes escalated.

❧ 4 ❧

Louisa Catherine Adams Campaigns
for the Presidency

Love's Labour's Lost

POPULAR HISTORICAL OPINION presents the Monroe administration as socially moribund, especially in contrast with the Dolley Madison years. Gone were the big weekly soirees and easy access to the executive mansion, and Washington residents and visitors felt the disruption keenly. These historians cite contemporaries who characterized the changes brought by the Monroes as "earthquake, upheaval and cyclone." To support their picture of the bleak social situation and the reaction of the populace, scholars of Washington City and the White House point to the "etiquette war" of 1819, the ladies' boycott of the White House drawing rooms and the subsequent bad feelings engendered by the Monroes, quoting Margaret Bayard Smith eight months after the Monroe inauguration: "Although they have lived seven years in Washington [when James served as secretary of state], both Mr. and Mrs. Monroe are perfect strangers, not only to me but all the citizens."[1]

Elizabeth Kortright Monroe garners most of the blame from historians for this state of affairs. In their depictions Elizabeth, whether from snobbishness or ill health (she may have suffered from epilepsy), retreated behind forbidding doors, and her reluctance to entertain proved a liability to her husband. The White House did indeed adopt more formal and aloof practices, but both James and Elizabeth decided on this self-consciously European style. James Monroe informed his cabinet that in order to win respect for the new nation among the world powers, he would place foreign ministers on a "European . . . footing of form and ceremony." No foreign minister could drop in on the president, as they had in previous administrations. The Monroes extended this tone beyond their dealings with the diplomatic corps to include many aspects of their administration, even contemplating "uniform dress" for cabinet members and other high officials.[2]

Despite the new, more reserved White House, the executive social calendar for the years 1817–25 reveals that the Monroes hosted many large social events, and observers report that they were more than well-attended. During the height of the season, the Monroes held drawing rooms every two weeks, dinners twice a week, and open houses on New Year's Day and the Fourth of July. James Monroe seriously considered ending the levees, but he never did, posting guards instead to control the huge crowds. Even during the last years of the second term, when Elizabeth Kortright Monroe made few personal appearances, the parties continued, presided over by the Monroes' older daughter, Eliza Monroe Hay.[3] The 1824 New Year's Day levee drew more people to the White House than had any event up to that point. In any case, the events cited by historians to illustrate the upheaval caused by Elizabeth Monroe and her reclusiveness—the etiquette war, the boycott, and Bayard Smith's assessment—occurred in the early years of the first term.

However, a far-reaching change in the capital's social policy and an ensuing social revolution did take place during the Monroe administrations. Viewing the revolution in isolation from politics puts the focus on the wrong kinds of social events and the wrong lady, and so fails to illumine the true significance of these events. It was not a lack of soirees that outraged the official elite; rather, it was the abrupt change in the calling patterns of the government families. Though Elizabeth Monroe spurred these changes, announcing that she would not call (and later, when no one called on her, that she would not accept calls), calling at the White House was not as crucial to political life as were the networks among congressional and cabinet families.[4] The real moving force that disrupted the social order, prompting the uproar, was the political team of Louisa Catherine Johnson Adams and her husband, Secretary of State John Quincy Adams.

Fortunately, when it comes to the Adamses' Washington career, both Louisa Catherine and John Quincy documented their activities extensively. These accounts cannot be relied upon to present objective truth or even their authors' actual motivations, but they do offer many intriguing perspectives on issues of the social and political culture. Though Louisa Catherine commented on and complained about the etiquette war in her letters and diaries, most of the information about the affair emerges in John Quincy's voice, from his diary and official papers. In all these documents John Quincy asserted himself as a partner to his wife and included her in his analysis to a degree not found in many other episodes in his life. So, while the following discussion relies heavily on John Quincy's words, we may discern Louisa Catherine's central role in the etiquette war, a role made even more definitive and detailed by her subsequent use of the affair.[5]

"EARTHQUAKE, UPHEAVAL AND CYCLONE"

The etiquette controversy centered around the problem of the first call: who would make the initial call on whom, thus determining who would occupy the subordinate position in the social hierarchy. In 1817 Louisa Catherine and John Quincy returned to Washington after a ten-year absence, having spent eight of those years abroad. In the months following their arrival, as John Quincy took up his role as secretary of state and Louisa Catherine began her social duties, they did not call on anyone systematically. Consequently the president of the Senate pro tempore, Senator John Gaillard, and a colleague called upon John Quincy in his office on January 5, 1818, and informed him of the Senate's unofficial, unwritten rule decreeing that senators would pay the first call only to the president (and, by implication, not to the cabinet families). According to his own account, John Quincy expressed surprise at this and informed the delegation, in the politest terms, that when he had been a senator, he and his wife had paid the first call on the department heads. He hastened to add that he "was ready to conform to any arrangement that might be proper," "suppos[ing]," however, that the senators' rules regarding their extent of their own obligation "did not extend to a requisition that the heads of department should first visit them." The delegation seemed to agree, and the men parted "in perfect good humor on the subject."[6]

Two weeks later, to cement this declaration of their family policy, Louisa Catherine officially allied herself with Elizabeth Monroe, declar-

John Quincy Adams, by Thomas Sully, 1825. (Courtesy of New York State Office of Parks, Recreation, and Historical Preservation, Philipse Manor Hall State Historic Site, Yonkers, New York)

ing that though she would return all calls paid to her, she would not initiate any.[7] The Adamses might have thought the matter settled, but the official elites of Washington did not. The policies of the two households caused many "heartburnings," and more than once John Quincy and Louisa Catherine made trips to the executive mansion to confer with the Monroes on questions of calling and socializing. Matters came to a head at the start of the 1819–20 congressional year, when the drawing room of

Mrs. John Quincy Adams, by Charles Bird King, 1824. (National Museum of American Art, Smithsonian Institution, Adams-Clement Collection, gift of Mary Louisa Adams, Washington, D.C.)

the president opened "to a 'beggarly-row of empty chairs,'" and only three ladies attended Louisa Catherine's first party of the season. At the same time a "friend" (political supporter) of John Quincy's spoke to President Monroe about the calling situation, "because it had excited some feeling among the senators, and because uses were made of it for political purposes."[8] Immediately, James Monroe called a cabinet meeting to discuss the issue.

On December 20, 1819, the cabinet met for two hours and came to no firm resolution. In John Quincy's account of his participation in this meeting and in two subsequent state papers (letters to President Monroe and to Vice President Daniel Tompkins, in his position as president of the Senate), he articulated a stand on behalf of himself and Louisa Catherine that seems reasonable, logical and, from a republican point of view, downright virtuous. In all three of these documents, John Quincy adopted the tone of a political naïf. According to his account of the cabinet meeting, John Quincy suggested that each cabinet member "should follow his own course" and "separate entirely the official character from the practice of personal visiting"—in other words, make calling a purely social activity, stripped of any political content or context.[9]

In his letters to Monroe and Tompkins, he continued this theme, reckoning that to visit every member of Congress at every session "would not only be a very useless waste of time, but not very compatible with the discharge of the real and important duties of the departments." John Quincy also managed to include a virtuous stand on etiquette in general, deeming the "introduction of such a system of mere formality" incompatible with the "republican simplicity of our institutions."[10]

John Quincy's public stance, as conveyed by the two state papers, confused many observers. Thomas Hubbard informed his wife, Phebe, of John Quincy's "very singular" letter, commenting, "I think it is ridiculous for gentlemen to create to themselves so much trouble and to notice a paltry question of etiquette in so grave and serious a manner." In Hubbard's opinion John Quincy was "descending from his proper level." Sarah Gales Seaton believed the secretary of state's pose of naïveté, forwarding a copy of his "curious" letter to a correspondent because she found it to "display the character of the man who *may* be our future president in a stronger light than all the public papers he has written." The letter demonstrated to Gales Seaton that John Quincy was "more of a bookworm, and abstracted student than a man of this world."[11]

Both Adamses professed themselves bewildered by all the fuss over private, social practices. John Quincy noted a visit by his wife to Elizabeth Kortright Monroe to discuss "affairs of etiquette in visiting, which, it appears, are affairs of high importance here," as though he had not spent a score of years in the diplomatic corps. Louisa Catherine was even more biting, remarking to her father-in-law, "You will at least have the happiness of living to see the day when the prosperity of the country has arrived at such a pitch of greatness, that the Congress can find no better subjects to regulate than the common and social intercourse of general society." But John Adams knew as well as Louisa Catherine did that his family was not part of "general society" and replied soothingly, "I can easily believe that the etiquette question has become an object of state," advising her "as discreetly as possible" to follow the course set by Mrs. Monroe.[12]

But these supposedly private documents do not necessarily reveal true feelings or opinions. John Quincy wrote his diary with both eyes firmly on his own posterity, and at this point in her life, Louisa Catherine sent her journal home to Quincy to be read aloud within the family. Putting aside their written statements of outrage and exasperation, it is clear that John Quincy and Louisa Catherine had other motives behind their disruption of the calling patterns. Seasoned politicians and diplomats that they were, they would not have risked alienating the political community unless they had higher stakes in mind. The motivations behind the etiquette wars may be discerned by a look at the larger social and political context in which they took place, as well as with the hindsight gained by examining the Adamses' later actions.

The social upheaval was part of the political turbulence of the late 1810s and early 1820s. Although it originated in the political structure of the federal government, the upheaval centered around the election of 1824. James Monroe, who took office in 1817, was generally expected to win a second term easily in 1820, so as early as 1818 the political focus shifted to his possible successors. The election served as both a cause and a symptom of the intense political atmosphere in Washington City during these years. In historical hindsight, this energy signaled a major shift in government, as the rudimentary political systems set in place during the first decades of the new nation struggled to accommodate the federal center's growing power. Though newspapers dubbed the first years of the Monroe administration "The Era of Good Feelings," such harmony, if it ever existed, did not last long.

The campaign to succeed James Monroe as president started early; without question, it was in full swing shortly after his second inaugural in

1821.[13] At the first presidential drawing room of 1820, people had already "teased" Louisa Catherine about how she would "behave in this same situation, as it was likely I should be tried in four years from this time." In the early nineteenth century, presidential cabinets swarmed with potential presidents, though the post of secretary of state was acknowledged by all as the most likely step prior to the presidency. John Quincy held that coveted post for both of James Monroe's terms. Two other front-runners also came from the cabinet: John C. Calhoun of South Carolina, secretary of war, and William H. Crawford of Georgia, secretary of the treasury. The other contender, Henry Clay, had been a runner-up to become Monroe's secretary of state but had settled for the position of Speaker of the House. At the beginning of President Monroe's second term there was another aspirant, depicted in popular cartoons as a dark horse coming up fast on the outside: General Andrew Jackson, the popular Hero of New Orleans and, by 1823, senator from Tennessee.[14]

Astute observers thus kept one eye on the cabinet and one on the Congress, which commanded focus in the capital as the center of federal power. Congress's power grew faster than its ability to contain or direct it, and this was especially true every four years at presidential election time. The United States had no system of national conventions to nominate presidential candidates until the 1830s, and the Constitution specified none. From the election of 1804 through that of 1824, congressional caucuses made presidential nominations. Anyone could recommend or endorse a man for president—local party leaders, members of a state legislature, groups of judges, lawyers, or other leading citizens, a newspaper, even a crowded western barroom—but the ultimate selection lay with "King Caucus" in Washington City. Though the caucus system had begun as a nominating agent, with the demise of the Federalist opposition the Republican caucus became, in effect, the electing power.[15]

Except for a close call in 1812, the caucus ensured an orderly, calm progression from one Republican president to another. But in the agitated atmosphere of the Monroe administrations, this rudimentary stability came under fire from legislators and voters who thought it too aristocratic. With no Federalist candidate, the caucus seemed to deprive the voters of all meaningful choice, and the process of backroom negotiation and deal making among elites gave the whole procedure an unsavory cast. Americans of all classes began to demand reform of the system along democratic lines.[16] This growing opinion, voiced by newspapers and pamphlets, plus the early plethora of presidential choices, contributed to the sense of political upheaval in the capital.

The members of Congress played another important role in the election of a president, especially in the 1820s. The early appearance of a large number of contenders made it seem likely that the election would end, as it had in 1800, in the House of Representatives. The consequences were obvious to everyone, as John Quincy wrote: "The only possible chance for a head of department to attain the presidency is by ingratiating himself personally with the members of Congress; and, as many of them have objects of their own to obtain, the temptation is immense to corrupt conditions." Inevitably, the possibility of House election "leads to a thousand corrupt cabals between the members of Congress and the heads of the Departments, who are thus almost necessarily made rival pretenders to the succession." No wonder the city's leading newspaper, the *Intelligencer,* moved from being a spokesman for the presidency to being a congressional organ: obviously the legislative branch held the key to the action.[17]

This influence over the executive branch, coupled with institutional growing pains, gave rise to much discord in the two houses of Congress. Louisa Catherine reported to John Adams that the members of Congress "grow more and more turbulent and a universal disgust is expressed at their conduct." She attributed their obstreperousness to there being "no decided party" or leaders "to take command of these very raw troops." Instead, legislators were "guided by . . . individual passions" or by "cabals and intrigues to gratify . . . personal ambition."[18]

Louisa Catherine's picture of a growing, fractious Congress confirms later historical estimates of the situation. No consistent leaders appeared because no one was prepared to follow consistently. Cooperation, conciliation, and compromise were scorned by a political culture that saw such "politic" moves as indicators of weak character or ulterior motives for gain. The unruly legislative body was capable of only the most parochial cohesion, that of the sectional "independent icebergs" formed in boardinghouses. With no sanctioned institutional ways to create cohesion, such as party leadership and loyalty, the early political community built its stabilizing structures through culturally approved associations and channels, such as custom and "unambiguous popular approbation."[19]

Social events incorporated both of these avenues and proved most effective in building coalition. "There is a party for every night of the week," Louis McLane informed his wife, Kitty, "and the Otises are at all of them." Thomas Hubbard announced to Phebe that "the Ladies" were "giving tea parties (vying with each other in the splendor of their tea table equipage)" and their husbands gave dinners. Whereas previous social seasons had begun in late December and lasted until February and March, during the years 1819–24 they began by late November and lasted into May.[20]

During the era of the early Republic, no one ran for national office; there were no speeches, rallies, or events. A candidate could write to the newspaper under the guise of supplying biographical information (as John Quincy did) or explaining a political position (as Calhoun did), but the chief method of assuring one's nomination was to arouse the zeal of one's political friends and, through a network of supporters, create a favorable image of one's self in the public mind.[21] Parties, balls, dinners, and White House drawing-room receptions were ideal for this purpose.

Within an atmosphere of entertaining, a strain of focused socializing emerged, mirroring the concentration on candidates and key legislators. As the 1824 election neared, society divided into "separate battalions," and social circles grew smaller even as candidates endeavored to attract more and more supporters. As early as 1820 Margaret Bayard Smith, who had once been socially promiscuous, visited only four families on intimate terms: "her candidate"'s family the Crawfords, her old friends the Calhouns, the Thorntons, and Mrs. Bumford.[22] Long before people used the word *party,* in the sense of "political party," they used the word's meaning of "social event" to suggest political cohesion, as Margaret Bayard Smith did when she spoke of having a "right down Crawford party," a "party" of "fifteen or twenty" theatergoers—"senators and members"—assembled to show public support for William Crawford.[23]

In the gendered world of the early Republic, social events were considered women's work, no matter what their political uses might have been. Despite formal androcentrism, social events were identified by women's names. As a result of Washington City's peculiar needs in that era, women found themselves central personages, sometimes to their delight and other times to their distress. The irony of their official political invisibility and unofficial importance, born of male political need, was not lost on them.

During the etiquette wars Louisa Catherine identified herself as a "plain individual having no claims to any station . . . on the contrary, being continually told that I cannot by the Constitution have any share in the public honors of my husband." So, she added sarcastically, "it is certainly very flattering to me that people should insist upon becoming acquainted with me and force me even against my will to visit them."[24]

Cabinet families emerged as the most assiduous exploiters of this system, investing time, money, and effort in entertaining the congressional families, spending much more of their resources on the cultivation of personal acquaintance than did the congressional community. Government officials spent as many hours engaged in social activities as they did performing their official duties, and anyone who neglected social obligations incurred bitter public and private reproaches. Personality and social attitudes provided the basis for rating a man's political prospects, and a successful candidate at least had to assume a facade of good spirits. When a newspaper scolded John Quincy for shirking his social duties, the secretary of state took this public rebuke seriously and cut short his day to counter the image of a "reserved, gloomy, unsocial temper."[25]

Socializing was a business from five o'clock onward, and both guests and hosts complained frequently about the arduousness of pleasure. Everyone complained about going to the parties that everyone else complained about giving, but go and give they did.[26] The intense politicking of the early 1820s stripped away any graceful pretense of pleasure, and parties scheduled during the election seasons demonstrated too much regularity and method to be expressions of sociability.[27] The secret of the incessant social machine lay in its important function within the political machine.

PARTNERS IN AMBITION

All of these elements of conflict had been in place since James Monroe's election in 1816. The capital was in the throes of change, ripe for manipulation and exploitation, when Louisa Catherine Johnson Adams and John Quincy Adams took up residence in 1817. Their arrival on the Washington scene represented a special political confluence of personality, place, and time. The Adamses possessed unique gifts for this particular context; in some ways, they and their new city were made for each other.

At age fifty, John Quincy Adams had already spent a lifetime in public service, having embarked on his first post in 1780, when he was fourteen. By becoming secretary of state—popularly known as the stepping-stone to the presidency—he was in a position to achieve his highest goal. At no time in their half century of marriage would the couple be as united in partnership as during the years 1817–24.

If Washington City could supply the Adamses with their highest goal—achieving the presidency—the political couple could help the struggling capital as well. To become a full-fledged center of power, Washington City had to overcome its republican fears of large government and acquire practices and structures as effective as those of other courts and capitals. In pursuit of their own goals, Louisa Catherine and John Quincy, fresh from their years in European courts, proved well equipped to introduce the kinds of courtly practices that could establish politically effective relationships and networks.

Indeed, the two may be seen to embody the contradictions of the capital in themselves. Both Louisa Catherine and John Quincy existed uneasily in their own skins and their relationship, both struggling with their unbecoming desires for fame and success, both under multiple burdens. Not only did the cultural milieu forbid open displays or acknowledgments of ambition, but John Quincy's family culture and Louisa Catherine's gender added their own strictures.[28] John Quincy came from a family in which overwhelming ambition for advancement and desire for fame and public honors competed with a rigorous ideal of public service. Even in a culture that demanded modest virtue from its elected officials and discouraged open avowals of ambition, John, Abigail, and John Quincy Adams were extreme in their ambivalence, seesawing between worry that their places in history might not be illustrious enough and horror that they might be caught caring.

For John Quincy, as for his father, politicking and cultivating favor were distasteful. In the Adams credo public office constituted a just reward for virtue and should come as a mandate from the people, an honor bestowed in recognition of a job so well done as to be universally recognized. Like Cincinnatus at his plow or George Washington in the fields of Mount Vernon, a public servant should be called from a virtuous private life by the electorate, to take up the yoke of public service.[29]

Louisa Catherine's ambivalence took the same (though exaggerated) form as that of other politically connected elite women: denying or disclaiming any interest in or taste for politics, usually immediately before engaging in a political discussion or action. But her constant disavowals only reinforce the impression that others regarded her as tremendously powerful. As the election neared, she was subjected to "queer questions" during parties and joking about her plans for being First Lady. She belittled such goings-on—"What a foolish thing popular favor is"—and her own influence—"if he or she court me for that purpose [office seeking] they are woefully mistaken if they imagine I had the least influence." However, even her grumps against her husband confirm that she had influence with him, though she cast it in a negative way: "I believe it would be sufficient for me to utter the name of any person with a view to an appointment to have them excluded all together."[30]

The topic of personal ambition infused the correspondence between the pair from the earliest days of their engagement, each accusing the other of ambition while denying it in themselves. The sheer weight of the subject in their thoughts belies their denials, which extended to the ludicrous extreme of each pretending that John Adams's election to president in 1797 mattered not at all: "the honor of the place" was "a mere bauble." These early exchanges set the tone for their lives together. For them, life was full of high aspirations and a good deal of denial and self-delusion.[31]

In fact, Louisa Catherine and John Quincy had their eyes on the prize, probably from the moment they learned of his appointment as secretary of state. For John Quincy, the presidency was the culmination of a life spent following his father's example, and it also became a high point for Louisa Catherine, who risked her health to sail to the United States to join him at this critical juncture and indeed suffered her last in a long series of miscarriages on board ship.[32] John Quincy knew what it would take for him to achieve the presidency, even as he scornfully described the process in 1818: "The government is indeed assuming more and more a character of a cabal, and preparation, not for the next presidential election, but for the one after—that is, working and counterworking, with many of the worst features of elective monarchies."[33] But even as he belittled the process, he acknowledged that personality and politicking ran the system, and that if he were doing it alone, he would be doomed to failure.

One of John Quincy Adams's best-known traits perfectly blended the personal and the political, albeit in a negative way. He seemed to lack charm or social grace, a defect that stemmed from his inability to interact easily with people. This aspect of his character earned him a considerable reputation and exasperated even the most unimaginative politicians to flights of inspired description. Though not a man to resort even to the threat of physical violence, he garnered comparisons to a "bulldog among spaniels . . . doggedly and systematically repulsive." Rufus Choate decided that "he had an instinct for the jugular and carotid artery as unerring as that of any carnivorous animal."[34]

Such assessments could be grudging testaments to John Quincy's tenacity as a politician as well as to his spectacular lack of charm, and he accordingly took a perverse pride in them. He knew he lacked even a modicum of graciousness: "I am a man of reserved, cold, austere, and forbidding manners; my political adversaries say, a gloomy misanthropist, and my personal enemies, an unsocial savage. With a knowledge of the actual defect in my character, I have not the pliability to reform it." Though John Quincy placed the blame for his public silence on childhood admonitions to be seen and not heard, he also seemed complacent and rather proud of this defect, which proved his virtue, making any personal honors seem like a just reward for unstinting service rather than a reflection of mere popularity.[35]

However, though such virtue would not go unrewarded in political theory, it had its drawbacks in actual practice. Up to this point in his career, John Quincy had enjoyed his greatest successes in appointive rather than elective offices; ironically, those offices were in the diplomatic corps. John Quincy proved a conscientious and thorough, if limited, minister. John Spear Smith, who accompanied the Adams family on their mission to Russia, wrote to his father that he and the other American men dubbed Adams "the Mute of Siberia." The young man lamented that his mentor was "an unfortunate appointment for this court. He has no manners, is gauche, never was intended for a foreign minister, and is only fit to turn over law authorities." Smith was clear about where John Quincy's greatest weakness lay, telling his father: "You would blush to see him in any society, and particularly at court circles, walking about perfectly listless, speaking to no one, and absolutely as if he were in a dream. . . . Dry sense alone does not do at European courts. Something more is necessary, which something Mr. A. does not possess."[36]

Yet John Quincy's American missions enjoyed considerable success in Berlin and St. Petersburg. The reason was simply the presence of a woman who had ample portions of the "something more" John Spear Smith prescribed. From her first sojourn in Berlin as a young bride until her death, Louisa Catherine enjoyed a reputation among diplomats and congressmen as a woman of great charm and attraction.[37] Though she often assumed a pose of weariness toward her social duties, her descriptions of "occasions" and "personages" reveal a delight in society and a love of people. Throughout her career she obtained places of favor in court circles on two continents by her talents in music, her ability to speak French, and her desire to reach out and please those around her. When it came to social occasions, Louisa Catherine was the diplomat of the family, and both Adamses knew it.[38]

In many ways Louisa Catherine had been as surely bred for a life in politics as her husband, though not so overtly. Born in London in 1775 to an American father and an English mother, Louisa Catherine spent the years of the American Revolution in France, thus acquiring a native fluency in French which would stand her in good stead in the courts of Europe. Her family were hardly aristocrats, rather mercantile arrivistes, and Louisa Catherine's memoirs, though recalling a childhood "fraught with bliss," present a picture of an anxious household struggling to attain and maintain a precarious social position.[39] Louisa Catherine and her seven sisters enjoyed an education that featured the "accomplishments"; music proved Louisa Catherine's particular talent. Their mother, Catherine Nuth Johnson, trained her girls to be charming hostesses, to run a large upper-class household, and she shared with them an extensive knowledge and love of the burgeoning material culture of the day.

Conscientious climbers, the Johnsons made their sumptuous London home a center for prominent Americans, including government officials who found themselves in England. John and Abigail Adams attended an evening party there when John served as the American minister to the Court of St. James's. As Louisa Catherine and her older sister, Nancy, grew into young ladies, they often entertained guests after an elegant dinner with songs, the pianoforte, and other instruments. In this household whose entertaining style resembled a diplomatic home, John Quincy met and married Louisa Catherine Johnson in 1791. He and his parents knew how important it was for him to make an advantageous match, and they often fretted about the ability of this petite, pretty, emotional creature to measure up to rigorous family standards. However, by the time the Adamses came home in 1817, John Quincy knew well his deficiencies and her assets. If the wider political culture and his own psyche demanded that John Quincy Adams had to appear as a man of "principle and modesty," Louisa Catherine was entirely ready to assume the task of "Smilin' for the Presidency."[40]

Louisa Catherine and John Quincy's diaries demonstrate their respective positions. John Quincy's account teems with testimony to his own lack of popularity, his astonishment at and distance from the electioneering around him. In January 1825, at a crucial point late in the electoral process, he even fell suggestively silent. The power of Louisa Catherine's account lies in its dailiness; unlike John Quincy's diary with its vague and sweeping proclamations, her words disclose a clear, specific pattern of actions that belie the family rhetoric. From the moment Louisa Catherine and John Quincy entered the capital in the fall of 1817, they labored together on a social plan designed to make John Quincy Adams president of the United States. The six years covered by Louisa Catherine's journals present a picture of steady campaigning that grew in intensity as 1824 approached, organized and orchestrated by a political team that acknowledged their respective strengths and weaknesses, exploiting the former and compensating for the latter.

DECLARING WAR

One of their first moves in the presidential game was to rework the social networks already in place, beginning with the calling patterns. Unless one clearly sees the relationship between the etiquette wars of 1818 and 1819 and Louisa Catherine's extensive involvement in the campaigning to elect John Quincy Adams president, in a context that included the subtle interdependence between politics and society, those wars appear isolated or confusing, and Louisa Catherine's efforts might be relegated to the "exceptional."[41]

At first glance the etiquette wars do not fit any master plan the couple

might have had, and they would seem to have worked against their interests. In John Quincy's official version in his diary and the two state papers, he appears as the virtuous, if naive, republican, and Louisa Catherine seems to be the retiring lady. To preserve their independence as private
persons, the couple were willing to risk offending the influential members
of Congress. However, even a cursory look at how the two spent their
time reveals that John Quincy Adams initiated calls all the time on his
rounds and reacted with guilt and promises to do better when publicly
criticized for neglecting his calls. For her part Louisa Catherine, in her
quest for the presidency, did not miss a single congressional member once
the campaign began in earnest.

Examined within a framework that takes the political use of social
events seriously, Louisa Catherine and John Quincy do not appear the
naïfs they wished to seem. By making their own rules, the couple asserted
themselves as social leaders, an important spot to occupy in a political
town that depended on its unofficial structures in the absence of official
ones. In doing so, they usurped the traditional function of the White
House and the president's wife and checked the presumption of a growing Congress, whose members thought that they could set the tone. In a
discussion with the vice president, John Quincy learned that some of the
members, especially the southern members, claimed the right of receiving
the first visit from cabinet ministers as an acknowledgment of a power
and status at least equal to that of the executive branch. John Quincy and
Louisa Catherine stole their march; candidates for the presidency were dependent on Congress, but if John Quincy ascended to the presidency, he
would possess a valuable commodity himself: disposition of cabinet posts
and other appointments. Legislators figured largely among presidential
appointees, and two out of three cabinet members (and thus potential
presidents) were former legislators.[42]

The disruption caused by the Adamses' refusal to participate in old
patterns worked. The split continued down the political pyramid, with
House and Senate families refusing to pay calls on any executive families,
even dividing among the two houses over who paid first call. The etiquette
wars reflected, in part, the growing pains of an increasingly self-important
Congress and a substantial shift in political power among branches of the
government.

There were other, more immediately practical reasons why the Adamses needed to establish themselves at the head of society. They had arrived in town virtual strangers to everyone. The calling patterns in place favored long-term residents, like Mrs. Crawford and Mrs. Calhoun, who had paid the first call, or had it paid on them, years before. According to custom, this familiarity allowed invitations to flow among all the important households. Social networks firmly in place, these established cabinet families interacted freely in the homes of congressmen and vice versa.

In his diary John Quincy acknowledged the use the women made of their networks, scorning William Crawford's statement that his wife and not himself "insisted on adhering to the system." From John Quincy's point of view, Crawford, "whose policy it is in all things to cringe among the members of Congress," "had a steady eye on the caucus."[43] Fearing that by using conventional methods they could never establish the intimacy their rivals enjoyed, Louisa Catherine and John Quincy preemptively seized the upper hand. However, refusing to follow customary usage was only the first stage, for the Adamses did not want to alienate people. The second and more important stage of their campaign was the reconfiguring of the social scene itself.

In his letter to the president and the letter intended for Congress, John Quincy careful flattered both houses, finding that "no republican principle" would justify honoring the members of the Senate without doing the same for the House, while denying that he ever had any expectations of a first call from anyone. He also devoted a long paragraph to praising the Senate as a body of "importance and dignity," reflecting that "if there is a body of men upon earth for whom more than any other I ought to cherish any feelings of attachment . . . it is the Senate of the United States." Because John Quincy had spent most of his career in the diplomatic service and the Senate held the power of appointment, he acknowledged his obligation: "Base indeed should I feel myself . . . [should I become] inflated by the dignity of the stations to which their . . . kindness has contributed to raise me." Perhaps in afterthought this seemed too obvious a flattery, for the passage appears only in the letter to the president. When John Quincy rewrote the letter for Congress, he eliminated this crude acknowledgment of the Senate's power to confer.[44]

The most significant line of the letter to Congress hinted at the change the Adamses proposed and which they would soon exploit. John Quincy stated that though he paid no visits of form, he was always ready to receive and return visits and would be "happy to invite to my house every member of the Senate, whether he had or had not paid me a visit." Perhaps significantly, this innovation did not appear in the letter to the president, only in the letter meant for Congress. This statement broke the custom that demanded a first call to initiate household interactions. In effect, the floodgates were open for the political use of invitations. After establishing this policy, Louisa Catherine and John Quincy could invite any useful family they chose to their house, and their ability or inability to visit would not act as a brake on the numbers they could include. This paved the way for an increasing politicization of social events that would have lasting repercussions on the growth of Washington both as city and as capital.[45]

"MY CAMPAIGN"

John Quincy could never have become president without Louisa Catherine's efforts as campaign manager.[46] Louisa Catherine launched what she called "my campaign" with the political savvy she had developed during a twenty-year career in European courts. Though male candidates for office did not campaign, they could make junkets to key areas outside Washington to discuss their plans with local politicos, often disguising their trip's purpose, as Jefferson and James Madison had done on their "Hessian fly" trip in 1791. John Quincy would not stoop even to that accepted level, but Louisa Catherine did. During the six years preceding the election, she traveled to nearby Maryland, where she had "respectable and distinguished" family, to secure her home state in John Quincy's camp. "As my connections in this state are of the most respectable and distinguished, I am most solicitous to them in his interest," Louisa Catherine promised; "Maryland, it is said, will be his."[47]

In February 1821, a decent interval after Monroe's second election, Joseph Hopkinson, a Philadelphia judge, came to dinner at the Adamses' to discuss presidential plans with John Quincy: no bargains, no corruption, just prospects. However, to an Adams the mere discussion of office seeking smacked of sin. According to his diary, John Quincy replied: "I would take not one step to advance or promote pretensions to the presidency. If that office was to be the prize of cabal and intrigue, of purchasing newspapers, bribing by appointments, or bargaining for foreign missions, I had no ticket in that lottery." He modestly asserted that "whether I had the qualifications necessary for a president of the United States was, to say the least, very doubtful," but on one point he stood firm. "That I had no talent for obtaining the office by such means was perfectly clear. I had neither talent nor inclination for intrigue."[48] Hopkinson left disappointed.

After the 1822 social season ended, Louisa Catherine spent the summer in Philadelphia, caring for her convalescent brother. Even while living in a boardinghouse, she created a salon, inviting newspaper editors, former congressmen and their families, and other local political figures, including Judge Hopkinson. Not surprisingly, all of these citizens became supporters of John Quincy. Encouraged by this show of popularity, Louisa Catherine tried to persuade John Quincy to keep her company for a week or so, as a loving husband might be expected to do, "and show yourself." John Quincy at first put her off with humor, but when she insisted—"Do for once gratify me . . . and if harm come of it, I promise never to advise you again"—he reacted angrily. He would not travel to Philadelphia "to show . . . how much I long to be president."[49] For all his harshness, John Quincy never told Louisa Catherine to stop working on his behalf.

Rather than push her husband, Louisa Catherine concentrated on cultivating his supporters. Encouraged by her efforts, Judge Hopkinson made another approach. In January 1823 he wrote a letter to her, but his message was aimed straight at John Quincy. Beginning rather fancifully— "Let me beg you to consider for a moment that you and I are sitting, with or without a bright moon, as you please, on the piazza looking into the garden, in familiar chat"—the persistent judge mentioned that he had heard "our friend" was adopting a "Macbeth policy" for the upcoming election:

> *If chance will have me king, why chance may crown me*
> *Without my stir.*

This short letter, deflecting criticism through being addressed to Louisa Catherine, lightly chided John Quincy for his indifference to a subject so important to his country's welfare and his allies' hopes. Indirectly, Hopkinson warned Adams that his attitude was "calculated to chill and depress the kind feeling and fair exertions of his friends." People could not continue to work for him for long, cautioned Hopkinson, without some encouragement from the candidate. In his desire to rise above the fray, John Quincy discouraged legitimate support. "We would not have him [the candidate] make corrupt bargains, or write, or procure to be written, skulking letters or addresses. But, on the other hand, there is a just and honorable support and countenance he may give to his cause and to those who maintain it, perfectly consistent with the purest pride and delicacy, and of which none would complain."

Hopkins ended his missive by dryly asserting that politics should not be left to chance or merit, but that "kings are made by politicians and newspapers; and the man who sits down waiting to be crowned, either by chance or just right, will go bareheaded all his life."⁵⁰ Typically, John Quincy's response to this letter was three times as long and laden with high-minded language. He pointed out that had Macbeth left it all to chance, he might not have been king, but then there also would have been no tragedy. The crux of the matter, for John Quincy, was that "the principle of the Constitution in its purity is, that the duty shall be assigned to the most able and the most worthy." Newspapers and politicians may point out who that is, John Quincy conceded, but in a republic the people—not chance or politics—shall choose. If a candidate allowed himself to become obliged in any way, even to a friend for the slightest of services, he rendered himself unfit for the job. Not one iota of kindness could a candidate accept lest he be lost to the world.⁵¹ This appears in his diary as his official stand on politicking for the presidency, but Louisa Catherine's unofficial papers paint a very different picture.

Not only did Louisa Catherine make extensive journeys several times during her campaign, but she also traveled from home every day to secure her objective. For all the fuss Louisa Catherine and John Quincy caused in 1817 with their refusals to call, Louisa Catherine used the reworked patterns like a professional. The etiquette war allowed John Quincy to appear as an incorruptible republican and Louisa Catherine as a private lady, but once they established these public stands, the couple applied method and dedication to this part of the family business. As she explained to John Adams, though the members of Congress visit "very freely," "it is understood that a man who is ambitious to become president of the United States, must make his wife visit the Ladies of the members of Congress first," adding sarcastically, "otherwise, he is totally inefficient to fill so high an office." Her next remark demonstrated that John Quincy knew this, too: "You would laugh could you see Mr. A. every morning prepare a set of cards with as much formality as if he was drawing up some very important article to negotiate in a commercial treaty."[52]

In spite of regarding these duties as "literally . . . the torments of my life," she turned society into a science, working long and hard, at one time paying twenty-five such calls in a morning and on another occasion covering six square miles in her travels. Notwithstanding that these visits made her "sick many times, and I really sometimes think they will make me crazy," on one occasion Louisa Catherine, in a move reminiscent of Dolley, spent two hours stopping at eight or ten boardinghouses to return a call. She finally gave up, "fretted and fatigued to death and almost unfitted by my anxiety to return the civilities shown me." She located her targets a day later and promptly issued cards of invitation to her soirees.[53]

Though Louisa Catherine did important work for John Quincy while out and about, her primary strategy for campaigning lay in home entertaining. Having guests to their home was obviously a priority for the Adams family. In 1823 they built an addition on their F Street house, consisting of a new twenty-eight by twenty-nine foot entertainment room, two halls, two back rooms, and five or six chambers. All this space would be used for social events by the end of the campaign. Though the Adamses constantly complained about expenses, their account books reveal that they dedicated a good deal of money to such affairs and other social necessities.[54]

Especially in the early years, Louisa Catherine gave dinner parties for the members of Congress. In 1819 she gave about one a week, for as many as twenty-two guests, a record that rivaled the White House schedule. In 1821, before the Adamses built the addition, Louisa Catherine worried about the "utterly insupportable" crowding and expense of trying to fit all the members into her social schedule, so she invited only the male politicians, without ladies, to her dinners. To Louisa Catherine's dismay, her example prompted emulation by the other Cabinet families and even President Monroe, "forgetting," she remarked tartly, "the difference between a salary of twenty-five thousand dollars a year and six thousand dollars a year." Though she seems to have suffered no censure, Louisa Catherine was informed by one gentleman that this habit of President Monroe's was "dangerous" and that if he should continue it "even his best friend would desert him."[55] Perhaps fearing a long congressional memory, Louisa Catherine took this warning to heart, and though she continued to give dinner parties, she turned her attention to a social form that she herself invented, one that accommodated women and proved more efficient and effective in winning friends for her husband.

Large parties and balls had always been part of her social campaign, but "Mrs. Adams's Tuesday nights" served quite a different purpose from her New Year's party of 1822, which five hundred guests attended. Though it might seem that Louisa Catherine's regularly scheduled soirees evolved naturally from the practice of giving frequent parties, she quite consciously instituted the subscription aspect that made them different and aroused controversy. In December 1819 she mentioned that she "open[ed] my campaign, having given a general invitation for every Tuesday during the winter." The innovation apparently "creat[ed] some noise and jealousy," but it turned the Washington spotlight firmly on the Adamses' F Street house at least once a week, "mak[ing] our Congress less dependent on the foreign ministers for their amusement" and, though she leaves it unstated, less dependent on other cabinet households. "My evenings," noted Louisa Catherine, "are called sociables. I wish they may prove so."[56] They did, and more so.

Though called "sociables" and "salons," Louisa Catherine's events (and the ones that followed her in imitation) were not centers of high-toned conversations about culture, with the setting and accoutrements mere backdrops for the primary business: a lively exchange of ideas. Louisa Catherine's soirees were big and showy, and the exchange was, if not of a baser coin, at least of a more practical, political one. The new Washington was clear on its priorities, and in the 1820s the residential elite discovered to their disgust that social events increasingly served political purposes. The prominent locals were not necessarily excluded, but the days were long past when Washington hostesses invited everybody in town to ensure an interesting and varied company. The new social events had a more pointed purpose than sociability.

Louisa Catherine's parties also differed in several politically significant ways from regular parties and even from the White House levees. One strength of Louisa Catherine's Tuesday soirees lay in their regularity through the years. Like Dolley Madison's drawing rooms, they provided a routine, dependable source of entertainment and access and by doing so carved out a significant niche on the Washington social scene. The season after Louisa Catherine's spectacular success with her Tuesday nights, other cabinet families imitated her, though Louisa Catherine's events remained the most popular. For these new events, unlike presidential levees and even other private parties, guests were not invited to a single occasion but to a whole series. The "subscribing" families committed themselves to attend one set of parties throughout the season, the choice of host and hostess almost inevitably dictating political alliance.[57] Thomas Hubbard noted with amusement that Mrs. Adams had given him "*fair* and what Mr. Storrs would call *legal* notice of her tea party," his language conveying the institutionalization of the practice and the level of commitment. Party-hopping was frowned upon, and those who did so were relegated from friend to the lower status of guest.[58]

Unlike a presidential drawing room, where conversation formed the principal amusement, Louisa Catherine's soirees featured more dramatic, performance-oriented, and entertaining activities, including card playing, music, and dancing. By the second year "Mrs. Adams's regular Tuesdays" were a fixture on the scene, and the house on F Street had achieved a status second only to the White House as the place of entertainment. In 1820 Louisa Catherine noted that her first Tuesday party attracted two hundred people, which she considered large for a first party; clearly she expected even more once the season got under way.[59]

Louisa Catherine's occasions and those of her competitors met many political needs, not the least of which was the invitation to evaluate the hostesses. William Cabell Rives assured his wife that she would not believe the metamorphosis of "little Mrs. Calhoun," who had been a dumpy, quiet woman the year before. In the election year she had "recovered her shape and exhibits herself fearlessly in every circle. . . . Dresses like a queen, trips along like a sylph, puts on a thousand fashionable airs." All to a political purpose, according to Rives, for "she has plainly caught the spirit of her husband's ambition and is looking forward to 'queen[ing]' it in good earnest." However, in any competition that focused on elegance, accomplishment, or semiroyal atmosphere, Louisa Catherine emerged the winner. The European-educated Louisa Catherine was the perfect hostess for a frontier town growing into a political capital. Her Continental polish always put her ahead of the pack in style, but her American father and connection to the Adams family ensured her republican respectability. John Adams knew she would make a splash in the town, assuring her that "your experience in Berlin, Petersburg and St. James's, your sense, wit, and perfect fluency and purity in the French language will hold you constantly besieged."[60]

Louisa Catherine's other acquirements met more practical needs. As far back as 1806, Rosalie Stier Calvert had noted to her sister in Europe that "music is an indispensable talent for a young lady. Dancing is even more essential." In spite of this, the Washington entertainment scene, especially the availability of musical talent, remained in a lamentable state. Anyone with any pretensions to accomplishment could perform, resulting in presentations bad to the point of comedy. Harrison Gray Otis regaled his wife with an account of a "droll duetto" at the home of British ambassador Charles Bagot and his wife, Mary, which featured a Dutch woman and her husband playing the clarinet and singing. Though Harrison Otis could declare, "I never saw such a figure of fun," such a fiasco might prove not as much fun for a chagrined hostess.[61]

In contrast, Louisa Catherine's musical talents were indisputable. The celebrated composer Thomas Moore had visited Louisa Catherine several times during her 1804 Washington sojourn, playing and singing with and for her. "He said that I sang beautifully," Louisa Catherine wrote her husband, "but I wanted *soul*." Accomplished upon the piano and harp, she took the performance upon herself if she could not secure the latest musical celebrity in town. With this ability, along with her "superb" dress and manners ("the most accomplished woman in America"), Louisa Catherine reigned as the charismatic figure in these settings.[62] In her quest to win popularity for her husband, she served as his surrogate. This was often literally true, as she sometimes presided over her company without him, though she did not care to do so.[63] With Louisa Catherine in the spotlight, John Quincy did not need to change his personality or habits. Like a good republican he could dress as though "he needed [no] finer

decorations than his talents" and continue to repel visitors with his taciturn style.[64]

In analyzing how the soirees worked, the party atmosphere cannot be
overestimated. These events allowed power to circulate, with the setting,
the activities, and the material context signaling to participants that "alternative circuits" were up and running.[65] The atmosphere of a private
party allowed politicians to interact in an emotionally cool atmosphere.
Men debated, shouted, argued, horsewhipped, and caned each other in
the House and Senate, but no one would stage such a public scene in a
home.

The sight of the lady of the house, performing and hostessing, the
displays of food, music, decor—all acted as the Adams family's open assertion of their right to rule. The early Republic had not abandoned deferential society completely, and Louisa Catherine's efforts referred directly
to this gentry tradition, as did the Washington emphasis on personal sociability as a criterion for rule. To have been invited to the Adams house
must have seemed flattering in the extreme to congressional families, especially impressing those from rural areas. To those of similar gentry backgrounds, the displays of material affluence and specialized knowledge of
how to manipulate it had the effect of aligning the Adamses with the upper-class visitors as "our kind of people."[66]

In assessing the suitability of a candidate, the lifestyle of his family
was part of the evaluation. Louis McLane had a chance to observe Mrs.
Crawford and her daughter at a Crawford family dinner party. The event
itself was very pleasant, "but alas!" Though the two ladies exhibited "all
goodness, they were never designed to the wife and daughter of a president." William Cabell Rives also regarded Mrs. Crawford as a lovely person, demonstrating a commendable "affectionate concern and confiding
tenderness" toward her husband and motherly affection as she took a
child onto her lap. But "she is plain, almost to coarseness and is without
any of the airs and graces, which seem appropriate to the wife of a president."[67] In other words, she was not a polished woman like Louisa
Catherine Adams.

Louisa Catherine strove to attract people to her home to ensure popularity and hence congressional votes, but the invited came for reasons of
their own: for entertainment, to ally themselves with a presidential candi-

date, and for other purposes specific to them. Like Dolley's drawing rooms, the Tuesday evenings at the Adamses provided an unofficial space for politicking. Louisa Catherine's success at establishing herself as the charismatic figure can be judged by how often the politicking focused on her. Throughout her career people attempted to solicit her for positions, but as the election neared, such visits increased. Senator Edwards called on her and complained about unfair appointments, threatening to resign. In the process of his petition, he also gave her "a good deal of information concerning Mr. Pope and his affairs which as far as wealth can go are prosperous even to surfeity but his political career is not successful." A steady stream of visitors, reported Louisa Catherine, came to beg her influence in procuring places, and though she disavowed any such power, she did not hesitate in applying to the president for a position for her brother-in-law William Smith.[68]

"The eye of the public is already on me," wrote Louisa Catherine in 1821, "and although I endeavor to give them as little opportunity of attaching me as possible, and continue to be as simple in my habits as nature originally intended me to be, yet I cannot escape." She was becoming a public figure: "I find the most trifling occurrences are turned into political machinery. Even my countenance was watched at the Senate during Mr. Pinckney's speech as I was afterward informed by some of the gentlemen." As the campaign progressed, Louisa Catherine became more and more a political animal. Her letters and journals sent to John Adams reflect this change; after 1820, the discussions of politics increase in both occurrence and length. Though she tried to maintain her image as a private lady, in her accounts Louisa Catherine revealed herself to be a canny political player, knowing when to thrust, parry, listen, or speak. On February 7, 1823, she remarked, with her usual disclaimer: "Mr. Clay is playing a new game. I always mistrust these sudden changes and though I do not interfere in politics, it is difficult for me to avoid knowing his actions which are talked of by everyone and which places a man in the light of a dreaded enemy to my husband."[69]

Three days later Clay's strategy focused on her: "Mr. Clay last evening took an opportunity of assuring me that it was his wish to be on terms of friendship with me and my family and expressed a hope that if he should not be able to come to all my Tuesdays that I should not believe it was in-

tended as a mark of enmity." The tide would turn several more ways be-
fore the final Clay-Adams rapprochement, but on this occasion Henry
Clay knew to whom he should turn to build bridges over political waters.
Others did as well. A month earlier Louisa Catherine recorded: "Mr.
Cannon after dinner gave me a hint that he would like an invitation to my
Tuesdays, and I gave it to him. This is one of the leading radicals who has
always been the most opposed to Mr. A."[70]

Gossip—the prime conveyer of political news—is the lifeblood of
politics. Circumstances change rapidly, and the uninformed political player pays the price in bad decisions and unpopular moves. Louisa Catherine's "morning-after" reports on her soirees and other social events document the many opportunities she encountered to gain or disseminate
information. At another family's entertainment, she learned from the
French ambassador (and before her husband) that the Adams-Onís Treaty
with Spain had been completed, "at which I was much rejoiced knowing
how Mr. A. had labored to get anything like an amiable arrangement between the two countries."[71]

John Quincy's diary, too, reveals countless instances of political talk,
offers, and information passed to and from him in a social context. On
one occasion at least, John Quincy himself planned a dinner party and,
Louisa Catherine grumbled, invited many more people than she would
have. John Adams, too, showed an appreciation of the importance of her
efforts, when he urged Louisa Catherine to retain her "Tuesday Campaigns" though often "fatiguing and perhaps dangerous."[72]

In a dynamic typical of the couple, John Quincy's positive assessments
of his wife's efforts often can only be discerned in his complaints when
things did not go well. At one dinner Louisa Catherine found herself "so
ill I could not attempt to sit at table," which "mortified" John Quincy. He
was also displeased when illness prevented her from receiving and calling
upon visitors. Louisa Catherine's willful neglect of her guests on another
occasion placed her "in great disgrace." John Quincy's mortifications reveal an intense dependence on a political partner who prevailed and usually persisted in the face of ill health. Along with dinner parties and other
events on the Adams social calendar, the soirees proved so crucial to the
election process that they continued in the face of family illness or the fu-
neral of a friend. But even a careful reading of John Quincy's diary does

not reveal references to these activities or their importance. Whether consciously or unconsciously, he did not systematically record these maneuvers in his undeclared political campaign. Some of the isolated events do appear—he does mention several Tuesday soirees and the occasional dinner—but only in Louisa Catherine's papers do they emerge as a clear pattern.[73]

The success of Louisa Catherine's Tuesday nights cannot be assessed apart from their political significance, for they cannot be considered as simple opportunities for pleasure. They served only to court favor, and for that purpose they unquestionably succeeded. At the peak of their social domination, the Adams family counted sixty-eight congressional members and their families as steady guests. John Quincy's personal popularity grew as his household's social popularity rose. In 1820 Louisa Catherine found herself one Tuesday evening "surrounded by many *friends* who grow warmer in their expressions of unity in proportion as Mr. A rises in popularity." By 1824 she could afford to be offhand: "This winter we are all the fashion." In a context where attendance meant allegiance, popular fashion and popularity were not foolish if they attracted guests to the Tuesday soirees. If, in 1821, John Quincy thought fit to assume a "very doubtful" pose in regards to his election, by 1824 he "seemed to be more gay and animated than I have ever seen him, which is a pretty good symptom that he is satisfied with his prospects, which are generally admitted to be pretty good."[74]

"ALL THE WORLD'S A STAGE, AND ALL THE MEN AND WOMEN IN IT PLAYERS."

Life in the capital had assumed an almost theatrical intensity after 1818.[75] The topic of the presidential election had increasingly obsessed the political community from the beginning of the Adamses' social campaign. The atmosphere of speculation, anxiety, and excitement communicated itself even to those far from the capital. John Adams conveyed this image of conflict to Louisa Catherine as early as 1822: "A man drawn by four horses or a carriage by eight to the four cardinal points of the compass are an admirable hieroglyphic of our approaching presidential election." During the 1823–24 congressional year, the uncertainty and anxiety surrounding the upcoming presidential election escalated in tension and narrowed in focus, with the "caucusing . . . eternal out of doors." In December 1823 Louisa Catherine, "wearied to death" with all the demands of her campaign, worried about her husband: "I have twice today been given to understand that the game is nearly up for him." She encouraged him to play cards for "relaxation and to keep him from thinking of" the approaching election.[76]

Whatever her internal misgivings, Louisa Catherine continued to work for the cause, receiving as many as forty-five members of Congress in one day, as part of a "continual reception." "I was in a fever before I got through and was very much tempted to wish them all safe at home, even while I was thanking them for their civility—all of which proves how little I am fitted for a public station."[77]

Her journal reflects this fatigue and anxiety. She reported any election rumor she heard, and her use of initials and dashes between words and sentences increased, as though she was too tired or paranoid or insecure to write fully. The last straw came at a "snarling dinner" in December, when even Louisa Catherine's gracious presence could not "prevent sharp speeches. Mr. Clay as usual assumed a very high tone and forced our secretary of war [Calhoun] completely in the background." At this low point the opportunity presented itself to make one grand gesture, and the idea for it came from the singularly "unsocial" John Quincy. Though he would deny with his last breath any talent for politicking, John Quincy occasionally revealed himself a canny strategist, as he did on this and several other occasions. On December 20, 1823, Louisa Catherine wrote, "It was agreed this day that we should give a ball to General Jackson on the eighth [of January, 1824]—I objected much to the plan, but was overpowered by John's arguments and the thing was settled."[78]

Perhaps because of her resistance, Louisa Catherine and John barely got the invitations out in time to take advantage of two crucial pieces of timing. First, for this gesture to have maximal impact, the ball had to occur before the upcoming caucus, which could be called in January or February. Second, in a political and family culture that demanded republican spareness, a lavish celebration needed a real occasion to justify serious expenditures of time and money, and George Washington's Birthday (traditionally the time for a ball) fell too late for the caucuses. The only suitable date was January 8, the anniversary of the Battle of New Orleans.

Like President Washington's birthday, January 8 had already become an occasion for commemoration; nearly every town in the United States held festivities to honor the victory.[79] In 1820 the Adamses' rivals the Calhouns had given a Jackson Ball in the capital at which they reigned as "among the most agreeable personages in this quarter." In 1824 Washington City already had a ball planned by the Washington Dancing Assembly for the ninth anniversary, to be held in the Carusi family's public assembly hall. Once she agreed to John's plan, however, Louisa Catherine determined to create an event that would outshine any other Jackson Ball, past or present.[80]

At first glance it may seem strange for one candidate to go to the trouble and expense of giving a ball to honor a rival. However, at this juncture the field of candidates was so large that it was not clear that Jackson, though gaining popularity daily, would be a leading contender. An openhanded, well-timed gesture might persuade the honored general to enlist on the Adams side. Electorally, it would be an unbeatable combination, with Adams carrying New England and the Middle Atlantic states and Jackson delivering the West and South.

As it turned out, by the end of 1824 Andrew Jackson became John Quincy's chief rival, but however the political chips fell later, John Quincy's idea to give a ball to honor Jackson was a master stroke. It would allow John Quincy to make a patriotic, republican stand, appearing to rise above personal interest in celebrating a national hero. In doing so, John Quincy could also take advantage of Jackson's popularity and ensure a share of the spotlight for himself. If sumptuous enough, the event would attract newspaper coverage and reach the distant constituency. Perhaps more important, given the presidential election process in place, a grand public relations event would involve the entire political community, a not unworthy consideration, because it seemed that the election would surely go to the House.[81]

Given the short notice, the guest list was the first priority, along with issuing the invitations. Deciding on the featured players in this performance proved easy. Louisa Catherine wrote out invitations to all the members of both Houses, except two representatives from Virginia, Alexander Smyth and John Floyd, whose "personal deportment" toward John Quincy could not be overlooked. To disguise the political nature of the congressional courting, Louisa Catherine and John Quincy also invited the department heads, as well as members of the local gentry.[82] In the end

Louisa Catherine sent out five hundred invitations, most of them personally hand-delivered. As interest in the Jackson Ball grew, members of both political and local elites called on Louisa Catherine, hoping to be asked. In her journal she marveled that the "number of persons who come to be invited on this occasion exceed belief."[83]

If political necessity cast the players in this drama, the other components were up to Louisa Catherine as director of this spectacle. It did not take her long to devise "a beautiful plan in my head which I shall endeavor to have executed," one which brought together and built on the elements that had already made her Washington's premier hostess. The parallels between the preparation and execution of the Jackson Ball and the similar process of mounting a theatrical production cannot be overstated: Louisa Catherine even had scripts for her event, in the form of etiquette books and dance instruction manuals, which contained sections on ballroom organization and behavior. These books outlined each aspect and activity, the roles of all the players, including the hostess, as both the director of the piece and a leading actor.[84]

As in a play, the setting and decor, music, dancing, and food acted as signifiers, ritual and material adjuncts that carried meanings far beyond their face value. In this case, she chose the complex of behavior and objects to further social and political relationships. Louisa Catherine had already given considerable thought to the importance of setting when she renovated the F Street house to accommodate her social campaigning. In the tradition of gentry entertaining, the house not only provided the stage setting for the performers but also was a player in and of itself, one which participants and observers assessed for its own beauty and charm.[85]

The day after John Quincy and Louisa Catherine agreed that they would host the ball, Louisa Catherine and her family began to construct the decorations. From December 22 to the very day of the ball, Louisa Catherine, her nieces, sons, servants, and community craftsmen wove lengths of laurel, wintergreen, evergreens, and roses into garlands and wreaths. Louisa Catherine based her decor on her experiences in European courts and her observations of the most stylish households in Washington, those of the foreign legations. At a ball given by the British minister the previous year, a man from Baltimore had chalked beautiful designs for the dance floor, and Louisa Catherine hired him for her ball. She drew the designs herself, and the chalking took a full day to complete.[86]

In addition to these decorations, Louisa Catherine also gave serious thought to the setting's structural problems. To accommodate the crowd, Louisa Catherine cleared the furniture out of two stories of the house, took all the doors off their hinges, and rearranged the rooms, converting John Quincy's library and study into the ballroom and turning her own dressing room into the family dining room. Concerned that the second floor, where supper would be served, would collapse under the weight of the crowd, she installed pillars to prop up the upper story. Louisa Catherine worried about the appearance of extravagance inherent in a guest list that required extensive house renovation, so she determined to conceal the pillars by "mak[ing] some sort of ornament, and this of itself will occasion more talk than I like. To this, however, I must take my chance and brave it as well as I can."[87]

As to music, Louisa Catherine had little choice; as she had for her soirees, she made a personal trip to the Navy Yard to hire eight members of the Marine Band. The band could have played their entire repertoire, the same selections with which everyone in Washington was all too familiar, but Louisa Catherine made some significant selections regarding dance music. Though John Quincy apparently waltzed beautifully, Louisa Catherine deliberately did not chose the controversial "valse" or any of the trendy Spanish country dances that had so impressed her (and shocked others) at the British minister's ball. Instead, she favored cotillions and (for later, as the crowd thinned) reels: dances that required group attention, group participation, and group cooperation.[88]

As January 8 drew near, preparations intensified and Louisa Catherine's diary entries drop off. However, the press and private journals took up the task of reporting on the event. The ball, as the Adamses had intended, became a media event unprecedented in Washington. The excitement built to a fever pitch, the flames happily fanned by constant newspaper squibs, both in prose and poetry:

> *Wend you with the world tonight?*
> *Sixty gray and giddy twenty,*
> *Flirts that court and prudes that slight,*
> *Stale coquettes and spinsters plenty . . .*
> *Belles and matron, maids and madams*
> *All are gone to Mrs. Adams.*[89]

Finally, the great day arrived. One scholar has identified six rituals contained in this kind of event, and the first was undoubtedly the entrance upon the stage of all the guests. They made their way to the Adamses' house, guided by bonfires lit two blocks around. "At half past seven . . . the guests began to arrive in one continual stream, so that in one hour even the staircase up to Mary's chamber [possibly the third floor] began to be thronged." Louisa Catherine and John Quincy, as the central performers, "took our stations near the door that we might be seen by our guests and at the same time receive the general."[90] As the guests embarked on the second rite, greeting each other, the sight that met their eyes was impressive indeed.

According to Charles Francis, the Adamses' seventeen-year-old son, home from Harvard for the festivities, "the effect was very beautiful." The laurel and rose garlands that everyone had labored over festooned each room, with "small illumination lamps" and "large bouquets" at strategic points. The newly inserted pillars were "wreathed all up in order to match," and John Quincy's bookcase, too heavy to move, was "covered with green, and on the top" sported "a whole forest of flower pots with pretty flowers" and more lamps. The chalked floors spread a rich carpet of spread eagles, flags, and the motto "Welcome to the Hero of New Orleans" before the guests.[91] A fragile extravagance, it would be wiped out with the first dance.

The arrival of Andrew Jackson at nine o'clock signaled the third rite: that of greeting the honored guest. "Everybody wanted to see him, everybody wanted to speak to him," related Charles Francis. "The ladies climbed the chairs and benches to see General Jackson," and Mrs. Adams "gratified the general curiosity" by "gracefully" taking his arm and introducing him to the guests that packed her rooms. As Louisa Catherine took her place as hostess by the general's side, she stepped into the spotlight, the representative of the house, her husband, her family, and all the political freight associated with the event. She had prepared for this moment carefully, choosing a "suit of steel"—a steel lamé—with "ornaments for head, throat, and arms" of "cut steel," the whole ensemble "producing a dazzling effect." Yet the effect was achieved with a material simpler than gold or diamonds, its aristocratic style commanding power and authority but its material maintaining a republican simplicity. John Quincy contented himself with a simple suit; in fact, he was the only male guest not in formal attire.[92]

With the announcement of supper, Louisa Catherine led the general to the head of the table, while John Quincy escorted an honored lady to the foot. Louisa Catherine had selected the food that lay before the guests as she had the other elements, focusing on the latest in style. She had many occasions, while serving at courts, to see the elaborate sculpted suppers that were the rage in Europe, and her table featured "natural and candied fruits, pies, sweetmeats, tongues, games . . . prepared in the French style and arranged with most exquisite taste." Andrew Jackson drank Louisa Catherine's health and left after supper to attend the more public and plebeian ball at Carusi's, "where he expected to be greeted by the *people* with great joy, but I believe he was disappointed and found very few persons there."[93] He should have read the newspapers: "the people" were "all . . . gone to Mrs. Adams's." At the house on F Street, the reels lasted into the early hours of the morning. Jackson's early exit seemed almost incidental to the effect of the event; the night belonged to Louisa Catherine.[94]

As closely organized and choreographed as the event was, one unexpected accident occurred. At one of the rare moments Louisa Catherine sat during the evening, one of the "illumination lamps" "fell upon my head and [the oil] ran down my back and shoulders." In the mood to read political meaning into anything that happened at the Adamses', the crowd roared at the "good joke." "It was said that I was . . . anointed with the sacred oil, and that it was certainly ominous." Ever the one to deny involvement in politics, she retorted "that the only certain thing I knew was that my gown was spoilt."[95]

The Adams ball—a social event and political phenomenon—remained unsurpassed in the annals of Washington City for years to come and represents Louisa Catherine's most triumphal demonstration of the political lessons she had learned. Years after the event, it was referred to not as the "Jackson Ball," of which there were many, but rather the one and only "Adams Ball." The Adams ball succeeded in making John Quincy Adams look irresistibly popular, especially to those who only knew his name from the newspapers. Louisa Catherine and John Quincy brought everyone important into the Adams home, reconciling their enemies, introducing new supporters, and weaving everyone more tightly into their circle. The guests at the event left indebted to John Quincy for hospitality, "a ball as a social gesture to be repaid."[96] Few could afford to repay in kind, and it is too crass to say they paid with a vote. Rather, the ball had subtle effects, taking the electioneering process to a new plane, one occupied by the Adams family alone.

A ball which involved very large numbers of people also served different purposes from the conversation and entertainment at Tuesday soirees. Rather than sitting to watch a single performer in a drawing room, guests at a ball took center stage themselves by participating in the chief activity: dancing. The dance styles of the era, as Louisa Catherine chose them, reinforced group identity, making the community work together in visceral ways. A ball dynamically engaged members of the Washington community in deferential networks, which allowed the reinforcement of statuses, ranks, and roles—especially necessary in a culture where "popular attention meant power."[97] The Adamses' use of the ballroom to achieve these ends was part of a long European political tradition. However much republican theory might have eschewed such displays and manipulations, a political capital needed a place in which to gather and to assert authority.

Ballrooms, as well as drawing rooms, are political spaces, with slightly different emphases. Display can be part of a drawing-room experience, as in Dolley's yellow parlor, and certain intimate, drawing-room-style politics could occur even at an event as splendid as the Jackson Ball. But the particular political atmosphere of a ballroom uses lavish demonstrations of material display and performance to assert ruling privilege. Hosts, hostesses, and guests occupy a larger stage and perform more intensely at a ball. Then as now, this focus on performance relies largely on objects: eating utensils, lighting, dress, food, and other material devices. The presence or absence of objects, designs, and materials offers the possibility of behaving in some ways but not in others.[98] In this case, the size and arrangement of the Adams house, the decor, food, and music allowed the family to create an event that included a large percentage of both official and unofficial elites, entertaining and impressing them, while putting the spotlight on the Adamses themselves as the leading actors.

A CUP OF HEMLOCK

Big feasts and celebrations signal rites of passage, and after the Adams ball, popular opinion in Washington City deemed John Quincy the likeliest candidate for president.[99] This opinion persisted even after the caucus met and made its decision the next month. Many members of Congress, whether from political motivations or sincere doubts, questioned the need for a caucus, and as a result, though the caucus announced William Crawford as its candidate, the number who attended—66 out of 291—made it unrepresentative and thus inconsequential. The doubts and fears of the preceding years had proved true, and the Republican party was splintering.

The conventional political narrative examines the election of 1824 for its thrilling, neck-and-neck photo finish and the mystery of John Quincy Adams's corrupt bargain. The familiar story acquires new dimensions when viewed in the light of the social and political context and, more specifically, the Adams campaign. As the national election neared, the players constantly positioned and repositioned themselves. Calhoun wisely stepped out, figuring that he was virtually sure to win the vice presidency and from that office could make his presidential bid later. Although William Crawford apparently suffered a series of strokes that confined him to his bed during most of this time, he remained a candidate until the bitter end, thanks to the unstinting efforts of his supporters. The results of the popular vote in the election of 1824 took a month to come in, from October 29 to November 22. Jackson won the most votes, with a total of 152,901; Adams received 114,023, Clay 47,217, and Crawford, 46,979. Though Jackson obviously was the people's choice, Adams had a geographically broader base of support. Naturally, John Quincy won handily in New England and in the Middle Atlantic states, but he also held his own in the South and the West in spite of the other candidates' regional advantages. Jackson, on the other hand, though sweeping the South and the West, gained no votes in New England.[100]

The predictions of caucus supporters—that the lack of a majority caucus nomination would result in the election being thrown into the House—proved correct. The electoral college voted in mid-December, with Jackson winning ninety-nine votes, Adams eighty-four, Crawford forty-one, and Clay thirty-seven. Because there was no clear majority, the top three candidates were presented to the House of Representatives for a final decision, and the wheeling and dealing began. In a House election the representatives of each state voted among themselves, and the majority position counted as a single vote. As the House leader, Henry Clay could roam among the representatives, state by state and create majorities among them. With his presidential hopes dead, finding himself in the role of kingmaker probably did much to soothe Clay's wounded feelings.[101]

The balloting in the House took place on February 9, 1825. It was going to be close, in spite of Daniel Webster's success in delivering the votes of the Federalists to the Adams cause and Clay's persuasion of the representatives from Ohio, Kentucky, and Louisiana to vote for Adams against their constituents' wishes. It still remained uncertain whether John Quincy Adams had a majority; he needed New York, and he needed it on the first ballot. Adams supporters feared that the longer the balloting went on, the greater the likelihood that the fragile structure of allegiances and deals they had constructed would crumble. Jackson's support was growing by the day, and even Crawford, though he had not been seen for weeks, was electorally alive and kicking. Organized under Martin Van Buren's skillful management (Crawford was Van Buren's first choice, Adams his second), seventeen New York representatives stood for Crawford and seventeen for Adams. The only undecided vote was Stephen Van Rensselaer, "a kindly, upright, simple old Federalist gentleman" and a guest at the Adams family dinner table.[102] He was also a bit of a political hack, not outstanding in any way, and the unexpected spotlight of history made him extremely uncomfortable.

Van Rensselaer boarded with the Crawford men; because lodgers tended to vote in blocs, his allegiance to Crawford seemed certain. That morning at breakfast he assured his messmates that nothing could persuade him to vote for Adams. However, upon his arrival at the Capitol, Webster and Clay cornered him, and those two, Van Rensselaer wrote later, "could not be resisted." At the crucial moment, according to legend (and Martin Van Buren), the old man bowed his head on the edge of his desk and appealed for divine guidance. When he removed his hand from his face, his eyes lit upon a ballot ticket marked "John Quincy Adams" lying on the floor directly in front of him. Van Rensselaer interpreted this as an answer to his prayers, picked up the ticket, and put it in the ballot box.[103]

The first ballot gave Adams a majority: thirteen states. Jackson only garnered seven and Crawford, four. Henry Clay stood to announce the election of John Quincy Adams as the president of the United States. Some observers clapped, and others hissed; Crawford's supporters yelled "treachery and cowardice," especially at the hapless Van Rensselaer. Poor Van Rensselaer's messmates did not take kindly to his defection, Senator Louis McLane commenting, "He has betrayed those with whom he broke bread." Senator John Randolph of Virginia concluded: "It was impossible to win the game, gentlemen. The cards were stacked."[104] And so it seemed, five days later, when John Quincy announced his choice for secretary of state: Henry Clay, a man known for his uncanny luck at cards.

Immediately a cry of "bargain and corruption" arose—from Jackson and his supporters, from Washington politicians, and soon from newspapers and political organizations throughout the nation. The grumblings had begun even before Adams's announcement, when it became clear that Clay had obtained votes for Adams from representatives whose states' voters had clearly indicated their preference for other candidates. To the other candidates' supporters and the disgruntled national electorate it seemed that the people had been robbed of their choice by Washington insiders. In this view John Quincy Adams had bought Henry Clay's help in securing a majority in the House by promising him the State Department, thus almost guaranteeing that Clay would be the next president. It was equally obvious to Adams supporters that such a dastardly deed was below their paragon of disinterested virtue. The ensuing fuss doomed Clay's political career—he never again came so close to the presidency— and certainly contributed to the failure of John Quincy's administration.[105]

The question lingers. Was there a bargain—corrupt or not—between John Quincy Adams and Henry Clay? John Quincy's diaries reveal that in January 1825 Henry Clay paid two private evening visits to the Adams home, one early in the month and one later. Clay assured John Quincy of his support and then asked if John Quincy could "satisfy him with regard to some principles of great public importance." John Quincy hastens to add, "But without personal considerations for himself." From these conversations it seems highly probable that the two men at the very least came to an understanding. It is easier to reconcile such a politically hazardous action with Henry Clay, often depicted as a temperamental bon vivant, drunk with personal power, an inveterate gambler, risking it all on an audacious move, than with the righteous John Quincy, given to statements such as "To pass through it [the election] with a pure heart and a firm spirit is my duty and my prayer."[106]

Armed with more sophisticated ideas of human psychology and motivation, especially the notion of denial, we can discern a John Quincy that "protesteth too much." Between the lines of his diary, we see that John Quincy was painfully hungry for the presidency and prepared himself psychologically for his ultimate agreement with Clay months before, as he spoke less and less candidly about himself in his diary.[107] However, these modern explanations only deepen the mystery. Given his strong family legacy of disinterested virtue, how could John Quincy have so utterly sold his soul?

Louisa Catherine's writings go a long way to solve this particular mystery and to alert us to women's roles in political processes. Her experiences help us to reconcile the paragon of virtue with the expedient politician. In this sense Louisa Catherine's words demystify John Quincy and supply a coherent context. Any understanding John Quincy reached with Henry Clay was not a sudden plunge into the icy waters of a political corruption hitherto unexplored but the culmination of a deliberate immersion in political waters that began in 1817, when Louisa Catherine and John Quincy saw the presidency within their grasp. Indeed, Louisa Catherine's evidence shows that John Quincy openly wanted and worked for the presidency, which makes it all the more believable that he would deal with Clay to get it. The "Clay bargain" came at the end of a long process, which blurred the social and political, the public and private.

The election of 1824 had fulfilled the fears of all who had hoped for a peaceful transition and electoral stability. It was contested, fierce, close, and very much a Washington event, the very circumstances for which Louisa Catherine and John Quincy had prepared in their campaign. The Adamses' story demonstrates that federal politics occupied a small world. The public and private combined to create a hothouse atmosphere, where home was a continuation of the public workspace. Dominated by a small group of political families, the national politics of the early Republic were, probably more than at any other time, local to Washington. Andrew Jackson lost the presidency in 1824, even though he was a clear winner in the popular vote. But he was not a Washington player, and once the election was in the House's hands, the personal and family networks counted more than votes from distant locales.

Combinations of political and personal alliances dominated political events on the national scene, and during the election the action of one individual, in this case Stephen Van Rensselaer, tipped the balance. Unwittingly, Van Rensselaer signaled the way of the future when he, as a Federalist and an Adams party guest, broke the boardinghouse bloc's parochial focus and cast his vote for a president with a national vision.[108] The new narrative of this turning point in the history of the federal government demonstrates once again the importance of the face-to-face in politics. Though conventional approaches to history often star Great Men and focus on the personalities of colorful characters like Henry Clay and John Randolph, a more accurate analysis of the role of the personal in politics can only be achieved by taking into account aspects of human interaction often not considered by conventional political history.

Face-to-face relationships prove crucial to any political system, and especially to a democracy. During the early Republic, however, the nation's leaders did not yet view their experiment as a burgeoning democracy. The early years of the U.S. federal government provided a brief window of opportunity, when some tried to create a nonpolitical, republican ruling style, one that would run like a virtuous machine, not dependent on the kinds of personal interests that prevailed in the European courts. Though politics' needs would overrun the republican experiment, during this brief window women of a certain class, race, and personal circumstance had a chance to take on important political functions, such as the ordering of relationships among individual people and groups—which is the function of etiquette.

In a political and cultural environment that feared structure and "politics as usual," a candidate found himself in a double bind. A man had to cultivate popularity to be effective in politics and to enjoy a long career. But on the other hand, too much personal popularity seemed suspect, as though he was compromising his character.[109] The Washington social and political system, as it was evolving through the 1810s and 1820s, allowed men to retain a certain republican aloofness and thus comfortable denial, while some of the obvious political duties could be taken over by their wives or other female relatives.

Two portraits show the Adamses at the height of their pre-presidential fame and, in Louisa Catherine's case, the height of her political powers. The portrait of John Quincy painted by Thomas Sully in 1825 is a head and shoulders view, three quarters, which would become the basis for a larger full-length work the next year. In this portrait he appears the sober republican. The background is a subtle wash of dull colors, and the subject is clad in an immaculate neck cloth and dark suit, which blends in with the monochromatic background. His eyes look past the viewer, and his tightly pursed lips give nothing away. The portrait is fairly small, a bit less than two by three feet.

Painted around the same time, Louisa Catherine's portrait by Charles Bird King clearly defines her as a powerful figure. It is large, a bit more than four feet by three, and is warmly and brilliantly colored. Louisa Catherine is sumptuously dressed, overdressed according to members of her family. Her costume for this portrait is not meant to be a faithful representation of her everyday sartorial style but an evocation of her "power suit." She sits before a luxurious drape, pulled aside to reveal a majestic exterior of rushing waters and towering trees. Her head is less in shadow than her husband's, and though her eyes are also looking to one side, we see more of her face. Indeed, from the angle of her body and her hands, she seems to be craning forward, as though to make herself more available to the viewer's eye. Louisa Catherine wears no jewelry, but she does have a turban wound about with gold material that sits on her head like a crown. She is holding her harp, a symbol of her cultural superiority and almost royal prerogative to power, asserting her right to lead American society. The instrument is bigger than she is, but she dominates the picture. Perhaps the most significant prop is the music book on her lap, opened to a song by Thomas Moore. Her choice for this election year? "Oh Say Not That Woman's Heart Can Be Bought."[110]

The pictures do not fool us: in the patriarchal world of the nineteenth century, only John Quincy was allowed to use his power in official ways. If the rich clothes that adorn Louisa Catherine in her painting were not painter's props, legally John Quincy owned even them. But in this era no one worked as an individual, and in politics the team approach—using both men and women—allowed the widest range of options to achieve family goals. The Adamses are a particularly useful couple to analyze within this framework. In Louisa Catherine's spectacular success in dealing with people and the use of social forms and John Quincy's equally spectacular failure in this arena, the Adamses present an almost exaggerated specimen of the political team. In other couples the responsibilities may have been more equally shared, more interchangeable, or not as clearly delineated. For the Adamses the contrast could not have been more marked: in the social and political world of the Washington elite, Louisa Catherine was all light and color, while John Quincy lived in a world of muted shadow.

By becoming the charismatic figures in the spotlight, and thus the focus of popularity or opprobrium, women provided the perfect solution to the problem of disguising the personal in the political. A man such as Thomas Jefferson could be the charismatic figure, but it was safer if a woman filled those shoes, as she could signify her husband and family in an artfully artless way, covered by the private world of women's social events. Women's power is often invisible because it has had to function on behalf of male power structures that do not recognize female participation as legitimate. Scholars are only now recognizing the ways women appropriate power back to themselves within these structures.[111] Ironically, one kind of power American women appropriated in Washington was that of visibility. But if a woman attracted the wrong kind of visibility, putting her charisma to the service not of her family (or her country) but of her personal ambition, she broke a sacrosanct rule. And when one woman did so in Washington City in 1829, all hell broke loose.

The Fall of Andrew Jackson's Cabinet

"O, what a noble mind is here o'erthrown!"
—WILLIAM SHAKESPEARE, *Hamlet* 3.1.150

I N A CULTURE committed to denying female political work, female
politicking paradoxically thrived precisely because of its unconsidered, unofficial nature. Through the private milieu in which women
like Dolley Payne Todd Madison operated, and the female techniques
used to gain political ends, conventional male political structures safely
contained such efforts while benefiting from them. Under the cover of
their roles as mothers and wives, the Washington ladies ensured that the
machinery of politics ran as usual.

Some women, however, make trouble. Perhaps the greatest sin committed by the woman at the heart of the infamous Eaton affair—Margaret
"Peggy" Eaton—was that she invoked a different, though traditional, female persona, that of "The Courtesan." This label has come about partly
through Margaret's own actions and partly through the reactions of her
contemporaries and of historians. How else to explain how she (and the
scandal around her) brought down the first cabinet of President Andrew
Jackson's administration and threatened the future of the young Republic?
By forcing issues of female ambition and sexuality into direct relationship
with an indisputably political event, Margaret illumined the covert female
political culture. Her exposure of the powerful conjunctions of public/
private, official/unofficial, social/political, and male/female shook her
world to the core. The Eaton affair, though centered around a woman, de-
fies the easy (if erroneous) categorization that other female political
affairs have allowed. In studying how an operation works, its breakdowns
can be as informative as its smooth running. The significance of the
Eaton affair lies in what it reveals about a system in dysfunction.

The years 1829–31, when Andrew Jackson ushered in the Age of Democracy and the capital's official community contended over Margaret Eaton, brought an end to this particular era of women in politics, or at least altered its course significantly. The resulting disruption brought to light many subterranean factors, much as a familiar cityscape's infrastructure might lie revealed after an earthquake. The end of this era of female politicking cannot be attributed solely to the Eaton affair; at least two other larger circumstances—one internal, one external—played significant roles. First, at the beginning of the Jackson administration, the political culture itself was on the verge of a transformation into a more democratic style, which accounted for some of the tensions in the Eaton affair. Also, in the wider culture the new middle classes were forming a "vernacular gentility" appropriate to their present situation and future aspirations: a kind of social democracy.

Both these changes depended on an increasing separation between a familiar public sphere and a newly formed phenomenon, a "private sphere," characterized by home, family, privacy, and women. These changes would not unfold smoothly in a town based on politics. The subsequent eruptions shattered the interlocking political and social worlds.

THE LIBERTINE VERSUS THE SAVAGE

Though Jackson's ascension to the presidency precipitated the political and social upheavals in Washington City, the fissures had begun to show soon after the election of 1824. Like his father, John Quincy Adams had the ill fortune to preside over a moment of disintegration and transformation in the two-party system. In the family tradition, John Quincy found himself on the disintegration side, in one of the weakest presidencies in the government's history.

His plan for the United States' future, which he unveiled during his first annual message to Congress, projected a strong, unified nation-state, with a federal government active in physical and moral "internal improvements." Though John Quincy's vision proved prescient, it found little resonance in 1820s America. Having offered a strong and definite program only to have Congress and the press reject it, John Quincy could do nothing but wait out his ineffective term.[1]

Deprived of her pivotal role as campaign manager, Louisa Catherine became increasingly depressed and spent her White House years absent

Born to Command: King Andrew the First, *broadside, 1832.* (Courtesy of Tennessee State Library and Archives, Nashville; reproduced from Stephen Hess and Milton Kaplan, *The Ungentlemanly Art: A History of American Political Cartoons* [New York, 1968], pl. II-23, p. 68)

emotionally and sometimes physically. She continued to entertain according to the standards she had set during her campaign, but she made only a few efforts to use her social lobby to help either John Quincy's inert presidency or his reelection effort.[2]

The seeming immobility of the Adams administration, embodied in its two leading characters, proved only a deceptive lull. The caucus failure of 1824 had signaled the breakdown of the Republican hegemony, and after the 1825 presidential election in the House, new voices of change clamored to be heard. Among other reforms, male voters of the emerging middle and working classes demanded more direct participation in presidential elections. The energy around this particular issue indicated a growing expectation of enlarged rights for the "common man."

The growing pains of the federal government, the democratic impulses abroad in the wider culture, and the struggle toward a two-party system would explode during John Quincy's reelection bid in 1828. One of the dirtiest campaigns ever in U.S. history, the contest posed the choice between the National Republicans, headed by President John Quincy Adams, and a new movement, which would come to be called the Democrats, headed by the Hero of New Orleans, Andrew Jackson.[3]

Fear drove the campaign rhetoric, fear expressed by supporters of both candidates and the press and focused on the notion that America stood in danger of losing its republican virtue. In this context the contradictory dangers of creeping aristocracy and rampant democracy emerged as prominent themes of the campaign. Jackson's supporters presented John Quincy as the ultimate aristocrat: European-educated, corrupt, and dissolute, unfit to rule a burgeoning democracy. Until Andrew Jackson informed his supporters that he would not war against women, they used British-born Louisa Catherine as proof of John Quincy's effete predilections. Stymied in that attempt, Jackson's friends seized upon an entry wrongly included in the 1826 list of presidential expenditures sent to the House committee on appropriations—a billiard table, balls, and cues—to depict a dissolute Adams White House. When the Adams press weakly protested that "gambling furniture" was "a common appendage in the houses of the rich and great in Europe," the opposition labeled the administration "aristocratic." Though President Adams eventually proved that the billiards set had not been purchased with public money, the enemy's images remained fixed in the press and public mind.[4]

These proponents of democracy also made much of the 1825 "corrupt bargain" between John Quincy and Henry Clay that had, with a grand sweep of lèse-majesté, overturned the will of the people in order to gratify personal ambition. At a Republican convention the young men of Halfmoon, New York, resolved that the upcoming election pitted the "cause of Jackson . . . *emphatically the cause of the people*" against an "*aristocracy*," "an unholy and selfish ambition" that exhibited "a *contempt of the free principles of our Republic.*" Anyone who passed over the "incorruptible" Jackson in favor of Adams doomed himself to follow a "corrupt and sinking administration."[5]

Jackson supporters could attack any words or practices smacking of aristocracy quite freely, because that kind of critique had been part of the American political vocabulary since Revolutionary days. In making a case against the encroachment of democracy, on the other hand, John Quincy's friends had to tread more cautiously and more covertly, no doubt remembering how the press had reacted to John Quincy's worry that the United States, "palsied by the will" of its citizens, would fall behind the other nations of the world.[6]

In the twenty-eight years since Thomas Jefferson's election, the term *democracy* had gone from being generally accepted as a synonym for "rule by the mob" to being, for some, a sacred political goal. In the 1826 congressional elections, the "Democratic Republicans" had won a majority in Congress. To avoid appearing to offend popular sentiment, the Adams campaign attacked Jackson's personal history; if this was to be an age of the common man, they were determined to show that this man, at least, was far too common.

Their strategy consisted of portraying Andrew Jackson as a savage, uncontrollably violent man. Their pamphlets cautioned the public not to be complacent about their choice for president, warning that Jackson was a disease from which the Republic might take years to recover. Henry Clay used General Jackson's military record, the source of his fame and proof of his patriotism, to depict the hero as a "military chieftain," potentially as tyrannical as Alexander, Cromwell, or Bonaparte. Moreover, not only was this backwoodsman a ruthless military leader, but he was an infamous private murderer as well, participating in duels and illegitimate executions, as illustrated by an infamous anti-Jackson handbill decorated with coffins representing his victims.[7]

A View of the Capitol at Washington City, *drawn by William Henry Bartlett and engraved by C. J. Bentley, 1837.* (Courtesy of the Kiplinger Washington Collection)

This personal part of the National Republican message found its most dramatic expression in relating the tale of Andrew Jackson's marriage to Rachel Donelson Robards. The two had married in 1791, mistakenly believing that her divorce from the abusive Lewis Robards was final. When they discovered the error three years later, they remarried. Rachel Donelson Robards Jackson went on to live a pious and respectable life, but the years between weddings allowed Adams supporters to depict the two as adulterers. Adultery was not their only crime; Jackson's enemies asserted that he had abducted Rachel from her legitimate husband, implying that Andrew Jackson was a man who took what he wanted, holding no brief for law or the sanctity of marriage.[8]

If, as one historian has characterized it, the 1828 election was a contest between power, represented by Adams and the establishment, and liberty, as represented by Andrew Jackson, in the final count "liberty found more friends than power." In December 1828 Andrew Jackson won 56 percent of the popular vote and 178 of the 261 electoral votes. To make it worse for John Quincy, the voter turnout for this election was higher than it had ever been, more than double that of the election of 1824, due largely to the implementation of state electoral reforms that allowed greater participation by the people.[9]

The people may have been elated by the election of "a man of the people," but the official and residential elites of Washington City greeted the news with dread. As the time of the president-elect's arrival in the capital neared, their anxiety heightened, a collective uneasiness originating in uncertainty. The election of 1828, like the election of 1800, seemed to usher in a new era, a revolution. Using activist supporters and the press, Jackson, like Thomas Jefferson, had campaigned largely on the negative attributes of the entrenched party and made a good case for change; but again like Jefferson, he had been a little vague on what that change might entail.

Only one of Jackson's policies seemed clear: to reform the federal government by banishing the present batch of office-holding rascals. This stand was not calculated to soothe official society. The prospect of immense job turnover attracted vast crowds of aspirants, who traveled to the city while the established officials became "fear-ants," a new word in the local vocabulary. Margaret Bayard Smith's letters from this time convey the impression of a "dull" and "gloomy" society, waiting with dread for what the new administration would bring.[10]

The composition of a presidential cabinet always prompted speculation and interest in the capital, and this was even truer than usual in early 1829. In the eyes of many, Jackson's lack of experience, coupled with his reputed temper and stubbornness, necessitated a strong advisory body. His critics hoped that "able men, statesmen" would "steer" and "restrain" him. For all his vaunted will, Jackson, according to Daniel Webster, "has not character enough to conduct his measures by his own strength."[11] Webster and others worried that the general's arrogance, passions, and prejudices would make him easy prey for a designing intriguer.

In early January 1829 Washington City learned that Rachel Jackson had died, news that carried a double burden. Rumor held that the slanders of the campaign had brought on Rachel's death, shocking and shaming the Washington community, who had been joking for months about the country woman smoking her pipe in the White House drawing room. They were afraid that this latest tragedy only gave more bitter ammunition to the president-elect, who already harbored resentment and scorn for metropolitan society. More seriously, Washington worried about the loss of "a wife who, it is said, could control the violence of his tempers," soothe his hypersensitivity, and in general had proved a "restraining and benign influence." Though most often "affliction . . . softens" the heart, sometimes it "sours," warned Bayard Smith, and "should it have the latter effect, the public councils and affairs will have reason to deplore this awful and sudden event."[12]

When Jackson announced his proposed cabinet in late February 1829, the political community reacted with shock and dismay. With the exception of Martin Van Buren, Jackson chose men of little national stature, mostly provincial politicians only lately come to Washington, and one close friend. Only Vice President John C. Calhoun had federal experience. Jackson included his friend and adviser John Henry Eaton as secretary of war; Calhoun supporters Samuel D. Ingham (from Pennsylvania), John Branch (from North Carolina), and John M. Berrien (from Georgia) as secretaries of treasury and navy and attorney general, respectively; and Jackson supporters Martin Van Buren (from New York) as secretary of state and William Barry (from Kentucky) as postmaster general.[13]

"A millennium of minnows" became the common judgment. With "all the talents of the Union" to chose from, Jackson opted to surround himself with "narrow minds, some of them hardly gentlemen and none of them . . . [with] much character and no principles, moral or political." Shortly after these appointments were made official, Bayard Smith and one of her most politically active friends, Letitia Porter, wife of the newly deposed secretary of war, sat by the fire and "tore it [the cabinet] all to pieces and predicted that it could not support the administration," which would soon "crumble to pieces."[14] If Jackson's cabinet nominations were supposed to provide a clue to the tone and effectiveness of his administration, the signs discerned by the Washington community were not good. By choosing such "lesser men," Jackson demonstrated his determination to rule his administration absolutely.

"PITY ME, MY FRIENDS, I WAS BORN AND RAISED IN WASHINGTON!"

One nomination in particular loomed most ominously over the future of the Republic. The proposed secretary of war, John Henry Eaton of Tennessee, was held to be a solid, if not spectacular, character and, taken by himself, fully deserving of a reward in the Jackson administration (though some said not one as important as a cabinet post). The problem lay in his recent marriage to a Washington City resident, Margaret O'Neale Timberlake, by which he had irredeemably removed himself from polite society.[15] Margaret's father, William O'Neale, had opened his first hotel in the new capital in 1796, and Margaret grew up surrounded by the important legislators and government figures of the time. Given the best education available to a girl in the infant city, young Margaret made a name for herself in her teens for her beauty and her attractiveness to men. At age twelve Margaret won the crown at a local dancing school competition, bestowed on her by Queen Dolley herself.

Even when trying to project herself as a prim, well-bred innocent, Margaret reveled in her sexual power, proudly declaring in her autobiography, "When I was still in pantalets and rolling hoops with other girls, I had the attentions of men, young and old, enough to turn a girl's head." According to her own account, the nephew of the secretary of the navy poisoned himself with laudanum over her, the adjutant general of the U.S. Army proposed (though "all the wooings of December could not win May"), and Major Belton and Captain Root nearly fought a duel for her—all before her sixteenth birthday.[16]

Though physical descriptions vary, all agree that Margaret Eaton was a stunning woman and remained so throughout her life. Her hair was variously described as dark or a rich auburn, in curls, and her eyes dark, fringed by heavy lashes. Her figure was splendid, "of medium height, straight, and delicate," and in "perfect proportion." She had a "broad, expressive forehead," a "perfect nose of almost Grecian proportions, and finely curved mouth, with a firm, round chin," completing a "profile of faultless outlines."[17] At age sixteen Margaret married a ship's purser, John Timberlake, whose financial fecklessness required him to spend most of his days at sea. Margaret continued to live with her parents, raising her two daughters (born in 1819 and 1825) and working in her father's hotel and barroom.

In 1818 John Henry Eaton, a young widower, came to Washington to serve as senator from Tennessee. He would stay for ten years, working in the political interest of his friend, mentor, and kinsman Andrew Jackson.[18] Eaton quickly ingratiated himself with the O'Neale-Timberlake ménage. He squired Mrs. Timberlake to social events, befriended the hapless Timberlake during his infrequent shore leaves, and acted as family guardian and patron. Eaton used his political influence to find Timberlake a job as purser and on occasion lent both him and William O'Neale money.

In 1823 Andrew Jackson came to Washington, also as a senator, in preparation for his presidential run in 1824. Naturally, he stayed with his good friend and fellow Tennessean, John Eaton, and came to know Margaret Timberlake and the O'Neales. He wrote to Rachel that though the whole family was "amiable," his particular favorite was Mrs. Timberlake, who "plays on the piano delightfully, and every Sunday evening entertains her pious mother with sacred music to which we are invited." When Rachel joined her husband for a brief stay in 1824, she also concurred in her husband's good opinion of the young matron.[19]

The Jacksons' good opinion notwithstanding, the association between Margaret Timberlake and John Eaton gave rise to Washington gossip early in their ten-year friendship. Elizabeth Kortright Monroe forbade the White House drawing rooms to Margaret, even though John Eaton had achieved some prominence in political circles. "Not an inspiring character and [of] violent temper . . . she has never been admitted into good society," recalled Bayard Smith during Margaret's later troubles, though she "is very handsome." The year 1828 proved a decisive and momentous one in the life of the couple. In April news came that John Timberlake had died at sea, possibly by suicide, possibly from illness. At this stage Margaret Timberlake's reputation prompted rumors that he had committed suicide because of his wife's affairs.[20]

Soon after the election that autumn, John Eaton wrote to his friend the president-elect, detailing the current slanders and expressing a wish to marry Margaret and "snatch her from that injustice of city gossipers who attend to everybody's reputation to the neglect of their own." Eaton was aware that such a move would generate more talk—"The impossibility of escaping detraction and slander was too well credenced to me in the abuse of those more meritorious and deserving than I ever could hope to be"—and gently hinted that despite his honorable intentions the timing might not be right for such a move.[21]

Jackson reacted promptly and succinctly: "Marry her and you will be in a position to defend her." John Eaton did—on January 1, 1829—and Washington murmured and whispered. Bayard Smith, no friend to the new Mrs. Eaton, observed crisply, "Tonight Gen'l Eaton, the bosom friend and almost adopted son of Gen'l Jackson is to be married to a lady whose reputation, her previous connection with him both before and after her husband's death, has totally destroyed."

Cruder reactions demonstrate that Margaret's sexual reputation extended beyond premarital indiscretions. The elegant Congressman Churchill Cambreleng of New York wrote to his friend Van Buren, misattributing an epigram of Montaigne: "Poor Eaton is to be married tonight to Mrs. T. . . . ! There is a vulgar saying of some vulgar man, I believe Swift, on such unions—about using a certain household [*illegible*] and then putting it on one's head." Louis McLane, a politician friend of Van Buren's, exulted, "Eaton has just married his mistress, and the mistress of eleven doz. others!"[22]

A month later, when Andrew Jackson proposed that his cabinet include John Eaton, it seemed the last straw for Washington society. Through the official channels of marriage and political appointment, Margaret Eaton could skyrocket to the head of Washington society. With the president and secretary of state both widowers, the lady of the president's closest friend in the cabinet would become, in effect, the leader of national society and the court circle. Washington had initially feared only a tyrannical reign; now it was to have an immoral one. During the election campaign the more sophisticated among them had probably not believed the rhetoric claiming that Andrew Jackson was bringing an adulteress, Rachel Donelson Robards Jackson, to the capital to head society. After all, there existed a quite respectable explanation for the Jacksons' marital situation, and Rachel had spent thirty years living a model life. But Peggy Eaton? Washington insiders and longtime residents had known her from the cradle and proved determined to put her in her place.

The official elite reacted with a speed and gravity that demonstrated the universal (though cloaked) acknowledgment of the close ties between society and politics. The same day the cabinet proposals appeared in the paper, a delegation of Washington insiders, led by Colonel Nathan Towson, hero of the War of 1812, paid a call on the president-elect to warn him of his peril. Though no doubt Eaton should receive a post of some importance in the new administration, Jackson should not give him a cabinet position, which would force Eaton and his new wife into direct social contact with the prominent ladies of Washington. When Jackson pressed for details, the men admitted that ladies would not receive a woman of Mrs. Eaton's reputation. Jackson reacted ferociously: "Do you suppose that I have been sent here by the people to consult the ladies of Washington as to the proper persons to compose my Cabinet?" Old Hickory's back was up, and he would not give in, especially not to the forces of slander that he believed killed his wife. According to Margaret's recollections, Jackson said to her, "I tell you, Margaret, I had rather have live vermin on my back than the tongue of one of these Washington women on my reputation."[23]

To a Washington City already jittery about the people's choice, Jackson's inauguration day hardly proved reassuring. The ceremony itself went well, even Margaret Bayard Smith declaring herself profoundly moved by the "moral sublimity" of democracy in action. Echoing her reaction to Jefferson's inauguration, she asserted that she would have been proud for any European to observe the peaceful transition of power in a republic: "Here, the dignity of man stood forth in bold relief . . . free and enlightened man . . . ennobled by nature—bold in conscious liberty."[24]

Unfortunately, things fell apart later in the day, during the White House festivities. The "majesty of the people" gave way to a riot that reminded Bayard Smith of the storming of the Bastille, an association that carried the threat not only of mob violence but also of political upheaval. The new president was nearly pressed to death by supporters who wanted to *"shake hands"* with him, and he eventually had to escape out the back of the official residence, retreating to his hired lodgings.

Fortunately, servants opened the windows of the White House rooms and put tubs filled with punch on the lawn to prevent suffocation and stampede within doors. The rabble broke several thousand dollars worth of glass and china in their struggle to get to the refreshments, which proved woefully inadequate for the number of people. "Ladies fainted, men were seen with bloody noses, and such a scene of confusion took place as it is impossible to describe," as the crowd swelled to two thousand, and men with dirty boots stood on upholstered chairs to get a look at Old Hickory.

Bayard Smith concluded her account with resignation: "Ladies and gentlemen only had been expected, and not the people *en masse*. But it was the People's day and the People's president and the People would rule." Like many a good republican, Bayard Smith classified the tyranny of the people as the "most ferocious, cruel, and despotic" possible. But she reflected another apprehension, particular to the official community at Washington City, by adding what she considered "the worst of tyrannies—the tyranny of licentiousness."[25] Andrew Jackson had brought democracy to the capital, represented both by the mob pushing their way into the White House and by the person of Margaret Eaton, the amoral, low-born barmaid, pushing her way into Washington's highest social circles. No one could do much about the incursion of the people, but Bayard Smith and others could certainly do something about Peg Eaton.

The ladies of Washington declared among themselves and to their husbands that she would not be received into their society. Rather than expose their households and children to her contaminating influence, cabinet wives and other hostesses decided to freeze Mrs. Eaton out. They would not call upon her, because to do so would open intercourse between families. They would not attend events that she attended, not accept any of her invitations, and certainly not extend any to her.

PETTICOAT POLITICS

The first official shot in what came to be known as the "Petticoat War" was fired at the Inaugural Ball, where the ladies of the administration, led by Floride Calhoun, wife of John C. Calhoun, cut Margaret Eaton dead, refusing to be introduced or to speak with her. Floride enlisted Emily Donelson, the young bride of Andrew Jackson Donelson, the president's adopted son and secretary and herself the official White House hostess; Deborah K. Ingham; Mrs. Branch, with her daughters, Rebecca and Margaret; and Mrs. Berrien and her daughters. The only cabinet wife who sided with Margaret was Mrs. Barry.

Floride Calhoun had made her feelings known earlier. Shortly after their New Year's wedding, the Eatons called on her, and she received them politely. According to social rules, well known to Floride, her return call would open social interactions between the families of the vice president and the secretary of war. Floride chose to eliminate that possibility by not calling. Rather than be forced into interactions with the Eatons, Floride and John Calhoun decided that after the inauguration she would return to their home in South Carolina, where she remained for the entire four years of the first Jackson administration.[26] Thus, though she absented herself from the scene early in the Petticoat War, Floride's initial stand provided one impetus for the events that followed, and her absence and silence spoke eloquently to the ladies of Washington City.

Soon after the unpleasantness began, Jackson received a letter from Dr. Ezra Stiles Ely, a clergyman in Philadelphia, charging Margaret with a variety of offenses, some of them quite serious. Ely began by stating that Margaret had a notorious reputation from girlhood and that the respectable folk of Washington had long barred their houses to her. He related that a gentleman had said at the breakfast table on the morning after the British minister's ball that "Mrs. Eaton brushed by him last night pretending not to know him; she had forgotten the time when she slept with him."

As regards John Eaton, Ely claimed that John and Margaret had traveled and lodged together before their marriage, and that Margaret had instructed the servants to call her children by the surname Eaton instead of Timberlake. In addition, Ely asserted that while her husband was at sea, Mrs. Timberlake had suffered a miscarriage as a result of a driving accident. According to Ely's supposedly impeccable but unnamed sources, the physician arrived to find Mrs. Timberlake attended by her mother, and together they joked that he was too late to see "a little Eaton."[27]

Andrew Jackson's letter of refutation was longer than his inaugural address. In it he dismissed most of the charges as baseless gossip, citing his own and Rachel's good opinion of Margaret and his personal knowledge of Timberlake's devotion to his wife and to his friend Eaton. The miscarriage story he dismissed out of hand as contrary to all good sense. Jackson took the accusations seriously enough to employ his own investigators to scour the hotel registers looking for incriminating entries (they found none) and to collect depositions attesting to Margaret's good character. In all, ninety-three pages of Jackson's papers are devoted to refuting these charges.[28]

In the meantime, through a visit to Ely, Margaret discovered a Washington minister, Dr. John Campbell, was the source of the miscarriage story. When Jackson confronted the clergyman, Campbell attributed the tale to a doctor long dead. According to Jackson, Campbell asserted positively that the miscarriage had occurred in 1821. However, faced with proof that Timberlake had been in Washington City during that year, the parson changed his mind and the date, to Jackson's disgust. In September 1829 Jackson called a cabinet meeting to review all the evidence, written and verbal, in his possession. He also delivered the verdict—"She is as chaste as a virgin!"—in his mind effectively closing the case.[29]

However, the "Eaton malaria" continued. Martin Van Buren, a widower, led the Margaret supporters. Not only did he call on the Eatons, the only man in the cabinet besides Barry to do so, and they on him, but he also gave several parties and balls in their honor, embarrassing the other cabinet members by tendering them invitations he knew they must refuse. As secretary of state and host to the foreign legations, he enlisted the European diplomats, some in the United States without their wives, to host social events and invite the Eatons. At one of these soirees, the wife of the Dutch minister, Madame Huygens, made a scene when she discovered that Margaret had been given precedence over her and threatened to retaliate by extending the Eaton boycott into the diplomatic corps. Jackson decided her remarks constituted an insult to the United States, and only Van Buren's diplomacy averted an international incident. Because of this incident, Andrew Jackson changed his official protocol and asserted that cabinet members would take precedence over foreign envoys.[30]

The initial group of cabinet wives influenced the other Washington hostesses around them, compelling them to choose between joining their growing camp or taking Margaret as their only female society. The domino effect worked; one by one, Washington parlors closed to Margaret. Many were nervous at offending the volatile president of the United States, but after all, the presidency commanded little practical power compared to the legislature and the cabinet. Though ostensibly about morals, the choice came down to politics. Women who depended on the social whirl to further their own and their families' interests joined the wives and daughters of the cabinet and Congress in the boycott.

Andrew Jackson continued to "force" Margaret's society on official Washington, counting her dinner invitations as seriously as he would skirmishes in a war. John Quincy Adams noted in his diary that cabinet families gave large dinner parties "to which Mrs. Eaton is not invited. On the other hand, the president makes her doubly conspicuous by an overdisplay of notice. At the last drawing room . . . she had a crowd gathered around her and was made the public gaze." One eyewitness described the treatment of the "Unofficial First Lady": "Fifty guests, one hundred candles, and lamps, silver plate of every description and for a queen, Peggy O'Neale, led in by Mr. Vaughan (the British minister) as head of the diplomatic corps, and sitting between him and the president."[31]

Margaret herself had no intention of retreating quietly. John Davis, representative from Massachusetts, stayed at a party longer than he wished "to see Madam Secretary of War dispose of herself." He reported that the lady in question bore "up with spirit and vivacity against the gaze of the multitude," a feat which required unparalleled "self possession." Though "her face was highly suffused," and the "marks of anxious thought" were easily visible, she achieved the "triumph she sought."[32]

With all her beauty, Margaret played the opposite of the charismatic figure, repelling rather than attracting. Her presence at a ball did not provide legitimacy for the new reign but rather rubbed her meteoric rise and newfound (unearned) status in the faces of official society. If other women had served as charismatic figures for the benefit of their men, achieving advantage for male public careers with displays of graciousness and refinement, Margaret Eaton's person seemed the focus and symbol of what Andrew Jackson stood for in his enemies' eyes: immorality and tyranny.

The opposition suffered the initial casualties in the Petticoat War. Jackson gave a dinner with mandatory attendance and placed Margaret at his right side, demonstrating that all the furor had only endeared her to him. But his official hostess, Emily Donelson, continued to side with the ladies of Washington. Though he adored his family and needed them around him, the politically inexperienced Andrew Jackson could ill afford to appear unable to control even his own house. After a prolonged tussle with her Uncle Andrew, Emily Donelson either left for or was sent back to Tennessee and was replaced as White House hostess by Mary Ann Lewis, daughter of Eaton supporter William B. Lewis.[33]

More seriously, as Van Buren's star rose, Calhoun's fell. Initially, Calhoun took the stand that though he harbored no personal animus against Eaton, this purely social matter fell strictly under his wife's control. No doubt he and Floride thought they had forestalled any involvement in this matter by her absence from the capital. Jackson grew increasingly impatient with this excuse; he had always ascribed the attacks against Margaret to the machinations of unscrupulous politicians. At first Jackson accused Henry Clay of engineering them, but because of the part Floride played at the beginning of his administration and her continued absence, John Calhoun fell under presidential suspicion.

Calhoun had good reason to feel nervous about getting on the wrong side of Old Hickory. He had a few secrets to keep from the president if he wanted to succeed to the White House. Contrary to Jackson's belief that only Monroe and Clay had condemned his actions in Florida during the Seminole campaign, Calhoun, as part of Monroe's cabinet, had also called for his censure. The second inconvenient piece of information was that Calhoun had anonymously written South Carolina's position on nullification, asserting the power of a state to nullify any federal law that it regarded as unjust. Ostensibly nullification applied to federal tariffs and taxes, but it could also safeguard slavery. Even in the 1820s politicians recognized nullification as the foundation of a secessionist movement and a threat to the sanctity of the Union, an ideal especially close to Jackson's heart. Though these differences between John Calhoun and Andrew Jackson had long roots, the Eaton affair brought them to the surface and further polarized the president and members of his cabinet.[34]

Jackson's initial cabinet meeting in 1829, where he declared Margaret's comparative virginity, was not his only attempt officially to control the spreading "malaria." In the beginning of 1830, Congressman Richard M. Johnson, probably with Jackson's blessing, attempted to act the peacemaker.[35] Though he tried to convince the cabinet members at least to appear to accept Mrs. Eaton, they all refused, on the grounds that the president (through Johnson) had no authority to force them into social intercourse. Johnson, taken aback, threatened them with dismissal but to no avail. Though at first Jackson reacted "like a roaring lion," the president shifted his position on the advice of his friends and a few days later retracted his insistence that the Ingham, Branch, and Berrien families visit Margaret, requiring only that they help him protect her from slanders.

He called all three men together and read them a memorandum stating, "I do not claim the right to interfere in any manner in the domestic relations or personal intercourse of any member of my Cabinet, nor have I ever in any manner attempted it." However, he claimed that encouraging the "attacks" on Margaret hurt the administration and indicated a "wanton disregard of my feelings and reproof of my official conduct." He warned the three men that he had no intention of parting with John Eaton and that "those of my Cabinet who cannot harmonize with him had better withdraw for harmony I must and will have."

The time for rapprochement seemed at hand. The three secretaries denied any ill feeling against Margaret and agreed with the president's goal of harmony. Jackson heard this part of their response but did not heed their addendum. Whatever they might be willing to do, the secretaries insisted, they "could not undertake to control their families." Jackson pronounced himself satisfied, and for the next few social events, there seemed to be an uneasy peace.[36] But the controversy was not solved by this second cabinet meeting, and the social boycott and ostracizing of Margaret continued.

If society had been divided into "battalions" during the 1824 presidential campaign, in 1829–30 it became opposing camps, undertaking two different truncated versions of social life. By the spring of 1831, Washington society had undergone a massive transformation, the city giving "every appearance of decline." Everyone became afraid to move for fear of offending someone important. The women who had thought that the all-important calling and social rounds could continue without including Margaret were proved wrong. Recent arrivals to the capital found "no society and no amusements"; residents informed them "things are much changed for the worse."[37] Jackson was proving himself a forceful and intransigent character, less easy to placate than in the first months of his administration.

Neither could Jackson accomplish anything with his cabinet frozen and no unofficial sphere. A group of Tennessee politicians called a secret meeting to discuss ways of forcing John Eaton from the cabinet, and one hundred congressmen threatened to abandon Jackson if the situation continued.[38]

Almost everyone in Washington City had some comment about the affair. Many men reacted to its growing significance with disbelief. In 1830

Benjamin Williams Crowninshield, former secretary of the navy, wrote to General Henry Dearborn, "You ask how are things in Washington, and I reply perhaps the strangest in the world, because for the first time, I believe the destiny of the nation hangs on a *woman's* favor, and yet strange, 'tis true."[39]

For all the sexual joking about Margaret Eaton, observers and participants took the events seriously, especially the affair's impact on the careers of Calhoun and Van Buren. As early as 1830 Jackson's former rival John Quincy Adams noted: "The Administration party is split up into a blue and a green faction upon this point of morals, but the explosion has been hitherto deferred. Calhoun leads the moral party, Van Buren the frail sisterhood; and he is notoriously engaged in canvassing for the presidency by paying court to Mrs. Eaton." James Gordon Bennett of the *New York Enquirer* was more definite in his prediction: "I think that John C. Calhoun has doomed himself to oblivion by his refusal to rehabilitate Peggy Eaton."[40]

In the spring of 1831, Martin Van Buren suggested a solution to Jackson: he would resign, perhaps forcing the troublemakers to resign as well. John Eaton protested that because he and his family had caused the trouble, he should be the one to resign. In the event, they both did. Secretaries Berrien, Branch, and Ingham were slow to take the hint, and finally Jackson had to force them to step down. With a play on Van Buren's well-known nickname, the *New York Courier* greeted the news: "Well indeed may Mr. Van Buren be called 'The Great Magician' for *he raises his wand, and the whole Cabinet disappears.*"[41] It was the first (and thus far only) time in U.S. history that a president lost an entire cabinet.

Both sides of the dispute and the major players (politicians all) had definite ideas about the origin and true meaning of the events in which they participated, each based on a strong desire to present a particular face to the world. The Eaton camp saw the affair as a carefully planned political plot. Reflecting his well-documented paranoia and suspicion of politics, Andrew Jackson insisted that the problem lay in "the great exertions made by Clay and his partisans [and then later, Calhoun] here and elsewhere to destroy the character of Mrs. Eaton, by the foulest and basest means, so that a deep and lasting wrong might be inflicted on her husband."[42]

Margaret herself remembered that John Eaton reassured her that the slanders "are intended to separate General Jackson and me. Nobody believes them about you. They are just employed for political capital." Thus, Margaret claimed in demonstrating her personal sexual virtue, "it was the designs of politicians which led to the slander of my fair fame, not any frailty of mine that came in as an element to change the course of the political history of this country." She cited as proof the cessation of the slander as soon as the political ends in question had been reached.[43]

In contrast, the two chief candidates for mastermind—John C. Calhoun and Martin Van Buren—insisted that the affair originated and developed not in some masculine smoke-filled room but just where it seemed to begin, in the parlors of the ladies. It was a mere social affair. According to Calhoun, the ladies of Washington excluded Margaret Eaton from society as a result of that "censorship which the sex exercises over itself on which, all must acknowledge, the purity and dignity of the female character mainly depend."

He reasonably pointed out that if the affair had been instigated and propelled by political considerations, he should have cultivated Margaret Eaton himself, as the winning side was apparent early on, at least for a man who wanted the sitting president's support for his own ambition. Martin Van Buren, too, characterized the "imbroglio" as a "private and personal matter which only acquired political consequence by its adaptation to the gratification of resentments."[44]

Though neither man could satisfactorily account for the social war's dire effects on the political scene, Calhoun and Van Buren were correct about the origins and energy behind the affair. Other than paranoid accusations, no evidence supports a plot on any side. On the contrary, a great deal of confusion reigned. Though some tried to take advantage of events as they unfolded, no individual could predict the sequence of events or the outcome.

At the initial cabinet dissolution, when Margaret Eaton's enemies were packing their trunks, observers assumed that she was behind the plot to banish her detractors. However, Washington City learned that when Van Buren and Jackson called on Margaret shortly after the resignations, they were received coldly.[45] The conclusion that the cabinet breakup constituted her victory became untenable as subsequent events demonstrated exactly how much she and her husband had lost.

Margaret had not wanted her husband to resign, fearing that it would mean her own banishment, and she was proved correct. As for Calhoun, he himself pointed out that had he been the author of all the disturbances, he proved a very poor plotter indeed.[46] Martin Van Buren was the chief beneficiary of the tempest, partly from circumstance and partly because he focused on very specific and limited goals.

The efforts of President Jackson, Van Buren, and other men and women to control the progress or outcome of the social war backfired because they misapprehended (or could not acknowledge) the inextricable intertwining of the two "separate" worlds of society and politics. Only if society and politics were intimately connected could men use the social world for political purposes or women affect politics by decisions made about society.

If male observers expressed astonishment at the profoundly political outcome of a social boycott, the ladies proved as confused as their menfolk when their actions became a political issue. On one hand, they did not realize that they could not stage a social boycott without affecting politics. On the other, Jackson and his administration did not acknowledge that a political community could not exist and, more important at that moment, a new regime could not be legitimated without society. Blinded by their own denial, both sides were naive in their assumption that politics and society could be separated.

A WORLD OF WOMEN

Untangling the many threads of the Eaton affair requires that we privilege private papers and actions—sources necessary to all analyses of the unofficial sphere—over official documents, even ones as intriguing as President Jackson's memorandum to the cabinet. In the case of this particular historical episode, however, private papers can only go so far.

Though Margaret Eaton stands as the central figure in this controversy, she left no reactions to the events as they were happening, and so biographical approaches to the Eaton affair have all necessarily lost her voice somewhere in the middle of the narrative. Like Elizabeth Merry, Margaret Eaton becomes a ghost in her own story, the invisible eye of the storm. Nor did any of the major instigators of the war—Floride Calhoun, Emily Donelson, Deborah K. Ingham, or any of the Branch or Berrien women—leave any useful papers directly addressing the topic.

Fortunately, Washingtonians, both residents and visitors, followed the events closely and left rich mines of reaction and analysis—including accounts of female action—that reveal a milieu of increasing female influence.

As part of the development of the raw city into a power center, women like Dolley Payne Todd Madison and Louisa Catherine Adams had pushed the capital in a more aristocratic direction. Through the 1820s Washington City increasingly resembled a European capital, a place for displays of power and pomp, one dominated by established and rising elites. At the very time when the founding generation was trying to eradicate all signs of aristocratic rule from the government, they felt compelled to ratify their new authority with signs and markers from Europe.[47]

Political society began to pay more attention to the formalities that governed personal interactions and official relationships. The growing use of ritual paraphernalia, such as special calling cards, carrying cases, and racks on which to display cards received, testified to a growing attention to ceremony. Accounts of social events reveal both the increased efforts to create ceremonial or theatrical occasions—such as Mrs. Adams's "splendid shows"—and correspondents' awareness of display as a criterion for political assessment and a valuable political commodity.[48]

John Varnum wrote to his brother-in-law, Leverett Saltonstall, that though he "see[s] no more of dissipation [in Washington City] than at Haverhill [Massachusetts]," his "parties are more splendid." This modest statement points to an important truth. Washington City social arrangements were moving in a different direction from those of the rest of America. While the politicians seesawed between rule by aristocrats and rule by the mob as their two options, the social arbiters of American life outside the capital struggled with the emergence of another alternative: the development of a broad middling segment, invested and involved in politics and culture.[49]

The early nineteenth century, in other words, saw the rise of vernacular gentility among the middle classes of the country. A large and rising group of families combined aristocratic niceties, some of them articulated and defined by the burgeoning market in consumer goods, with democratic expectations to create a middle-class culture. Soberness, simplicity, tastefulness, and restraint all emerged as hallmarks of this new democratic style. The cultural life of the proponents of vernacular gentility concentrated on the personal and the private and found its greatest scope in the home and family circle.[50]

In contrast, Washington City was becoming a more traditional metropolis, modeled after the power centers in Europe. Display, luxury, consciousness of public gaze, and the public nature and intention of sociability were its distinguishing features. Homes retained their public, political functions rather than closing their parlors for intimate, private consumption. Legislators and visitors recognized the contrast between Washington life and their own experiences at home, and old-timers remarked on this trend, noting, for instance, "that the president [Adams] has set up a splendid court in a style superior to Mr. Monroe's."[51]

While some found this growth exciting, amusing, and quite legitimate, a critique also emerged. It flowered fully in the 1828 election rhetoric against the "aristocratic" John Quincy Adams, which, though focused specifically on the president, excoriated the style of life at the White House and, by extension, in Washington City. From the first days of the Monroe administration, observers noted the "germ of an artificial system of court manners" beginning in the capital. European influence, whether brought to the capital by foreign legations or by traveled Americans, proved "repugnant to the fastidious custom of our people." After observing one typically theatrical entertainment, one aghast legislator wailed to his wife, "What a horrible pass of mummery and false refinement are we getting to, in this republican country of ours?"[52] Scenes such as these provided Jackson the opportunity to present himself (as he believed) as a man unused to the ways of capitals and courts and thus a Washington outsider.

One did not have to observe mummery in person to be kept abreast of the state of affairs in Washington City during the late 1810s and early 1820s. Newspapers, periodicals, and manuals of style kept a close eye on the development of what they called "Etiquette!" a word often written as a headline in all capitals. "We are disgusted in hearing this word so frequently used at Washington City," fumed one editorial, cautioning its readers that if usages once just a "matter of *courtesy*" grew into an *"established order,"* Americans were going to be as bad as the Chinese, knocking their heads on the floor in the "imperial presence." The dreaded "etiquette" threatened to turn "*honest* and *reflecting* republicans" into a "breed of courtiers and race of hypocrites."[53]

If, in 1819, "gentlemen" began taking formal leave of the president, what could be next but the "kissing of hands"? And, "as our manners retire from republican simplicity, so will vice prevail," particularly the political vices, such as patronage, which lead to "posts of honor and profit." Soon the United States will not have to look to Europe for any fashion, "for if we continue in the like round of dissipation, gaiety, and extravagance, in a little while we shall give the *ton* ["tone," or style] to Europe."[54] To the newspaper-reading audience, made up mostly of "plainer folk," who shook hands and contented themselves with a game of cards or conversation around a fire, these accounts presaged a growing gulf between the rulers and the ruled.

No matter how dire the state of affairs in other cities, Washington's excesses proved more extreme and, because of its status as the center of national political power, more dangerous. With the country at large moving increasingly toward the leveling of the ranks noted by travelers such as Alexis de Tocqueville, Washington proved the opposite: "There is no place in the United States," solemnly intoned *A Description of the Etiquette at Washington City*, "where there exists so many distinctly marked grades of society, as at the city of Washington, during the session of Congress."[55]

Other towns depended on many types of enterprise, conducted in offices and shops; Washington City had only government. To outside observers who did not perceive the connection between the heavy social calendar and politics, Washington City was a town with little business and endless social activity. One writer advised his friend to depart from a city ruined by overwork—"over-trading" and "over-speculating"—and take up residence in Washington "where all is frolic and gaiety." There, the writer warned, he would find dangers in "over-dressing, over-eating, and over-balling."[56]

Political satirists used the increasingly luxurious material culture and attention paid to formal ceremonies simultaneously to trivialize for humorous effect and to impute extreme danger. In their hands the smallest luxury prophesied peril to the Republic. The satirical and fictional Fudge family saw a "state's disasters" in the "marble pillars and pilasters" of the capital's new buildings. What hope was there to retain republican virtue when a nation's "well-earned glory" was "struck to death with four-pronged forks"?[57] Women, of course, became symbols of these "effeminate pleasures"; satirists tied female craving for foreign luxury to a sexual preference for foreigners. Women were so mad to ally themselves with any kind of aristocrat, according to the fictional Fudges, that in a proxy ceremony one of them married a mere leg.[58]

The focus on women, though negative, indicates their important roles in an aristocratic culture, an importance enhanced by the circumstances of Washington City, which also needed to sustain a visible commitment to republicanism. When women took over many of the politicking functions of a power center as they did in the first decades of Washington City, they found themselves at the focus of criticism.

Beside the fictional representations of women dizzied by aristocratic foreigners, many eyewitnesses noted the increasing importance of women in the capital in the mid- and late 1820s. William Cabell Rives, a man accustomed to aristocratic behavior Virginia-style, related with amazement that the wife of the minister from Lübeck, Bremen, and Hamburg "has introduced an exotic style of manners that far transcends anything we have seen in the metropolis." Specifically, she had demonstrated a new mode of entering a social event, sweeping past her husband and preceding him into the room, "ducking and bowing all the way." The baroness took center stage, while "fifteen or twenty feet in the rear, comes on Monsieur, her husband, shuffling and padding like a Shetland pony." He climaxed his account with the revelation that the baroness was an American by birth, "a Miss Astor of New York." Even Rives, who thought of women "as important personages in every department of life," was appalled at such public recognition and honor.[59]

Even at the beginning of a congressional session, when the majority of ladies had not yet arrived in Washington, those who attended stood out, "dressed in the most extravagant and expensive manner." In these years, once official business got under way, correspondents and other observers openly noted women as influence peddlers and patronage seekers. William Rives gently mocked the "gilded" Mrs. Livingston who was cultivating the "backwoods" Rachel Jackson, in the "hope that General Jackson . . . would find a handsome office for her husband."[60]

Men learned that it paid to cultivate all members of a political family.

The efforts of Nathaniel Silsbee, representative from Massachusetts, did not escape John Varnum's notice. Though Varnum did not give parties as a rule, preferring to meet people "daily and familiarly," he noted that Silsbee "has been so attentive to my wife, whenever he met her . . . that I must invite him and a few other senators" to a dinner party.[61]

Like men, who more openly embraced party activities as the decade went on, women allied themselves in partisan ways, to the extent that William Rives divided his acquaintance of ladies into those who were (or were likely to become) "administration ladies" and those who were not. Washington City was gaining a permanent class of officials and "official women," whose engagement in politics colored their everyday life. As Bayard Smith noted, even in charitable societies "the ladies have elicited as much rivalship and party spirit, desire of precedence and authority as are found in political associations."[62]

WEAPONS OF WAR

Viewed within the context of Washington City, the specifics of the Eaton affair illustrate the power and place of women and social events in the early Republican United States. The events of the social war took place in social situations, in the unofficial space that proved so crucial to the development of Washington City and the federal government. As in earlier years, both men and women played important parts; and both male and female roles, powerfully gendered, proved crucial to the sequence of events.

During the Eaton affair, however, the same kinds of social events that had brought Washington City together, that had furthered politics, contributing to the growth of a federal structure, reversed their accustomed function and served to tear apart rather than integrate the community. Rather than being occasions for intimacy and coalition building, dinner parties furnished each side with opportunities to rally supporters and diminish or banish detractors. In the early months of the boycott, the opposing forces occasionally attended the same large, crowded balls. Instead of putting pleasure and display to the service of inclusion, these events now made possible shows of division.

Where Louisa Catherine and John Quincy had made use of the larger-than-life theatricality of a ball to make strong positive statements about

their right to rule, the ladies of Washington used such occasions of public display to make strong negative symbolic statements of their own.
During the Inaugural Ball no woman spoke to Margaret, not even at the
supper table.[63] Where the Adamses' well-orchestrated group dances embodied messages of cooperation and coalition, the ladies' movements at
these large events sent other signals. At a grand ball given by Sir Charles
Vaughan, the bachelor British minister, the women at Margaret's supper
table wielded "that instinctive power of inattention to whatever seems
improper to notice" and snubbed her.

To make their ostracism even more conspicuous, every dancing set that
Margaret approached "instantly dissolved into its original elements." The
ladies' refusal to call, to initiate social intercourse with Margaret, lay at
the heart of the affair, but their public "marked and universal neglect and
indignity" were important in advertising their stand. They forced her to
withdraw from society, and each public absence was a victory for them.[64]

In studying the formation of a federal structure and its ruling classes,
re-visioning social events (such as calling practices and soirees) and social
spaces (such as parlors and ballrooms) aids in description and analysis. In
the Eaton affair one particular activity stands as both event and "space":
gossip.[65] Most obviously, the furor around Margaret's actual or purported
behavior was furthered and enlarged by talk. Recent scholarship has discussed the psychic space of the "gossip circle" as one in which people
come together to engage in "emotional speculation," to build bridges and
ties. The space carved out by the act of gossiping also allows exclusion
and the formation of boundaries, a place for participants to "weave their
web of story."[66]

Gossip, "the world's talk," helps to define and create the world's shape.
When Andrew Jackson assumed the presidency in 1828, the established
Washington elites worried about the changes he would bring to a city and
political system still not entirely formed. By concentrating on creating
Jackson and his crew as outsiders, they reinforced their own solidarity as a
group. Gossiping about the Eatons provided reassurance, a way for the
old guard to circle the wagons, creating a safe and exclusive space. The intimate bonds created by gossip brought the comparative strangers of the
official elite together and actively shaped the social structure, not only reflecting "pre-existing sensibilities" but also creating and maintaining

them. The Eaton affair as "gossip event" recorded and related a series of narrative developments and also furthered them.[67]

Gossip has long been useful to politics; Thomas Jefferson's *Anas*—his "gossip log"—shows that he had mastered that political technique. At all levels of power, Washingtonians used gossip and talk to shape and enhance their own status. Gossip adapts itself for political use so well because it straddles the divide between public and private, official and unofficial. In its liminal position, gossip takes private matters as its subject and yet paradoxically serves the purposes of social control and political outcome.[68] Politics and gossip are both fundamental human activities, and both challenge the artificial separation of the social from the political.

Like the unofficial sphere itself, gossip's off-the-record quality renders it both useful and hidden. This covert quality may account for its historical neglect as a source for political history. Gossip has seemed too imprecise for official purposes, appearing in the documents of the unofficial sphere, in personal papers. Its very power stems from the naturalness of conversation, an association with nature that seems to place it beyond analysis. Gossip usually has been dismissed as personal, trivial, female, or any of the other codes that signal unimportance. The charge of trivial will not hold, because gossip focuses on "specific personal particulars" and also reveals the "shared understandings" of specific groups.[69]

Gossip's long-held link to women and to sexuality must also be blamed for its neglect as a historical source. At the same time that gossip is regarded as female and therefore trivial (or at least private), people have long acknowledged the power of the tongue to threaten the community. Sexual topics, the province of women, often dominate gossip, but even when it concerns a nonsexual topic, gossip exudes "a faint flavor of the erotic." The gossipers act as voyeurs, asserting a private, hidden power. Women have long been feared for their capacity to loose sexual excess, among the populace, and gossip's power has inspired similar fears about unchecked license. Like a whore, an unchecked tongue can corrupt, responding to the basest of human desires. Indeed, no other activity, save sexual license, has suffered so nearly universal condemnation.[70]

Gossip's association with women and triviality may seem to be another charge to lay at the feet of sexism. However, good reasons exist for the femaleness of gossip. The "territory" created by gossip proves especially appropriate for dispossessed people, voices excluded from the official world of white men, so gossip proves crucial when studying women. Prevented from power holding and lawmaking, women in early America (along with slaves and servants) used gossip to shape society-wide conformity. The numerous laws "governing the tongue" in the early days of the American colonies testify to the power of slander and gossip granted by women and men alike. Men used gossip as one possible option to exert social control; for women, it was the essential, perhaps the only method of gaining or protecting their interests.[71]

The Eaton affair followed the classic pattern of gossip events. It centered around the talk of women, around concerns of sexual reputation. To the participants the main issue was one of community standards, a traditional motive for gossip. In the uproar created by the ascension of Andrew Jackson and all that he represented, gossip functioned as a way of reestablishing order and drawing boundaries. Like humor, gossip can be seen as displaced aggression: though the ladies of Washington City might not dare to criticize a public man, they could focus on a nearby woman.[72]

Margaret Eaton was the woman closest to Andrew Jackson and in many ways was representative of his regime. For all his paranoia, then, Jackson was correct when he concluded that an attack on Margaret was an attack on him. He went wrong in thinking that the attack came from male quarters. "That Eaton Woman" became the symbolic bearer of Jacksonian democracy in the capital, and by their treatment of her, the elite women and men of the capital delivered their verdict on Jackson.

"Politics is men's gossip" goes the old saw, and in looking for documentation of gossip and its effects, the best sources lie in that realm delineated as male: newspapers, written by men, intended for men, where respectable women could not be named. Until late April 1831 the capital had managed to keep the details of its conflicted situation to itself. Of course, personal correspondents from the city reported on events in the Eaton affair as they unfolded, and in the early months a few out-of-town newspapers obliquely referred to these personal accounts. However, the generally obeyed prohibition against discussing women openly in the newspapers assured that as long as the situation in the capital was unofficial, the rest of the United States knew little of it. Once the affair generated official documents, however, all that changed. Americans outside of Washington

City first learned of the contretemps when newspapers printed Martin Van Buren's letter of resignation and Andrew Jackson's reply and then, a few days later, John Eaton's resignation, with the president's acceptance.[73]

In newspapers everywhere, these documents were presented to the public accompanied by shocked, wondering editorial comments. No one knew what to make of the news from Washington City, for the participants' letters themselves provided no clue. The resignations and replies were eminently civilized, masked documents and, when searched for specific causes and motivations, proved meaningless. If Martin Van Buren and John Eaton so deeply regretted having to leave the administration, and Andrew Jackson was so sorry to see them go, then why did they resign?

The first reactions from the press reflected horror at the extremity of the event. Washingtonians from outside elite circles stood in the streets "gaping," "as if uncertain what to believe, but all greedily drinking in the news." Did this event signal the end of Jackson's presidency or, even more ominous, the end of the American government? The Senate confirmed all cabinet officers; by demanding their resignation, did Jackson intend to end that role and establish a presidential dictatorship? The unexpected and unsettling nature of the event drew comparison to an "explosion," a "thunderclap on a cloudless day," a "grand blow up."[74]

The cabinet breakup, a first for the United States, was a regular feature of European politics, a fact which contributed to the sense that it could not really be happening. "It resembles a proceeding of some theatrical European government; it seems to us a dramatic recitative, like those between Napoleon and his resigning or dismissed ministers," ventured one editorialist. Comparisons to monarchies inevitably brought up the undue influence of women. The Washington *National Journal* hearkened to the "reign of Louis XV when ministers were appointed and dismissed at a woman's nod and the interests of the nation were tied to her apron strings."[75]

When Secretaries Ingham, Branch, and Berrien tendered their resignations and then left the capital, the mystery and the controversy deepened. Enlightenment finally came when the three politicians went back to their respective hometowns and embarked on a bitter letter-writing campaign, tearing into Jackson and John Eaton and bringing Margaret's name into print and national prominence for the first time. John Eaton replied, and the rhetoric escalated in heat and nastiness, including threats and dueling challenges.

"The Great Ones at Washington make all the news in these dull times," Massachusetts visitor Bradley Cummings reported to his journal, with the newspapers printing "letters, challenges, and etc., from the head folks there; it really is disgraceful to the country." In June 1831 a steamboat named *Andrew Jackson* exploded, providing an instant metaphor for the situation in Washington City and inspiring much purple political prose. The steamboat "started under prodigious high pressure," according to one wit, "and was built without a safety valve. The late accident is said to have happened because an 'incompetent boy had charge of the engine.'" The ship of state, continued the writer, had *"an incompetent old man in charge of the political machine, without the strength to blow off the steam or to supply the boiler with water."* The writer ended by warning the passengers to "Keep clear. . . . It will burst!"[76]

As the details filtered out through the spring and summer of 1831, and it became apparent that a woman ("the apple of discord") was involved, the resulting discussion across the country revealed the same anxieties centered around women and power, the separation of public and private, and the intersection between politics and society that had perplexed and worried Washingtonians earlier in the spring. In spite of the Jackson camp's best efforts, the writers and speechmakers of the United States openly focused on the "woman business" as the central concern.[77] Consequently, Americans took sides, their groups framing themselves as either "Pro–" or "Anti–Peggy Eaton."

The newspaper war demonstrates how deeply gender issues were implicated in the political culture.[78] It shows how seriously the country was expected to take the Eaton affair, revealing a pervasive trepidation surrounding the fate of the Republic and the roles of women in determining it. Closely following the explosion of the *Andrew Jackson*, another steamship, the *Bellona*, was refused landing in the United States, stimulating another apt metaphor for the doings in Washington. "Bellona—Goddess of War" became a favorite public nickname for Margaret, especially after the story of her snubbing by the Dutch minister's wife. Other appellations, "The American Pompadour," "Cleopatra," "Helen of Troy," "Czarina of Russia," and "the 'Malign Influence,'" hearkened to images not merely of women but of aristocratic women famous for acquiring illegitimate power by sexual means.[79]

The example of Margaret Eaton and Andrew Jackson, though startling and surprising when finally revealed, seemed to confirm rules and laws as ancient as Aristotle's and as freshly articulated by political thinkers such as Rousseau, who proclaimed that "never has a people perished from an excess of wine; all perish from the disorder of women." The root of this disorder lay in women's boundless sexual passion, an appetite being redefined during this era but still a part of ordinary political vocabulary.[80]

The public press could only hint at the more salacious verbal speculations on the source of Peggy Eaton's power, as observers reported that John Eaton looked "jaded": "whether this be with fatigue of body and mind, we leave others to determine." More usually, however, women in politics inspired fewer themes of lust than those of deviance and disease; images of "pollution," "foulness," "degradations," "perversions," and others appeared frequently.[81]

In this general climate of anxiety, centering around the very idea of a woman close to (political) power, political observers and journalists attributed a great deal of personal authority to Margaret. Here the mythical, power-mad, evil woman of legend and rhetoric blurred with the actions and personality of a real person. In the first few months, newspapers and the public viewed the cabinet breakup as Margaret's fault and her victory, part of some as-yet-unrevealed plot. Was not the result that all her enemies had left Washington and that her ally, Martin Van Buren (as was announced in April), had attained the post of minister to Britain?

The vocabulary the press used to discuss Margaret underscored the impression of executive usurpation. A rumor reached Jackson's ears that John Calhoun was calling Mrs. Eaton "the real president of the United States." To a New England newspaper, Mrs. Eaton was the "commander in chief not only of fashionable society" but of the country as well. Those who publicly attributed power to Margaret included not only Jackson's enemies, who might wish consciously to exaggerate cultural fears, but also Democrats, who, both as individuals and as a party, feared dependence on a woman.[82]

In letters to the editors, the displaced secretaries and others widely circulated the notion that Jackson's "deplorable infatuation" allowed Margaret control over presidential patronage, and she used her power to
threaten those who were not her partisans. The cabinet dissolution was
part of her plot to increase her power, as positions in the new cabinet
were "most disgracefully purchased by subserviency to Mrs. Eaton." Not
one merely to exert gentle influence behind the scenes on behalf of her
family, "she is not content with the triumph which she has achieved in the
person of her husband, she wishes to mark distinctly her influence—or in
other words, she wishes it to be understood that her influence predomi-
nates."[83] In the newly burgeoning private sphere of the nation's middle
classes, such a desire for distinction seemed perverse and unwomanly.

In 1830 Bayard Smith, who had always enjoyed favor with the preceding
administrations, complained, with no sense of incongruity, "Our government is becoming everyday more and more democratic, the rulers of the
people are truly their servants and among those rulers women are gaining
more than their share of power."[84] Bayard Smith certainly did not criticize
the "little influence" of decent women such as herself, which had ensured
her favor with all the past presidential administrations. By "women" she
did not mean ladies.

In ironic comparison with other women in Washington City, Margaret
Eaton seems to have exercised very little personal influence at all. Contemporaries and historians have uncovered only two attempts to obtain
jobs, two instances that Margaret herself discussed. Unlike some of her
enemies, Margaret was not a political wife, deeply interested and involved
in the affairs of the country. There is no particular evidence to suggest
that she wanted to enter society in order to play politics, and the attempts
to exclude her injured her personal, not her political, pride. She noted in
her autobiography that "it was believed that I had the ear of the president
and could influence appointments as I chose." Considering how little she
really accomplished, her assessment—"If I had been a designing person,
how I could have enriched myself!"—seems accurate.[85] One can only
imagine how a more politically astute and focused woman, such as
Catharine Akerly Mitchill, might have behaved had she been as close to a
sitting president.

However, because the newspapers and the culture denied any legitimate involvement for women in the public sphere at all, even Margaret's puny efforts could be made to appear significant. This is especially ironic considering the extensive patronage activities undertaken by the very women who lined up against Margaret and the strong family and cultural traditions that supported such efforts. Neither side in the debate over Margaret Eaton's role in the government mentioned other women's activities. The imperative to deny women's work in the polity transcended the needs and particulars of this one case.

In the press, observers outside Washington expressed confusion over the connections between capital society and the workings of politics. No matter that every city was ruled by a group of elite families (including their women), tied together and perpetuated by economic and social ties. The press and public insisted on the strict separation of political and personal relationships in Washington City. This theme of "officialness" grew from an obsessive fear of a strong executive and a powerful federal government, which, unfortunately for the president, dovetailed nicely with another apprehension particularly focused on Andrew Jackson.

THE TYRANT AND THE TART

The fear of tyranny, of federal power run amok, manifested itself in the newspapers' collective concern over the official regulation of private life, an anxiety so available in the culture that the three discontented ex-secretaries used it to frame their banishment from the capital. From their first letters in local papers, Berrien, Branch, and Ingham cast the events of the affair as heroic resistance to the ultimate tyranny.[86] The president of the United States dared to regulate an aspect of life far above politics, one sanctified by being the sole responsibility of pure-minded women, even to the extent of making private life a measure of official competence.

Samuel Ingham, aware that his wife played a leading role in the ostracism of Margaret Eaton, insisted that there had been no official disharmony in the cabinet, that is, among the men themselves, and that was all that counted. In spite of this, the president, and the president alone, dissolved the cabinet, because the members in question were not "decidedly for V.B. and Mrs. E. and expressly hostile to Mr. Calhoun." Ingham, Berrien, and Branch insisted that their socializing had no "official connection" with Jackson; each averred that the "charge of the family was a sacred trust, belonging exclusively to myself" and presumably to their wives.[87]

All three ex-secretaries declared firmly, in the face of administration evasion, that they were fired only because their families refused to associate with Margaret Eaton and refused to allow the president to force them to do so. The extent of this unholy abuse of power was most visible in the story of Richard Johnson's visit to each member of the cabinet. In their version of events, Johnson, acting as intermediary for the president, offered a compromise: if their families paid a call on the Eatons and invited Margaret to their large parties, they could exclude her from intimate intercourse. When the men balked, Johnson threatened them with dismissal. They refused, and Jackson asked for their resignations.

That the two events were separated by more than a year mattered little. The ex-secretaries used this incident for all it was worth, invoking the rhetoric of the private space. If Jackson believed that society and politics should be separated, and that families occupied the private sphere, how could the cabinet families be compelled by the president to do anything? Even more to the point, if families had nothing to do with public life, then how could anyone suggest that the refusal to socialize with Margaret Eaton had anything to do with politics? That all of this came to pass, according to the former cabinet members, could only be blamed on Jackson's attempt to exert total control.[88]

Any participant could invoke the trope of the separation between public and private to reinforce a point, conveniently ignoring the realities of the political process. What right had Jackson to dismiss the officials, queried the secretaries, echoed by their supporting newspapers, when each had managed their respective departments very well? Their work—in the official sphere—remained unaffected by the dearth of dinner parties or calling. Of course, in taking refuge in this strict construction argument, the ex-cabinet officials conveniently ignored another important aspect of their job, that of acting as the advisory body to the president. This task required harmony, Jackson rightly insisted, not to mention trust, a perfect example of how personal politics needed to be in order to function smoothly. For all of his ill judgment throughout the affair, Jackson rightly interpreted the social use of Peggy Eaton as a statement of either faith or mistrust in his leadership.

The depictions of Jackson as a dissipated tyrant contrast sharply with the images presented during the 1828 election campaign. Then Jackson had been the backwoodsman, the savage of the frontier, whose wife smoked a pipe. Humorous anecdotes and tall tales appeared to illustrate these points, and these continued into his White House years. One purported to tell the story of Jackson's reception of a European ambassador: the minister, who did not speak English, was in eminent danger of being roughed up by the narrow-minded provincial president and his common Irish porter, but for the timely intervention of the White House chef, who was French.[89]

With the Eaton affair, another image of Jackson began to supplant these embarrassing, cruel, but essentially nonthreatening depictions. The new image focused on the danger of tyranny, representing Andrew Jackson as an emperor, an aristocratic pasha, controlled only by his passions (including lust), and thus, although an abuser of power himself, easily led by a sexually alluring woman. During the campaign Henry Clay and others had expressed concern that the election of Jackson might bring about a military dictatorship, headed by a man under the sway of prejudice.[90] The new images of Jackson incorporated this worry and extended it, as if to say that all that had been predicted had come to pass, and it was even worse than anyone had thought. The "military chieftain" turned into aristocratic tyrant, the slave of passion was transformed into a royal puppet: all of these images seemed confirmed by every aspect of the Eaton affair and by Jackson's attempts to build a strong presidency. Taking on the Bank of the United States, challenging states' rights to nullify, dispensing patronage according to his will, and peremptorily dismissing a Senate-confirmed cabinet—all played into the public fear of a strong, federally minded executive.

These royal images inspired illustrators as well. Before very long cartoons and broadsides appeared featuring "King Andrew the First," in ermined robe, crown, and scepter, with the power of veto in his hand, trampling the Constitution underfoot. The more the affair "resembled the artifices of European courts," the more public writers responded.[91] *The Lay of the First Minstrel*, a forty-six-page epic poem, made no overt reference to Margaret but presented Jackson as a royal tyrant, surrounded by courtiers, liars, and wizards and unable to face the truth or honest working men.

Margaret Botsford's contribution, *The Reign of Reform, or Yankee Doodle Court*, featured as a main character the "Princess of Influence," controlling the uncontrollable monarch.[92]

In a travesty of the role of the charismatic figure, Margaret Eaton quickly became the target for criticism of the administration, taking the literal focus and the metaphorical heat for the president. Instead of attacking Andrew Jackson directly, critics and the press attacked her, a tactic not calculated to soothe Jackson's paranoia, because they had used Rachel Jackson's character and questionable marriage for the same purpose. Comparisons with Rachel's situation had been apparent from the first rumblings of the Petticoat War, and though some might question any similarity between the two women, the public commentary contained striking convergences. The scandal about Rachel Jackson had also occurred at a time of political change and upheaval, becoming an issue which transcended state and sectional lines. Discussions of both of these "illegitimate" women reflected directly on the legitimacy of Andrew Jackson's rule. In a culture where marriage provided the model, and seduction tales served as political warnings, adultery and promiscuity represented political chaos. In less than three years, Andrew Jackson's enemies could prove that he had allowed two women to wreak serious havoc.[93]

The heated rhetoric around Margaret, with its attributions of extensive political power, derived from the necessity to reconcile the event's obvious political importance and women's centrality to it. Surely the chaos in Washington politics could not be the result of what it seemed to be: a social war between women. It was far more believable to postulate a Machiavellian figure behind the throne, even if that figure was a woman herself. A female archvillain was easier to believe than a political culture that depended on the work of women and broke down when deprived of their support. Relatively free from having to depend on the work of women and social events, unlike the practical world of politics, the newspapers served as purely rhetorical organs. Their point of view emerged from the discourse loud and clear: women had no business anywhere near politics, and (reflecting the growing middle-class ideology) the public and private spheres had to be absolutely separate.

As editorialists and observers tried to puzzle out what had happened, sorting rumor from fact, pictures (specifically political cartoons) took on the most controversial aspects and the full metaphorical burden of incorporating both the topic of women and the new information coming from Washington and the disgruntled ex-secretaries. In some ways newspapers, male organs, could gossip, using pictures to substitute for spoken "tittle tattle." Humor allows its users both to express outrage and to contain it, and the political cartoonists of the day provided the best vehicle for treading the shadowy terrain of the Eaton affair. A political cartoon, David Claypoole Johnston's "Exhibition of Cabinet Pictures," depicts a gallery of pictures all relating to the state of things in Washington.[94] Peggy Eaton and other women dominate the pictured political events, sometimes as actual characters, at other times symbolized by the garment closest to their nether regions, the petticoat. In some cartoons the petticoat served the most obvious function, as in "Washington Course," which depicts Jackson in the race for reelection, tripping over a petticoat someone has left on the track. As Jackson stumbles, he cries, "Devil take the petticoat, I say, I thought I could clear it."

This suggestive, all-purpose metaphor for a whole range of issues surrounding women released the editorialists from the problem of female names and allowed creative articulation of the issues in the case. The new design for the "Arms of the U.S.," which presents an eagle in a corset, with petticoats for wings, illustrates the fear of female power. In "The Washerman," Jackson is shown next to a washtub, desperately trying to clean a petticoat, worrying, "It seems to me the more I rub this, the worst it looks." A nearby washerwoman agrees, advising that he needed a liberal whitewashing and a sprinkle of lime to do the job right.

Most of the pictures in the "Cabinet Gallery" derive their bite from humor, but some are truly ominous. In "Unity of the Late Cabinet," a woman in a short petticoat stands in the foreground, with her back to the viewer, while cabinet members fight over her. Ostensibly a silly illustration, it hints at the potential for personal violence, reflecting the dueling challenges that John Eaton issued in the summer of 1831. Even more pointed, in another one of the pictures the same woman in the same foreground position presides over a conflagration. Titled "The Destruction of Troy," it thus explicitly indicts the female in question, invoking not only the fall of ancient republics like Rome or the more recent terrors in France, but also the burning of Washington City, which almost brought down the capital and the Union.[95] In important ways the projection of cultural fear onto rhetorical women distracted from the real women themselves, the "petticoat politicians."

THE SOCIAL MACHINE

Why did the ladies of Washington City think they could do something about Margaret Eaton? The answer lies in their own concerns with the Republic and with new ideas percolating throughout the country. Times were changing, and Washington, though unlike any other city in the country, was not immune to those changes. All over the United States, men and women of the elite and rising middle classes debated, in words and actions, the meaning of society in what was rapidly becoming a democracy. Comparatively open social mobility had unleashed a universal scramble for distinction, resulting in a situation more deplorable, according to some, than the rigid class hierarchies of Europe. The German nobleman Francis J. Grund hypothesized that Americans would be better served if their society "had as many distinct and established orders of society as in England," instead of a single one based solely on wealth. For instance, he hazarded, women would not be always trying to outdo each other, and the result would be fewer heartaches and bankruptcies.[96]

The problem of how to define society was compounded in a city ruled by politics. Frances Trollope professed herself weary of "election fever," the madness which "irritates every temper . . . substitutes party spirit for personal esteem, and, in fact, vitiates the whole system of society." These issues perplexed Washington City's official families and local gentry as well. How much should an official position guarantee social position? Could there be a private and an official society? Should an individual's station in private society—high or low—carry over into the official society? Americans recognized that the answers to these questions can never be trivial, especially in a democracy which postulates that all are equal, and in which the problem of rules and hierarchies carries broad philosophical implications.[97] The era was gone in which known, established elites ruled (and made rules for) both society and government.

Margaret Bayard Smith vacillated between positions, at one time writing that the "drawing room circle . . . ought to be coextensive with the sovereign power," and at other times that society should be home-centered and indubitably private. By the time of the Eaton affair, she absolutely supported the ladies' right to make decisions in the "drawing room circle."[98] Louisa Catherine Adams held to a more consistent opinion on the topic. She stoutly believed that office should not be a guarantee of social position and remembered her early years when members of society in American cities "had not yet clothed themselves in the buffoonery of the modern democracy."

Echoing Grund, Louisa Catherine averred that a set of well-defined and rigid distinctions would satisfy people and stop the scrabble. A lack of social standards based on family and breeding made money the sole social criterion. Commenting on the United States, she bitterly observed the paradox of democracy: "In all countries poverty is an evil, in this it is a crime." Ironically, the very lack of standards rendered American society more exclusive than that of England and France, because in such well-defined societies there was less chance of the "permanent disarrangement of the ranks by the occasional admission of the low-born aspirant" and less need "for a jealous guarding of the barriers."[99]

Perhaps in search of a natural system of distinction, Americans increasingly divided the world according to public and private spheres, ratifying each with a gender correlate. Activities involving families and social relationships, centered in family homes, were becoming private and the sole province of women. In return for being banished from the marketplace, and for the house losing its public functions, white middle-class women were promised enormous influence over the men who actually controlled the public sphere. Their public relationship with the powerful members of their society was not with men as such, but with husbands, brothers, and sons. New cultural strictures decreed that they could not step beyond the household, but that their moral and cultural influence, carried outward by the men of the house, could be quite powerful indeed.

Women were exhorted to take this sacred duty seriously. The growing refinement of the vernacular gentility movement created not only modes of association but a standard of exclusion.[100] Women had to remain ever-vigilant to keep society moral, and in return for this responsibility, they had the right to rule it. These ideas were part of the Washington scene, present in the thoughts of women such as Margaret Bayard Smith and Louisa Catherine Adams and included in the lexicon of women new to the scene, like the female members of the Berrien, Branch, and Ingham families, who joined Floride Calhoun in excluding Margaret Eaton. Washington women added these new notions of female authority to the aristocratic privileges that members of political families (male and female) had already assumed.

As social leaders of the U.S. capital, Washington City's women felt a particular responsibility. The First Lady headed the society of the entire nation, and her proximity to the president meant she could "influence the destiny of nations." In a culture that increasingly prized "purity" above all else in a woman, it seemed only right that all the women of the White House circle should be epitomes of virtue.[101] In this scenario Margaret represented a double horror: an impure woman infecting local "good society" and, by Washington's unique extension, the society of the entire nation.

By the mid-1820s the parts of Washington City not directly connected to the federal government were assuming more of the characteristics of an ordinary city, and a parallel society was developing, based in the residential elite. No longer could all the interesting people in town barely fill one room, nor was society confined to an occasional brave display, huddled against the wilderness. The time for discrimination, as practiced by the other societies in the United States, was at hand, and the ladies of Washington occupied the perfect position to claim their natural hegemony over society.

In their zeal to establish themselves as sole arbiters of the private sphere, however, the ladies of Washington could not see the stumbling block that also proved invisible to the Eatons and Andrew Jackson, one that ironically defeated both sides in the Petticoat War. Washington's political needs demanded society, and anyone who did not recognize that overwhelming urgency was doomed to frustration. Until the Jackson administration, Washington's social and political needs had meshed quite nicely. In the beginning, anyone vaguely qualified was included to keep society lively. Dolley Payne Todd Madison's experience with the local gentry showed that this made good political sense as well, keeping the gentry money and influence physically and emotionally invested in the capital. Inclusion was Dolley's goal, and in those first few years society benefited. As the 1820s went on, the government structure still needed to include and accommodate as many players as possible, with the political sphere expanding with each congressional session. But society, which thrives on exclusion and hierarchical groupings with little regard for political usefulness, also grew during this era. For the first time in the capital, the needs of society and politics diverged.

The old notions of gentry aristocracy, as embodied by Dolley Payne Todd Madison, had focused social events on the public good, which allowed for political usage. The new vernacular gentility focused on family and valued propriety over public dignity, respectability over eminence, and private standards over political expediency.[102] In this formulation women's influence may perform a general public good or public virtue function, but it cannot serve anything as crass or specific as a political purpose.

At this juncture one may wonder why the women of Washington would trade their real political power over appointments and legislation for the hazier cultural power of the private sphere promised to women in less political circumstances. In other words, why would they allow themselves to be shunted to the arena of the apparently irrelevant? First, a large number of the ladies who allied themselves against Margaret Eaton—especially the administration wives—had spent no significant time in the city and thus had not availed themselves of Washington's peculiar situation.

Second, and more important, the local ladies, led by Margaret Bayard Smith (among others), denied that their participation in politics had ever been political or public. They had always seen themselves as private, their work on behalf of their husbands and families as extensions of their roles as wives and mothers, and their aid to non-kin supported by the tradition of benevolence. The depth of their denial, which appeared constantly in individual disclaimers, intensified during the Eaton affair. They had no consciousness of what they were giving up, or that there was even a choice to be made. Though they had never before tried to exclude as politically charged a person as Margaret Eaton, they saw the problem as rightfully theirs. They could not see that the times and context of the problem had changed.

It might be more accurate to say that they could see but could not accept the encroachment of democracy in their midst. This era of the political community abounds not only in denial of society's and women's roles in politics but also in anxiety. The fears about Jackson and all he represented grew more intense after the election of 1828. Washingtonians were seeing their culture change from that of a growing aristocracy of families to something else. "Our society is in a sad state," complained Bayard Smith, a state she traced directly to the ascendance of Andrew Jackson and women like Margaret Eaton. During the big White House social events, such as the Fourth of July and New Year's Day celebrations, no longer did the "old and settled population . . . mix in the present political circles." Once the most enthusiastic attendees, the local gentry and the older community left these celebrations to the "democracy," the sight of which struck some "with disgust." Rather than condemn "their wives and daughters . . . to mingle with the very lowest of the people," Washingtonians like Smith stayed home.[103]

Even on ordinary days at the White House, "persons of all ranks visit very sociably," related Bayard Smith, "for never before was the Palace so accessible." She went on to describe a democratic dream, unheard of in earlier administrations: "In return, the family accept all invitations and visit the citizens in the most social manner, and live on more equal and familiar terms, than any other presidential family has." Lest anyone think Bayard Smith approved of such "all men are created equal" behavior, she added, "All my sympathies attach me to the ex-party."[104] Many Washingtonians held Andrew Jackson to be responsible for and Margaret Eaton to be representative of these negative changes. Therefore, they could not have been surprised that when they decided to exclude Margaret, they found themselves face to face with the general himself.

Throughout the affair Andrew Jackson expressed anger at and contempt for the women of Washington. Much of his outrage stemmed from the frustration that he, the man who had defeated redcoats, Indians, and Spaniards, could not prevail over a handful of ladies. We may conclude, however, that the source of his frustration lay not in his powerlessness but rather in his inability to apprehend the complexities of the situation. Jackson had never lived in a community large enough to have society, and his political experience was limited to the truncated, male-dominated versions prevalent on frontiers. Most of his professional, nonfarming time had been spent in a military context, all male, with well-understood chains of command.

The situation was quite different in the capital. As scholars of the

London social scene have demonstrated, modern urban societies, faced with complex economic and cultural issues, had begun to rely on the impersonal, sifting, machine-like quality of society. In order to mediate between the competing claims of social authority and democratic mobility, the American middle class established new codes of civility that dictated social relations with all kinds of "others." The increased numbers of participants and the gradual shift from patronage and familial arrangements to individual achievements in determining membership in the social elite required such a machine, as surely as did the increasingly participatory and democratic political scene.[105] And, because years of party-building activities had to pass before the participants and architects of the system could even recognize it as such, the women and men who used the social machine and referred to it could not fully grasp its function.

Jackson's inability to understand the workings of this machine became apparent in his first days as president-elect. When he came to take up office in 1829, he saw no reason to call on President John Quincy Adams, the man who had orchestrated the attacks on his beloved wife. From the viewpoint of personal honor and preference, his decision made sense, but his pointed snub outraged Washington's official community. Though they could not articulate it, the political community knew that social rituals held political society together, neutralizing personal taste for the higher goal of getting things done. Jackson's violation of this code only highlighted his unfitness for high office.[106]

At many junctures Andrew Jackson and the ladies operated at cross-purposes, doomed never to understand each other. For Jackson the central and only issue was Margaret's virtue, specifically, the question, Did Margaret Timberlake Eaton have an affair with John Eaton and/or sex with other men before and during her first marriage? With zeal and focus the president set out objectively to disprove the opposition's case. Having done so, he could not understand why it would not go away. Though at the beginning of the fuss Andrew Jackson had clearly seen the women of Washington as the cause of Margaret's ostracism, the evolving affair convinced him that the cause must be something more important, something originating in male minds. A deep look at the world of the women reveals that Jackson was not fighting individuals but rather a Hydra that made the Bank of the United States look like a garter snake.

Jackson was right about one thing: Margaret's sexual behavior lay at the heart of the ladies' case against her. But the women of Washington did not approach the situation like opposing counsel in a court of law. The only evidence available to them was the reputation Margaret had acquired in the years before 1828, which resulted in her exclusion from good houses. The ladies insisted that the burden of proof was not on them; society had passed judgment. The only question open to them was, Should they allow themselves and their children "intimate intercourse" with a woman who had been excluded from society years before? Should they, as individuals, defy the machine of society's judgment?

Margaret Bayard Smith, who had been present in town when the initial judgment had been made, spoke from personal knowledge and declared firmly that vice should not be countenanced. But the women new to Washington, who did not know the facts for themselves, depended on female-dominated social networks to set the course for the relationships crucial to political society. If they defied the proper procedure, they, too, would be ostracized, a politically and personally disastrous outcome. From a modern vantage point, it may seem politically suicidal for an aspiring family to have sided against the president, but in the years 1829–31 Jackson had only begun the work of transforming the presidency into a powerful office. The all-important social networks among legislative and cabinet families were more crucial to a political family trying to obtain or retain a toehold on the federal scene.[107]

The cabinet wives and Emily Donelson used this peer pressure to swell their ranks, proving "very amiable" in visiting and recruiting all the "strangers" to join them. Thus the problem of who to believe and who to follow became more fiercely divisive, as Eliza Johnston, wife of a Louisiana senator, discovered. She personally thought the decision to exclude Margaret "very arbitrary," but she still felt "compelled . . . to leave her visit unreturned."[108] The machine was performing its exclusionary function, protecting its old members and guiding its new ones.

Throughout the summer of 1831, the Eatons remained in Washington. Though they were officially sidelined by the cabinet resignations, their presence continued to create disruption. On September 19 they left for Tennessee, to everyone's relief. With the Eatons safely out of Washington, attention turned to Andrew Jackson's new war against the Bank of the United States, and life went on. After suffering defeat in his race for the

Senate in 1834, John Eaton accepted an appointment from President Jackson as governor of the Florida territory. In 1836 Jackson appointed Eaton minister to Spain, and the idea of Peggy at a royal court offered Washingtonians much amusement.[109]

Every war story ends with an accounting. Though the story of Calhoun's fall and Van Buren's rise compels political analysis, the body counts and casualty rates must include the real antagonists: Andrew Jackson and Margaret Eaton versus the ladies of Washington. With the final picture of Margaret on a boat to Spain, banished to a royal court, it may seem easy to declare a victory for the ladies of Washington. Indisputably, in spite of Andrew Jackson's best efforts, Margaret Eaton never entered Washington society, at least not in the 1820s and early 1830s. Indeed, Margaret saw her banishment from Washington, leaving her enemies in possession of the field, as her defeat.

But like all the other dichotomies under examination, victory and defeat are not so easy to assess in social wars. The confusion and denial that pervaded the entire event rendered the outcome complicated to both contemporaries and historians. It is not even clear who lined up on which side in the battle between democracy versus aristocracy. Was Andrew Jackson the harbinger of democracy or a military tyrant? Did Margaret embody a democratic nightmare—the ultimate plebeian climber—or was she a sophisticated "American Pompadour"? Were the ladies of Washington old-fashioned elitists or the most modern democrats of all, insisting that Margaret's fitness for society be a product of her own merits and not that of merely marrying into a position, like royalty?

The contradictions loom because the real polarity is not acknowledged: not democracy versus aristocracy, but rather politics versus society. Nor is it profitable to use an adversarial framework. Everyone shared the same paradoxical goals; both Andrew Jackson and the ladies of Washington City wanted to keep the social sphere sacred and private and to use social events and interactions to make political statements and effect political change.

It is probably safe to say that the affair backfired on everyone. Though Margaret and Andrew Jackson seem to have been the losers in 1831, the long-term picture indicates a more lasting victory for the president and the ideals of democracy. Jackson did not achieve Margaret's inclusion, but he did succeed in breaking up the "phalanx of ladies," or perhaps more accurately, the affair subdued them. After 1831 and for the rest of Jackson's term, the Washington social scene never fully recovered from the cessation of society that had spurred the cabinet dissolution. Official White House parties were small and modest events. Some members of the new cabinet, fearing a repetition of the affair, did not bring their families or "keep house," and thus deprived official society of an upper tier. Bayard Smith commented, "In fact, our social relations are as completely changed as if we had removed to another city—I really feel again like a stranger in Washington." In the new democratic society that Washington adopted under Jackson's influence, wealth became an important, if not the sole, determinant of position. Even Washington Brahmins like Martha Jefferson Randolph felt "as if I had lost caste—so completely do I find my position in society changed."[110]

Ironically, the women of Washington had reached their zenith of power to effect change with their treatment of Margaret Eaton; though they won their battle, they lost the war. Confident and sure of their positions during the fracas, afterwards they may have questioned the usefulness of the exercise. Women of politically powerful families had always seen their efforts as cooperative ones; they acted not as independent agents but for their families' good. After the dust settled, it was clear that however principled the stand adopted by Floride Calhoun and the other ladies, their families' influence had suffered an enormous blow. That women could have such an effect on government seems not to have been empowering but rather unsettling in the long run.

In the culture's debate over women in the polity, people acknowledged that female influence could often act as a mediating force, stabilizing politics. As Louisa Catherine had put it in the midst of her campaign to win the presidency for her husband, "The ladies are hailed with pleasure as the medium which is to soothe and calm the turbulent spirit which is likely to be roused by party feeling." This function was perceived as especially necessary as the rise of the two-party system led men to extreme talk and actions. Obviously, the ladies of Washington had not performed that role during the Eaton affair, and this may have made them more wary of entering the political fray. Margaret Bayard Smith continued to report on social tiffs but explicitly requested discretion and warned, "Mrs. Eaton's affair, at the beginning, was but a spark, but what a conflagration it did cause."[111]

Paradoxically, though both sides used the separateness of the private sphere from politics to bolster their positions, they were confused and lost, doomed never to understand each other, because they ignored the political dimension. Denial is never total. Andrew Jackson, who ostensibly wanted society to remain utterly separate from politics, knew he needed social harmony in his cabinet and ended by firing them for social sins. The ladies, who disavowed public power, denying that they had the intention of "control[ling] in any way the etiquette of this place," found themselves with the power to shake the federal government profoundly.[112] The women of Washington wanted it all to be about morals; because of the intersection of politics and society, they could not have it that way. Andrew Jackson, too, wanted his politics separated from general society; he could not have it his way, either.

Reluctantly, Jackson realized that his administration could not function without the cooperation of the arbiters of society. The ladies enjoyed the importance they had earned as social players in the capital, deriving their power from society's intersection with the male province of politics. But they also desired total power in "woman's sphere," as their culture defined it, whose source of power stemmed from its separation from the public. In their zeal to exclude a sexually dubious woman, they refused to see the effects of their action: withholding legitimacy from Jackson's regime. In their zeal to impose the new middle-class ideology on the capital, the women of Washington forgot their primary task of creating a ruling class. Jackson and Margaret represented not only the coming of democracy but also the breakdown of the republican aristocracy in which the women of Washington had flourished. Margaret acted as a circuit breaker, disrupting the flow of power.[113]

The irony lies in the women's part in their own destruction. The women had won the right, if they chose, to preside over a dominion stripped of political power. With the arrival of new attitudes about private spheres, the suppressed power of aristocratic women, and the changed character of social events, Washington City fell more into line with the rest of America. Consciously and unconsciously, Andrew Jackson had brought democracy to Washington City.

For all the pyrotechnic language surrounding the Eaton affair, the re-sulting profound changes resemble less an explosion than a long-term shift, a sea change. Andrew Jackson did not single-handedly banish the politicking of elite white women from the nation's capital, nor did he sev-er politics and society. The two arenas were far too dependent on each other for any event to separate them utterly. But Jackson's actions did make a statement about how some social events were to be considered, and he stemmed the power that the women demonstrated they could de-ploy. Andrew Jackson's actions continued and legitimated the denial of the intersection between politics and society, a denial that still taints po-litical histories, whose authors seem oblivious to the part played by women and social events. The denial inherent in the political culture of the early Republic could only be sustained at great cost, and the ladies of Washington paid the price. One cannot solve a problem without recog-nizing and admitting it exists, so the issue of society and politics in a re-public was never fully resolved.

The most important de facto outcome of the affair—that women did not have the power to dictate who belongs in society as long as politics depends on society—freed the political community to decide that social events in Washington, among the official elites, would be completely dic-tated by political needs. As the years went on, the residential elite formed a high society of their own, but the Eaton affair finally determined that Washington was to be nothing but a political town. If the rest of the na-tion was engaged in reframing woman as the dependent of a man's world, Washington City was casting society as subservient to the public, political arenas. Social events would have no purpose other than politics. The resi-dential elite could base their society on exclusion and the criteria of blood, education, family, and breeding, but, freed from any other obliga-tion, government society need only grow as the political structure needed it. Because of the Eaton affair, and many other circumstances, the poten-tially useful linkages of society and politics would remain mostly unex-ploited until after the Civil War.[114]

Conclusion

"It is not the fashion to see the lady the epilogue."
—WILLIAM SHAKESPEARE, *As You Like It*, epilogue, 1–2

"IN ORDER to form a correct idea of the American government," opined the aristocratic democrat Baron de Grund, "it is absolutely necessary one should stay some time in Washington; and frequent, not merely the fashionable society, but the company of those sturdy members of Congress, who ... actually represent the opinions, habits, and sentiments of the different sections of the country." He declared that "Washington is the miniature picture of the United States," and that spending some time in the capital would impart to a visitor "a better estimate of the character of the American people than many years' residence in different parts of the Union."[1] Sometimes the city of Washington accurately reflected the nation it governed, as Baron de Grund thought; at other times, life in the capital seemed to be moving in quite a different direction from the rest of the country. But at all times, because it was a city created for politics, there was no place like Washington.

During the capital's first thirty years, Jefferson and his followers had engaged in an experiment to construct the unworkable, a government of republican virtue, an antipolitical, antipower political power. The republican obsession with public virtue and fear of corruption meant that public men rejected the connections, the acting on mutual interests that makes politics work. However, government and politics needed the kind of face-to-face interactions that republicans abhorred. In an absolute state, after all, the emperor or the queen can just order things done, without seeking consensus or even advice. But a democratic politics depends on agreement, on coalitions of people who can be persuaded to see that their interests lie together, and therefore, "Politics is the essence of self-government."[2] The personal relations that had seemed the hallmark and the stigma of court life proved even more necessary when building an antimonarchical system from the ground up.

Despite the republicans' best efforts, in those first decades of the nineteenth century the federal government at Washington City and the United States changed mightily, moving in a political direction recognizably modern, with structures and institutions based on consensus, the cooperative implementation of power, and assertion of state authority in visible, material ways. The government evolved from a small, weak entity into a powerful, complex bureaucracy. The office of president mirrored that change, growing into a strong executive tool under Andrew Jackson. Democracy became the ruling idea of the political culture, and the expanded electorate formed a two-party system. More generally, across the United States people imagined their common destiny as lying within a new nation.

Elite white women of political families played crucial parts in these developments. Their goals were identical to those of the official males, who were their husbands, sons, brothers, and friends: to legitimate the new nation both in the eyes of the world and in the eyes of its citizenry (a process we would recognize with hindsight as nation building); to create a New World, where republican virtue and simplicity not only would dictate the government but also would infuse and transform every aspect of American life; and to materialize the theoretical blueprint for government, making the Constitution concrete. During their reign the ladies of Washington played a central role in turning the country town on the Potomac into a focus for nationalism, a practical government, and an authentic capital for the new nation.

In the family business of politics, public men had to appear republican, sober, and unpolitical, while the traditional political tasks of patronage, networking, and material display often fell to the female members of the family. Like the work of male politicians, women's actions combined various degrees of short-term interests (such as obtaining a job for a friend) with larger, long-term goals (such as transforming the President's House into a national symbol). Women in Washington were not doing anything particularly new, but the emphasis had changed. In Europe and during the colonial era, gentry men and women played politics, dispensed patronage, and displayed material superiority. In republican Washington, however, for a brief window of time, the public men could not participate in these activities, but their womenfolk could.

Women and men of political families handled the explosive issues of power and politicking in a republican environment by cloaking the power in female garb and by denial. Individuals of both sexes appropriated masculine and feminine behavior when it served their interests. Men could maintain public virtue in the official sphere while working cooperatively and politically behind the scenes, perhaps during a family dinner. Covered by cultural taboos against female political involvement, middle-class and elite women used a veil of respectability to work aggressively toward their political goals. Perhaps the most crucial contribution of this alternative culture lay in building the bonds of interest and face-to-face interaction that had always characterized politics and that proved crucial for democratic self-governance.

Ironies abound. Washington women used old-fashioned court behaviors to create the new structures that would support and nurture a new kind of government: democracy. The new democratic system would eliminate the political avenues of elite women, elevating lower-class men over women of all classes. After 1832 the political culture shifted toward the middle class, though only men gained a new voice in national affairs, with no outlet for female politicking (at least not rhetorically) in the intensifying private sphere. However, as Elizabeth R. Varon has demonstrated, the speed at which male voters took to the party system and its deep penetration into ordinary life can be traced to middle-class women's embrace of partisanship. Again, by incorporating partisanship into the everyday, by using food, clothing, entertainment, and material culture, women endowed the new party system with natural qualities.[3]

Ironic, too, is the realization that these titanic political accomplishments were not seen as feminist, radical victories but as the family work of conservative wives, mothers, sisters, and daughters. Indeed, the story of women in Washington is in many ways the story of the triumph of a class, rather than an oppressed gender. These women came from both the North and the South, enjoyed more education than most women and men of the time, and shared the same prospects and values as their male relations, visions of a future with increased educational expectations, market consumption, and other privileges of living well in a growing nation. In pursuit of these goals, and amid disclaimers and denials, they formed and acted upon political identities closely tied to their personal and class identities.

The marriage of women's history to the mainstream political narrative has revealed that gender is a primary category of historical analysis, as deeply embedded in political, social, and economic relations as class or race. Gender, as one of "the recurrent references by which political power has been conceived, legitimated, and criticized," invites us to rethink the basic premises that constitute historical interpretation. History has always been the study of power, and gender provides a language and a geography of power.[4]

The people of this particular past saw power in deeply gendered ways, and anyone who seeks to understand their time must do likewise. Words such as *women* and *etiquette* encountered in the sources should spur us to deeper analysis, even (and especially) when the participants insist on the inherent frivolity of these issues. More likely than not, we may uncover a profound political and/or cultural discussion, much as the furor over "Lady Washington" and her "levées" concealed a grave anxiety about the place of aristocracy in a Republic that both repudiated the notion and craved the legitimacy it imparted. More generally, using gender for political analysis demonstrates that power is configured in more ways than we have imagined, that governments depend on many kinds of relations between women and men, and that politics does not depend wholly on who has the vote.[5]

From the start Washington City had its chroniclers, usually letter writers eager to describe life in this invented city to the folks at home. Before the government had officially removed to Washington in 1800, even before construction began, travelers from all over sent out descriptions of the setting, maps of the city, and any news or gossip they could garner. Americans and Europeans knew that they were observing a process unlike any they had ever seen: the invention of a new city, a new government. Unbeknownst to them, it was the creation of the capital of a modern nation-state.

From 1800 on, Washington City never lacked for reporters and storytellers, but the honor of the first and one of the best must go to Margaret

Bayard Smith. Though she wrote prose pieces (published and unpublished) and novels about life in the capital, her letters to her female kin stand as her primary literary vehicle for presenting and puzzling out the social and political implications of Washington City. To date, her writings have been published very partially, most notably by Gaillard Hunt in 1906 as *The First Forty Years of Washington Society.* Hunt did a thorough job sifting through Bayard Smith's voluminous correspondence with her two sisters, Jane Bayard Kirkpatrick and Maria Bayard Boyd, and with members of her husband's family. In making his selections, he included the mentions of "Great Men" that he knew would interest his readers and tried to eliminate all the tedious details of the relentless social round that dictated the lives of the Smiths and their neighbors. As Laurel Thatcher Ulrich points out, however, it is the very "dailiness" that reveals the rich particularity of history, and Bayard Smith's writings prove the point irrefutably.[6]

Hunt's selections, and his own interpretations of them, gave later historians the false impression that Bayard Smith wrote, as a proper lady should, "only" about social life in Washington, eschewing discussions of politics. But taken as a whole, Bayard Smith's writings present a picture of life in the capital in which politics and society were intricately and inextricably bound together, where social structures, by necessity, had to substitute for governmental ones—in other words, a real-life, real-time depiction of the theoretical points of this book. Indeed, I could not have come to my scholarly conclusions—could not have cast off the blinders of my own cultural prejudices about public and private—without Bayard Smith's work.

Throughout the nineteenth and early twentieth centuries, other women (and some men) thought and wrote about Washington City, the White House, and, most pointedly, about the role of society in a republic. Elizabeth Ellet, Rufus Griswold, Anne Hollingsworth Wharton, Margaret Botsford, Geraldine Brooks, Mary Cable, Samuel C. Busey, Madeleine Vinton Dahlgren, Florence Howe Hall, Laura C. Holloway, Katharine Anthony, Ethel Stephens Arnett, Charles Hurd—their names and works pepper the notes and bibliography for this book. More importantly, because no good story is complete without ghosts, this book is haunted by these authors' urgency and conviction that women's social work was important.

However, they did not have the language or framework to be able to say how or why women mattered, nor could they articulate the consequences of women's social work. As a result, some of their writings have a defensive tone. Elizabeth Ellet began her *Court Circles of the Early Republic* boldly, albeit invoking the authority of an influential male: "Lord Napier remarked to a distinguished lady in Washington, that a book descriptive of Society in the National Capital ought to be written; and that a faithful record would give a better idea of the spirit and character of the period than any history."[7]

Ellet thus embarked on her story with a sense of mission—the only illustrations that appear in the work are of women—but ultimately, she could not assert the importance of her female subjects except by recounting their relationships with men and could not describe them without resorting to the formulaic adjectives of her culture. "Gracious, refining, beneficent"—high praise indeed, but as stubbornly unrevealing (and thus resistant to analysis) as the paeans on the tombstones of colonial goodwives.

Thanks to the work on women and gender done in the late twentieth century, I did not have to make the impossible case that "a faithful record" could be "better" than "any history"; I could see stories of women and social life *as history.* I am proud to take my place, then, with the pioneers of both centuries, to stand with Elizabeth Ellet as a historian of society and to keep company with my colleagues and teachers as a historian of women and gender.

This book cannot even feign to be the latest (let alone the last!) word on the intersection of society and politics, and the roles of women, in Washington, D.C. The past is rich territory for this kind of analysis, as any recent review of the literature reveals, and several forthcoming studies mentioned in the notes will deepen our knowledge and increase our fascination with the subject. And the present guarantees that this book is only a recent installment in a long saga of Washington City, and that historians and political scientists ignore questions of etiquette and the unofficial sphere at their peril. Indeed, I undertook this project in the face of two government shutdowns, instigated by a Speaker of the House piqued at an Air Force One seating arrangement.

When I began my research, the Clintons had been in the White House long enough to change the culture of Washington, along ominous lines according to the older political elite. The Clinton administration had adopted a "college-dorm" work style, calling out for pizza or Chinese while "pulling all-nighters." Articles and editorials in the *Washington Post* warned these newcomers that the business of politics took place only partly in the office, and that at five o'clock the smart pol left the office for home, changed his shirt, and went out to dinner.

The assumption that the person leaving the official sphere had only to change his shirt, of course, underlines another reason that examinations of the official/unofficial sphere will compel and intrigue future scholars. As this book has pointed out, though men and women can appropriate actions and ideas from both sides of the male/female divide, unofficial space and official space have always been deeply gendered. For the first time in history, however, the cast of characters is beginning to change, switching gender identities back and forth, like players in a Shakespearean comedy.

Slowly but surely, we modern Americans are beginning to accept women in official capacities, whether as CEOs or politicians. After all, with access to education, women can now achieve the qualifications needed for these offices. And one cannot blame women for their eager embrace of official, sanctioned, undisguised power. However, that brings up the other explanation for why political men are not changing their shirts and attending Georgetown dinner parties. No one is at home to give them, and the rich realm of the unofficial is being abandoned.

If women are learning to occupy official positions of power, it is less clear that men are learning to adopt roles in the unofficial spaces needed for the political process. For one thing, the qualifications required to be a master of the unofficial sphere are less clear than a record of elected office or an MBA. It is much easier to imagine a qualified woman serving as president than to reckon what her husband (the "First Gentleman"?) would be doing. Would he take his place, like Dolley Madison, at the head of official (and national) society? Could he use his role as loyal spouse to achieve what Eleanor Roosevelt did? Men have not shown such eagerness to prove themselves masters of the unofficial sphere, and one can hardly blame them. Except . . . .

Except that politics is a fundamental human activity, and good politicians recognize this. Politics, if it is to transcend the realm of the abstract, if it is to connect with the humans it serves, must encompass and use all arenas of human life. The unofficial sphere can introduce issues, minimize risk, and bring life and emotion to the formation of public policy. In a democratic politics it can build bonds of loyalty and trust between politicians and bind citizens more closely to the national mission. Those who serve as personnel for the unofficial spheres of the twenty-first century, then, will have important roles to play and, if this history is correct, a long line of distinguished predecessors to emulate.

When Thomas Jefferson arrived in the capital in 1801, he relished the prospect of building both a new kind of city and a new kind of government from the ground up. Women (and their politicking ways) had a very definite, very delineated place in his world concept: on the margins. With Margaret Eaton on a boat to Spain and the ladies of Washington retreating into their homes, it would be a neat device to state that Andrew Jackson accomplished what Jefferson could not, the separation of women from the political sphere.

But Jefferson was almost immediately defeated by forces he could not control, and Jackson soon would be. Even more than other groups, like Indians and slaves, women could not be segregated or kept to the side for long, less because they had tasted the rhetoric of liberty and more because politics (like history making) cannot exist in the "unsocial brains of needy bookworms."[8] Politics includes the best of humanity in the form of altruism. Political impulses are also rooted in the most base selfishness, the exploitation of resources and of people for personal profit. Women, as people, possess and act all along this human spectrum. Answering the question, Where are the women? produces not politically correct history but correct political history.

Notes

ABBREVIATIONS

Proper Names

AJ   Andrew Jackson
CAM   Catharine Akerly Mitchill
DPTM   Dolley Payne Todd Madison
HGO   Harrison Gray Otis (husband to SFO)
JBK   Jane Bayard Kirkpatrick (sister to MBS)
JM   James Madison
JQA   John Quincy Adams (husband to LCA)
JWR   Judith Walker Rives
LCA   Louisa Catherine Adams
MAM   Margaretta Akerly Miller (sister to CAM)
MBB   Maria Bayard Boyd (sister to MBS)
MBS   Margaret Bayard Smith
ME   Margaret Eaton
PGH   Phebe Guernsey Hubbard
SFO   Sally Foster Otis
THH   Thomas H. Hubbard (husband to PGH)
TJ   Thomas Jefferson
WCR   William Cabell Rives (husband to JWR)

Archives

AAS   American Antiquarian Society, Worcester, Massachusetts
MHS   Massachusetts Historical Society, Boston
DLC   Library of Congress (District Branch), Washington, D.C.
NYHS   New-York Historical Society, New York

Manuscript Collections

MBS Papers Margaret Bayard Smith Papers, Manuscript Division, DLC
CAM Papers Catherine Akerly Mitchell Papers, Manuscript Division, DLC
AJ Papers   Andrew Jackson Papers, Manuscript Division, DLC
APM   Adams Papers Manuscripts (on microfilm)
HGO Papers Harrison Gray Otis Family Papers, MHS

INTRODUCTION

1. Stephen Sondheim, *Pacific Overtures*, Revelation Music Publishing Corporation and Rilting Music, Inc., 1975, 1976.

1. PRESIDENT THOMAS JEFFERSON IN
WASHINGTON CITY

1. Melish, *Travels* 1:193; Foster, *Notes,* 11.

The choice of Shakespeare for the epigraphs is fitting for a study of the early federal government and the creation of the capital. Many felt the excitement of the republican experiment, as well as the anxiety, and they viewed the daily happenings as unfolding events on a national stage. In particular, the dramatic juxtaposition of the highborn and the low, their respective nobility and drollery, the episodes of pageantry and display, the struggles for power and preeminence that characterized Washington City life struck many visitors and residents as reminiscent of the history plays (and the comedies) of the Bard.

2. Hurd, *Cavalcade,* 16; Ebenezer Mattoon to Thomas Dwight, 2 March 1801, Dwight-Howard Collection, MHS.

3. Thomas H. Hubbard to Phebe Guernsey Hubbard (wife), 7 Dec. 1818, Thomas Hubbard Collection (unprocessed), DLC.

4. Adams, *History* 1:30; Albert Gallatin to Hannah Nicholson Gallatin (wife), 15 Jan. 1801, cited in Adams, *Life of Gallatin,* 253; Young, *Washington Community,* 31, 29. These figures do not include military personnel, a small number of federal workers serving the District of Columbia, or local officials, magistrates, clerks, etc. Total population for Washington in 1800 was 3,210; by 1830 it had risen to 18,826 (Green, *Washington: Village,* 21).

5. MBS to Susan Bayard Smith or Mary Ann Smith (sisters-in-law), 5 Oct. 1800, MBS Papers.

6. MBS, Journal, Oct. 1800, MBS to JBK, 16 Nov. 1800, Samuel Harrison Smith to Susan Bayard Smith or Mary Ann Smith (sisters), 10 Oct. 1800, ibid.

7. MBS, "Notebook," 1837, ibid.

8. LCA, "Adventures of a Nobody," Nov. 1803, LCA to JQA, 16 and 22 Sept. 1801, APM, 269, 401.

9. Henrietta Liston letter, 9 Sept. 1796, cited in Arnebeck, *Fiery Trial,* 385; Prince d'Orleans, cited in ibid., 434–35; Warden, *Chorographical and Statistical,* 32–33.

10. MBS to JBK, 16 Nov. 1800, MBS Papers.

11. Mannix, "Albert Gallatin," 75; Foster, *Notes,* 84–85; Green, *Washington: Village,* 21.

12. MBS to JBK, 16 Nov. 1800, MBS Papers.

13. Carson, *Ambitious Appetites,* 9–10; Albert Gallatin to Hannah Nicholson Gallatin (wife), 15 Jan. 1801, NYHS.

14. HGO to Sally Foster Otis (wife), 15 Feb. 1801, HGO Papers. See Earman, "Boardinghouses, Parties, and the Creation of a Political Society," 1, refuting James Sterling Young's vision of Washington as a place where "selfless public servants lived in monklike quarters during their tenure in the swampy federal city . . . [and where] the branches of government remained physically and socially separate and political parties had little meaning or influence."

15. Elkins and McKitrick, *Federalism,* 169, 171; Bowling, *Creating,* 79.

16. TJ, "Notes and Calculations," in Boyd et al., *Papers of TJ* 6:364–65.

17. Kern, paper presented at "New Horizons in Jefferson Scholarship," Oct. 4–5, 1996.

18. Burstein, *Inner Jefferson,* 278; Smelser, *Democratic Republic,* 6, 12; Foster, *Notes,* 155–56.

19. Ellis, *American Sphinx,* 31–34, 58; Burstein, *Inner Jefferson,* 31–33; Mannix, "Albert Gallatin," 80.

20. Howe, "Republican Thought," 149, 165; Lewis, "Blessings," 117; Freeman, "Slander," 28; Sharp, *American Politics,* 228; Smelser, "Passion," 391–419 (characterizing the early Republic as an "Age of Passion").

21. *Connecticut Courant*, 20 Sept. 1800, cited in Lerche, "Political Smear," 480.

22. TJ to Joseph Priestly, 21 March 1801, to John Dickinson, 6 March 1801, in Ford, *Writings of TJ* 8:21–23, 7.

23. Banning, *Persuasion*, 51, 55–57, 71–72; Ellis, *American Sphinx*, 42–43, 131–33. William Plumer, senator from New Hampshire and a Federalist, called his own party "the Court party" (Brown, *Plumer's Memorandum*, 453). See also William Maclay, "Journal," cited in Banning, *Persuasion*, 119: "In 1801 . . . the 'Country' came to power."

24. Banning, *Persuasion*, 273.

25. On 20 Feb. 1801, when Congress elected Thomas Jefferson, the *Aurora* intoned: "On [this] day the sun of aristocracy set, to rise no more" (cited in Banning, *Persuasion*, 270).

26. Warren, *History* 3:279–80.

27. Rousseau, *Emile*, 59; TJ, *Notes*, 280; TJ, "Hints to Americans Traveling in Europe," 19 June 1788, in Boyd et al., *Papers of TJ* 8:264–77.

28. Ellis, *American Sphinx*, 171; Foster, *Notes*, 8.

29. "Cornelia," *National Gazette* (Philadelphia), Dec. 1792, cited in Shields and Teute, "Jefferson," 2.

30. Banning, *Persuasion*, 59.

31. Ibid., 83. See also ibid., 117–18, 121, 183, 227; Ellis, *American Sphinx*, 121.

32. On manners and politics, see Banning, *Persuasion*, 201; Buel, *Securing*; Pocock, "Virtues, Rights, and Manners: A Model for Historians of Political Thought," in *Virtue, Commerce, and History.* For emphasis on these issues, see Freeman, "Affairs of Honor"; Shields and Teute, "Court"; Shields and Teute, "Jefferson."

33. TJ, *Anas*, in Ford, *Writings of TJ* 1:156, 165–67. See also Ellis, *American Sphinx*, 255–56; Sisson, *American Revolution of 1800*, 138.

34. "Queries on a Line of Conduct to be Pursued by the President," in Fitzpatrick, *Writings of Washington* 30:319–21; Alexander Hamilton to George Washington, 5 May 1789, in Syrett and Cooke, *Papers of Hamilton* 5:335–37.

35. Even in 1881 one historian of the "Republican Court" explained: "A degree of stiffness and formality existed at those receptions that we of this age can scarcely understand, accustomed as we are to the familiarity and freedom of the present-day gatherings" (Holloway, *Ladies of the White House*, 35). See also Griswold, *Republican Court*, 269–70; Truman, *Group Portrait*, 19.

36. Ellet, *Court Circles*, 30.

37. Abigail Adams, cited in Ellet, *Court Circles*, 30; Griswold, *Republican Court*, 215; Ellet, *Court Circles*, 19–20.

38. Shields and Teute, "Court," 3–6; Truman, *Group Portrait*, 26; Griswold, *Republican Court*, 313–14, Ellet, *Court Circles*, 33.

39. TJ, *Anas*, ed. Sawvel, 126–27; McCormick, "First Master," 172; Ellis, *American Sphinx*, 90–97; McLaughlin, *Monticello*, 193. See also Lewis, "Blessings," 115. Cf. Teute and Shields, "Jefferson," 27–28.

40. See Hunt, "Introduction"; Deneys, "Political Economy of the Body"; Cameron, "Political Exposures"; Hunt, "Many Bodies of Marie Antoinette"; Maza, "Diamond Necklace Affair Revisited." British political historians also are beginning seriously to consider elite British women as more than the transmitters of wealth and genes in nation building. See Colley, *Britons*, 227–73, and Colley, "Female Elite."

41. Goodman, *Republic*, 90–135. For John Adams's vivid word picture of the effect these Parisian "learned Ladies," see Ellis, *American Sphinx*, 90.

42. TJ to George Washington, 4 Dec. 1788, in Boyd et al., *Papers of TJ* 14:330.

43. TJ to John Banister, Jr., 15 Oct. 1785, ibid., 8:635–37; TJ, *Autobiography*, 1188.

44. The two protoparties of the era had very different relationships to the idea of female partisanship. See Zagarri, "First Party," 127; Varon, *Mean to Be*, 72.

45. TJ to Anne Willing Bingham, 11 May 1788, *Portable TJ*, 922–23; TJ to Eliza House Trist, 18 Aug. 1785, in Boyd et al., *Papers of TJ* 8:403–4. Ironically (or, knowing Jefferson, unconsciously), these ladies were prominent salonnières in the United States (see Shields and Teute, "Jefferson," 11–13).

46. Ellet, *Court Circles*, 63–64; Shields and Teute, "Jefferson," 17. In his reply to "Etiquette of the Court of the U.S." in the *Aurora* (Philadelphia), Jefferson declared that he had "buried levees, birthdays, royal parades and the arrogation of precedence in society by certain self-styled friends of order, but truly styled friends of privileged order" (TJ, *Aurora*, 13 Feb. 1804, cited in Malone, *First Term*, 500).

47. Malone, *First Term*, 374–76; Adams, *History* 2:363–64; Peterson, *New Nation*, 725–30. Plumer noted the use of wine at these parties, observing that "even two glasses of wine oftimes renders a temperate man communicative" (Brown, *Plumer's Memorandum*, 543).

48. Smelser, *Democratic Republic*, 3; Ellis, *American Sphinx*, 191; Young, *Washington Community*, 168–70, 190–91.

49. My ideas about Jefferson's dinner parties were formed during long discussions with Joanne B. Freeman. I thank her for her intellectual generosity. Ellis believes that Jefferson's intense desire to avoid conflict undermined his goal of promoting personal bonds through these dinners (*American Sphinx*, 191).

50. Freeman, "Jefferson and Political Combat." In 1793 Jefferson used his dinner table to deliver a political rebuke to New Englander John Trumbull (Trumbull, *Autobiography*, 173–75). My thanks to Joanne B. Freeman, who drew my attention to this story and shared her views with me. See also Burstein, *Inner Jefferson*, 223.

51. Brown, *Plumer's Memorandum*, 458, 428, 299. Teute and Shields note that by dispensing with levees, Jefferson banished forms that defused conflict; party-based dinners only increased animosity ("Jefferson," 20).

52. Freeman, "Affairs of Honor," paper presented at Yale University; Ellis, *American Sphinx*, 279.

53. McLaughlin, *Monticello*, 233; Brown, *Plumer's Memorandum*, 21; Buel, *Securing*, 92, 243–44, 288; Freeman, "Slander," 40.

54. For examples of these visits, see Brown, *Plumer's*, 193–94, 333–36, 465–71, 491–92, 516–18.

55. Brown, *Plumer's Memorandum*, 333, 471. The pose of gossiping with friends allowed early Republican politicians to practice rudimentary party politics (Freeman, "Slander," 30; see also ibid., 33, 40).

56. Lewis, "Blessings," 111, 133; TJ to James Monroe, cited in ibid., 113; TJ to Martha Jefferson, 28 March 1787, 17, 31 May 1798, 23 Nov. 1807, in Betts and Bear, *Family Letters*, 35, 161–62, 164, 315. Lewis also points out how the "expressions of love" increased as the conflicts, worries, and tensions of public life accelerated ("Blessings," 112).

57. Rousseau, *Emile*, cited in Kerber, *Republic*, 24; Lewis, "Blessings," 135.

58. Lewis, "Blessings," 132, 134, 135, 138. Though she does not go as far as I do, Lewis states, "In rendering a vision of private life, Thomas Jefferson was necessarily constructing the public world as well" (ibid., 111).

59. Adams, *History* 1:144; Buel, *Securing*, 135, 288. Alexander Hamilton used the word "womanish" (Hamilton to Edward Carrington, 26 May 1792, in Syrett and Cooke, *Papers of Hamilton* 11:439). Hamilton's "explicit exercise of authority" called attention to himself in ways Jefferson found distasteful and untrustworthy (Ellis, *American Sphinx*, 128–30).

60. Buel, *Securing*, 92. The two proto-parties appropriated each others' styles as needed (ibid., 214, 243). For women as master politicians of the home, see Lewis, "Blessings," 136.

61. Ellis, *American Sphinx*, 105, 183, 191–93, 282, 301. Banning describes republicanism as an "ideology that taught that power was a monster and governing was wrong" (Banning, *Persuasion*, 273).

62. Ellis, *American Sphinx*, 189.

63. TJ to Thomas Jefferson Randolph, 24 Nov. 1808, in Betts and Bear, *Family Letters*, 362–65; Lewis, "Blessings," 133–34; TJ to Walter Jones, 5 March 1810, in Ford, *Writings of TJ* 9:273–74. See also TJ to Francis Wayles Eppes, 21 May 1816, to Martha Jefferson, 4 April 1790, 7 Jan. 1798, 28 April 1793, in Betts and Bear, *Family Letters*, 415, 51, 151–52, 115.

64. TJ cited in Ellis, *American Sphinx*, 190; Lewis, "Blessings," 136.

65. Brown, *Plumer's Memorandum*, 213. On Rousseau, see Okin, *Western Political Thought*, 144.

66. The perfect republican mother and wife are presented by Kerber, *Republic*, and Lewis, "Wife," respectively.

67. Teute and Shields, "Jefferson," 8–9. They cite the poetry of Annis Boudinot Stockton, a noted New Jersey salonnière, who published two paeans to Washington. Ellis calls Jefferson's an "inconspicuous presidency" (*American Sphinx*, 191–93).

68. Lipset, *New Nation*, 18–22.

69. Ellis, *American Sphinx*, 178; Smelser, *Democratic Republic*, 16; Cable, *Avenue*, 26. At this time actors wore green to signify rube characters.

70. Brown, *Plumer's Memorandum*, 550, 193, 212.

71. MBS, Notebook, DLC; also in MBS, *First Forty*, 5–7.

72. MBS, Notebook, MBS Papers; also in *First Forty*, 7–8.

73. This "feminine style" was not limited to Jefferson; see Lewis, "Ambivalence," 140–45. For another story to counteract the image of Jefferson as a "violent demagogue," see MBS, *First Forty*, 11.

74. Young, *Washington Community*, 163–70.

75. Ellis, *American Sphinx*, 178–80, 184–86, 198–99.

76. Rufus King to James Madison, 10 April 1802, in King, *Rufus King* 4:100–101. King was right: Jackson eventually did come to the United States and then left in three months, establishing the record for fastest achievement of persona non grata status.

77. Lester, *Redivivus*, 12.

78. Elizabeth Merry to Thomas Moore, n.d. [after 26 Nov. 1803], in Moore, *Memoirs* 8:50–52.

79. Anthony Merry to George Hammond, 7 Dec. 1803, cited in Lester, *Redivivus*, 18.

80. Augustus John Foster to Lady Elizabeth Foster (mother), 30 Dec. 1804, Augustus John Foster Papers, DLC.

81. Lester, *Redivivus*, 32–33.

82. Ibid., 33.

83. Louis André Pichon to Charles Maurice Talleyrand-Périgord, 5 Feb. 1804, cited in Adams, *History* 2:368–69. This was not a full diplomatic dinner, which would involve inviting the whole corps, because the chargé of Denmark had not been invited.

84. Anthony Merry to George Hammond, 7 Dec. 1803, ibid., 2:372.

85. Anthony Merry cited in Jacob, *Elites*, 25.

86. Pichon to Talleyrand, 5 Feb. 1804, cited in Adams, *History* 2:368–69.

87. Anthony Merry to George Hammond, 7 Dec. 1803, cited in ibid., 372.

88. Brant, *Secretary of State*, 164.

89. Pichon to Talleyrand, 5 Feb. 1804, cited in Malone, *First Term*, 381.

90. Pichon to Talleyrand, 13 Feb. 1804, cited in Lester, *Redivivus*, 41.

91. "Cannons of Etiquette," in Ford, *Writings of TJ* 10:47–48; Lester, *Redivivus,* 39.

92. Lester, *Redivivus,* 34–35; 78–79.

93. Ibid., 98.

94. *Aurora* (Philadelphia), 25 Nov. 1802, cited in ibid., 24; TJ to Robert Livingston, 18 April 1802, in Ford, *Writings of TJ* 8:143–47.

95. The documents are cited in Lester, *Redivivus,* 50, 87, 76–77.

96. Ibid., 96. That Anthony Merry might have decided that Jefferson was pro-French from his dinner-table behavior is my own interpretation.

97. Ibid., 90, 97. Though Lester discusses party rancor, real and imagined, he makes no connection to the Merry affair, and he claims no historical importance for the affair.

98. TJ to James Monroe, 8 Jan. 1804, in Ford, *Writings of TJ* 8:290–91.

99. MBS, *First Forty,* 46.

100. Eleanor Parke Custis Lewis to Elizabeth Bordley Gibson, 23 March 1806, in Brady, *Beautiful Nelly,* 67; Lester, *Redivivus,* 10, 22; Thomas Moore to his mother, Sept. [?] 1803, in Moore, *Memoirs* 1:134; Augustus John Foster to Lady Elizabeth Foster (mother), 20 July 1806, Augustus John Foster Papers, DLC.

101. MBS, *First Forty,* 45–46.

102. Adams, *History* 2:361; MBS, *First Forty,* 46.

103. The other wives of Europeans—Sally McKean Yrujo, who married the Spanish minister, and Elizabeth Patterson Bonaparte of Baltimore—were good Republican daughters and thus unlikely to give Jefferson much trouble.

104. Foster, *Notes,* 55, 21.

105. Freeman, "Slander," 28–30, 32. For Freeman, the "grammar of political combat" included gossip, dueling, and social events.

2. DOLLEY MADISON TAKES COMMAND

1. Few, "Diary," 1 Oct. 1808, 349; Latrobe cited in Furman, *Profile,* 52. See also Klapthor, "Decorate," 156.

The epigraph refers, of course, to the glamorous and doomed ruler of Shakespeare's Egypt. Dolley Madison, as glamorous and as powerful (if not as despotic), enjoyed a better fate. In the play one of Cleopatra's attendants pronounces this benediction; Dolley, too, inspired such adoration in those closest to her. Perhaps the epigraph's greatest significance lies in the power of its construction. A man fomenting a revolution in language, Shakespeare often blended the older Anglo-Saxon forms with the newer Latinate derivations just coming into vogue. "Lass"—the homeliest of nouns—followed by the elegant, exotic "unparalleled" can take the reader's breath away with its jagged power. As this chapter demonstrates, Dolley's talent lay in a similar ability to mix old forms and new, juxtaposing seemingly contradictory elements in her culture to powerful effect.

2. Anthony, *Dolly,* 198; Furman, *Profile,* 56.

3. Lipset, *New Nation,* 34; Young, *Washington Community,* 181, 185–86.

4. Lipset, *New Nation,* 35; Ellis, *American Sphinx,* 121, 178–79.

5. Young, *Washington Community,* 157–78.

6. Rives, *Biography of JM* 3:63.

7. "Society is the handmaiden of politics, especially in a capital city" (Hall, *Social Usages,* v).

8. McGerr, "Political Style," 865–66.

9. Ibid., 865.

10. Also noted by Shields and Teute, "Jefferson," 7. Michael Warner describes republican authority as "peculiarly depersonalized" (*Republic,* 39, 43).

11. Bloch, "Gendered Meanings," 44–45; Zagarri, "Manners," 209. For contemporary documents that confirm the tie between women and luxury, see Edmund Burke, *Philosophical Enquiry into the Origin of Our Ideas of the Sublime and Beautiful* (1775), and Mary Wollstonecraft, *Vindication of the Rights of Woman* (1792), cited and analyzed in Jones, *Eighteenth Century*, 2–6. Many observers of the American social scene report the supposedly widespread female fascination not only with things foreign but also with foreigners; see, for example, Grund, *Aristocracy*, 70–71.

12. Zagarri, "Manners," 195, 199, 201–2, 204, 205 (citing James Wilson, "Lecture on the Study of the Law in the United States" [1790]), 206; "Remarks on the Manners, Government, Laws, and Domestic Debt of America," in *The American Museum* (Philadelphia), March 1789, cited in ibid., 205. See also ibid., 193, 197–201, 210–11. For the influence of the Scottish Enlightenment school on the founders' ideas, see Howe, "European Sources of Political Ideas in Jeffersonian America" and "Why the Scottish Enlightenment Was Useful to the Framers of the American Constitution."

13. On female republican virtue, see Kerber, *Republic*; Lewis, "Wife," 689–721; Bloch, "Gendered Meanings," 37–58.

14. Anti-Federalists and Warren cited in Bowling, *Creating*, 21, 11; Sloan cited in Willson, *Friendly Relations*, 96–97. On the fear of centralization in state capitals in this period, see Zagarri, *Politics of Size*, 83–104.

15. MBS to Maria Bayard, April 1802, MBS Papers; Rosalie Stier Calvert to Isabelle van Havre (sister), 30 Dec. 1803, 20 July, 26 Sept. 1806, to H. J. Stier (father), 25 Jan. 1805, in Callcott, *Riversdale*, 72, 109, 145, 149.

16. Jacob, *Elites*, 24–25; Foster, *Notes*, 47; Rosalie Stier Calvert to H. J. Stier (father), 21 June 1805, in Callcott, *Mistress*, 122–23.

17. Bushman, *Refinement*, 40.

18. Lipset, *New Nation*, 62, 112.

19. Gillette, "Introduction," iii; Green, *Washington: Village*, viii. "Permanent seat of empire" comes from an 1810 House of Representatives committee report on a petition for banking charters (ibid., 33–34).

20. Adams, *History* 1:30–31; Jacob, *Elites*, 2; Young, *Washington Community*, 26, 27.

21. During this era the executive mansion went by several names: the "President's House," the "Executive Mansion," the "President's Palace" (Earman, "Boardinghouses," 7). A British minister used the term "white house" in the spring of 1811, and the Baltimore *Whig* employed it in 1810: "'White house' may be considered the 'people's name'" (Bryan, "Name," 306, 307).

22. Young, *Washington Community*, 5.

23. *Temple*, 2–3.

24. Hunt-Jones, *Dolley*, 34–35; Shulman, "Dolley," 53. Bushman, *Refinement*, discusses the public nature of house building and decorating and the great concern men had with material life.

25. Truman, *Group Portrait*, 21; Hunt-Jones, *Dolley*, 36.

26. Benjamin Henry Latrobe to JM, 10 March 1809, JM Papers, DLC.

27. Cited in Klapthor, "Decorate," 157; Hunt-Jones, *Dolley*, 36–37.

28. Raley, "Interior," 568.

29. The "anthemion and husks" is a flat radiating pattern featuring honeysuckle flowers and thought to be of classical Greek design (Benjamin Henry Latrobe to DPTM, 22 March 1809, NYHS; Benjamin Henry Latrobe to DPTM, 21 April 1809, New York Public Library).

30. Hunt-Jones, *Dolley*, 39.

31. Ibid.

32. Raley, "Interior," 570; Truman, *Group Portrait*, 21–22; Gerry, *Diary*, 180.

33. Hunt-Jones, *Dolley*, 42–43, 88–89.

34. Ibid., 43–44; Shulman, "Dolley," 53–54.

35. Shulman, "Dolley," 54.

36. Daniel J. Boorstin points out that democracies are "conspicuously weak" in ritual, and for such cultures architecture plays the role of ritual; for him, the White House is the pinnacle of "architecture-as-ritual" ("Roles," 3–4).

37. Gerry, *Diary*, 179–80; Henry Dearborn to Albert Gallatin, 19 May 1809, cited in Brant, *President*, 33; Smith, "Attractions of Exclusion."

38. Shulman, "Dolley," 53; Klapthor, "Decorate," 157. For considerations of gender and nationalism, see Waldstreicher, *Fetes*, 232–42.

39. Earman, "Boardinghouses," 11; Jackson cited in Willson, *Friendly Relations*, 98; Few, "Diary," 349; Carson, *Ambitious Appetites*, 2; Ellis, *American Sphinx*, 172.

40. Simon, "Construction," 6; Young, *Washington Community*, 21–24; Jacob, "High Society," 10.

41. Simon, "Construction," 6.

42. Carson, *Ambitious Appetites*, 79; Ellet, *Court Circles*, 80–81; Jacob, "High Society," 3; Jaher, *Urban*, 9.

43. Jacob, *Elites*, 3, 8. For the "We's" and "They's" of Washington City, see Jacob, *Elites*, 29–33.

44. Carson, *Ambitious Appetites*, vii; Busey, *Pictures*, 332, 338.

45. Albert Gallatin to Hannah Nicholson Gallatin, 22 Jan. 1801, NYHS.

46. Young, *Washington Community*, 50, 53, 60–63, 68, 78–80.

47. Jacob, *Elites*, 27–28; see also Jacob, "High Society," 11.

48. Virginia representative John Randolph of Roanoke decided that "not one" of his New England colleagues "possesses the slightest tie of common interest or of common feeling with us" (cited in Adams, *John Randolph*, 275).

49. Foster, *Notes*, 56.

50. Paullin, "British Diplomats," 249; MBS to Mary Ann Kirkpatrick, 9 Feb. 1807, MBS Papers.

51. Richard Hofstadter's hypothesis that there were no political parties in the early Republic remains conventional wisdom, reinforced by the work of scholars such as Ronald Formisano; James Sterling Young's "boardinghouse bloc" discovery is based on this contention. Rosemarie Zagarri points out, however, that the political men and women of the time identified "parties," "party fever," and "party spirit," aligning themselves and others in one of two camps ("Petticoat Politicians and Concurrent Patriots"). Other scholars also see the proto-party activity as significant; for example, see Bogue and Marlaire, "Mess and Men," 207–30; Cunningham, *Jeffersonian Republicans*, Earman, "Boardinghouses."

52. Rosalie Stier Calvert to H. J. Stier (father) 5 May 1808, to Charles J. Stier (brother), 10 March 1815, in Calcott, *Mistress*, 184, 278 (see also ibid., 194–95, 232); Smelser, "Passion," 392–93; Samuel Latham Mitchill to CAM, 29 Jan. 1806, in Sung, "Letters," 177.

53. Furman, *Profile*, 61; CAM to MAM (sister), 11 Jan. 1809, CAM Papers.

54. Anderson, *Imagined*, 55–56.

55. Samuel Latham Mitchill to CAM, 13 Feb. 1807, in "Dr. Mitchill's Letters," 752; Gerson, *Velvet*, 158; Anthony, *Saga*, 80–81; Boller, *Wives*, 38.

56. Young, *Washington Community*, 158. On the Constitution's provision of a "wholly inadequate vehicle for presidential leadership," see ibid., 157–58, 170, 209–10.

57. MBS to Susan B. Smith (sister-in-law), March 1809, MBS Papers. The season lasted from the first Wednesday in December until the middle of February (Jacob, *Elites*, 18).

58. Goodwin, *Dolly Madison*, 93. Dolley gave more formal dinners than any other president's wife in history (Hurd, *Biography*, 50). They continued as a major form of political entertainment until the 1930s (Shulman, "Dolley," 59; Arnett, *Incomparable*, 166).

59. Klapthor, *Cookbook*, 45; Seaton, "Diary," 12 Nov. 1812, in Seaton, *William Winston*, 85; Anthony, *Saga*, 82; Rosebush, *Public Wife*, 72; Anthony, *Dolly*, 197.

60. Boller, *Wives*, 38; Seaton, "Diary," 12 Nov. 1812, in Seaton, *William Winston*, 85; Anthony, *Saga*, 82.

61. According to Shields and Teute, elite women of other cities, inspired by the seeming simplicity of the Republican Court, were giving small, intimate parties that focused on conversation and genteel displays ("Court").

62. Ibid.; Mayo and Meringolo, *Public Image*, 12.

63. Caroli, *First Ladies*, xvi, 7, 32; Truman, *Group Portrait*, 17, 18, 21, 23; see also Hunt, *We Were*, 59–60.

64. Anthony, *Saga*, 48. See also Colley, "Female Elite," 16. In republican America, a man could publicly eschew aristocratic honors, but his wife's possession of the appellation "Lady" would signal to others his high social standing.

65. Truman, *Group Portrait*, 18.

66. Bushman, *Refinement*, 208–9, 227. Holly Cowan Shulman, the best modern scholar of Dolley, characterizes her style as a "middle ground" between Republican simplicity and Federalist high fashion ("Dolley," 52).

67. Europeans found elite southern society, in which Dolley was raised, the most urbane society in America as well as the most personally welcoming (Foster, *Notes*, 108; see also Schlesinger, *Learning*, 7; Jacob, *Elites*, 38; Klapthor, *Cookbook*, 45).

68. Shulman, "Dolley," 56. In creating these ceremonies Dolley enlisted the help of Jean Pierre Sioussat, the first master of ceremonies in the White House. See McCormick, "First Master," 170–94; Brown, *Dolley*.

69. Ellet, *Court Circles*, 83.

70. MBS, *Gentility*, 150.

71. Washington Irving to H. Brevoort, 13 Jan. 1811, cited in Brant, *President*, 239; CAM to MAM, 2 Jan. 1811, CAM Papers.

72. Trollope, *Domestic Manners*, 194–95; CAM to MAM, 8 April 1806, CAM Papers.

73. CAM to MAM, 11 Jan. 1809, 2 Jan. 1811, CAM Papers; MBS to JBK, 13 March 1814, MBS Papers.

74. Abijah Bigelow to Hannah Gardner Bigelow, 29 Dec. 1810, in Bigelow, "Letters," 312; Bagot, "Exile in Yankeeland," 35.

75. Truman, *Governmental Process*, 322, 324.

76. Caroli, "Changing Role," 180.

77. Jacob asserts that "there had never before been such easy access to the president" as during the Madison regime (*Elites*, 18). See also Clark, *Life*, 201; Anthony, *Saga*, 82; Seaton, "Diary," 12 Nov. 1812, in Seaton, *William Winston*, 86.

78. Brant, *President*, 99, 260, 435.

79. James Milnor to Thomas Bradford, 12 Dec. 1811, Milnor Papers, DLC; Arnett, *Incomparable*, 181.

80. Sophia May, Diary, 23 April 1812, SM Papers, AAS; DPTM to Anna Payne Cutts, 27 March 1812, in Clark, *Life*, 130.

81. Brant, *President*, 433, 465.

82. JM to TJ, 23 April 1810, in Madison, *Papers* 2:321.

83. Young, *Washington Community*, 157–59.

84. DPTM to Anna Payne Cutts, 27 March 1812, Clark, *Life*, 130; John A. Harper to William Plumer, 13 April 1812, Plumer Papers, DLC.

85. DPTM to Phoebe Morris, 29 July 1812, DM Collection, Dumbarton House. While Anthony Morris was in Spain, he may have begun negotiations with Spain for Florida, which the Adams-Onís Treaty secured two years later in 1819 (*Dumbarton*, 8).

86. The 4 March 1809 *National Intelligencer* called Dolley the "Presidentess" on inauguration day. Senator Samuel Latham Mitchill referred to Dolley as both prospective "Presidentess" and "Lady President" in his letters to his wife, Catharine Akerly Mitchill (Samuel Latham Mitchill to CAM, 25 Jan. 1808, 23 Nov. 1807, CAM Papers).

87. Brooks, *Dames*, 31; Truman, *Group Portrait*, 21. For the rise of the congressional nominating caucus and its effect on the presidency, see Smelser, *Democratic Republic*, 318.

88. For James Madison's decision to go to war and Dolley's role in it, see Furman, *Profile*, 61, 68; Means, *Woman*, 70; Anthony, *Saga*, 86–88; Anthony, *Dolly*, 212; Arnett, *Incomparable*, 111; Boller, *Wives*, 46; Caroli, *First Ladies*, 15–16; Goodwin, *Dolly Madison*, 142. On Dewitt Clinton as a "spoiler," see Brant, *President*, 452–59; Goodwin, *Dolly Madison*, 93.

89. Freeman, "Dueling," 289–318; Brant, *President*, 263; Anthony, *Saga*, 86.

90. Daniel Webster, cited in Boller, *Wives*, 43. The necessity for the individual to learn to control "passion" in order for the modern court or government to survive is discussed in Elias, *Civility*, 241–42, 258–59. See also Freeman, "Affairs of Honor."

91. Jonathan Roberts cited in DePauw and Hunt, *"Remember,"* 149. See also Arnett, *Incomparable*; Anthony, *First Ladies*; Shulman, "Dolley."

92. Sung, "Letters," 171; MBS, "Inaugurations—1806," 534.

93. DPTM to Anna Payne Cutts, 12 May 1812, cited in Arnett, *Incomparable*, 209; Shulman, "Dolley," 51.

94. Davidoff, *Best Circles*, 14–15.

95. Phoebe Morris to Anthony Morris, 17 Feb. 1812, DPTM to Phoebe Morris, 10 May 1811, DM Collection, Dumbarton House. See also other letters cited in *Dumbarton*, 5, 8, 17.

96. Smith, *Entertaining*, 49; Dean, *Hostess*, 121–22; Caroli, *First Ladies*, 16; DPTM to Joel Barlow and wife, 15 Nov. 1811, DM Papers, DLC.

97. Shields and Teute compare the French salons with the Republican Court in "Court." See also Carson, "Complicating Categories"; Arnett, *Incomparable*, 113; Hunt-Jones, "Dolley," 35. Catharine Akerly Mitchill reported John Randolph's scathing comments; see CAM to MAM, 1 April 1806, CAM Papers.

98. Anthony, *Saga*, 94; Muller, *Darkest Day*, 68.

99. MBS to JBK, 13 March 1814, MBS Papers. See also Lewis, "Ambivalence," 122.

100. Shulman, "Dolley," 52.

101. Lenore Davidoff and Catherine Hall warn against artificially separating the realm of emotion and morality from that of "rational activity," in their case, market forces (*Family Fortunes*, 13, 16–17, 21–22, 112).

102. Klaus, "Smartest," 37.

103. Jackson cited in Brant, *Secretary*, 89; Truman, *Group Portrait*, 23.

104. Lipset, *New Nation*, 30. For the crucial role of the charismatic leader, see Freeman, "Affairs of Honor." See also Freeman, "Aristocratic Murder." On George Washington as a charismatic figure and women's use of him as such, see Shields and Teute, "Court"; Shields and Teute, "Jefferson," 8–11.

105. Young, *Washington Community*, 191.

106. While visiting James at Montpelier, Margaret Bayard Smith described him as "sportive" and his anecdotes as "very droll, and we often laughed very heartily." However, she noted, "had a single stranger or indifferent person been present," he "would have been mute, cold, and repulsive" (MBS to MBB, 17 Aug. 1828, MBS Papers; see also MBS, *Gentility*, 153–55).

107. Sarah Ridg, Diary, 8, Ridg Papers, MMC, DLC; MBS, "Inaugurations—1806," 533.

108. Seaton, "Diary," 2 Jan. 1814, in Seaton, *William Winston*, 113; Pope cited in Anthony, *Saga*, 87; Brant, *Secretary*, 465; Caroli, *First Ladies*, 14; Anthony, *Saga*, 84.

109. MBS to Susan B. Smith (sister-in-law), March 1809, MBS Papers.

110. Seaton, "Diary," 2 Jan. 1814, in Seaton, *William Winston*, 113; MBS to Susan B. Smith (sister-in-law), March 1809, MBS Papers; Phoebe Morris to Anthony Morris, 17 Feb. 1812, DM Collection, Dumbarton House; Klapthor, *Cookbook*, 47; Harriet Otis, Journal, 1 Jan. 1812, HGO Papers.

111. Remember Jefferson's anti-dress reaction in the Merry affair. See also Colley, "Female Elite," 16–18. Military historians have also long realized the importance of dress and uniforms; see Woodham-Smith, *Reason*, 56–57, 133, 173–74.

112. Colley, "Female Elite," 17.

113. JWR, "Autobiography," WCR Papers, DLC.

114. Seaton, Diary, 12 Nov. 1812, in Seaton, *William Winston*, 85; CAM to MAM, 11 Dec. 1808, CAM Papers; MBS to Susan B. Smith (sister-in-law), March 1809, MBS Papers.

115. Cohen, "Aesthetics," 481.

116. Jaeger, *Courtliness*, 258.

117. Arnett, *Incomparable*, 1.

118. *Dumbarton*, 2; Seaton, "Diary," 5 March 1813, in Seaton, *William Winston*, 98. See also Arnett, *Incomparable*, 211–12.

119. Ingersoll, *Second War* 2:206–7.

120. Brant, *Secretary*, 451; Seaton, "Diary," 1 Jan. 1813, in Seaton, *William Winston*, 91. This passage is often quoted to defend Dolley from the charge of "rouging."

121. DPTM to Edward Coles (cousin and presidential secretary), 12 May 1813, cited in Clark, *Life*, 152.

122. Arnett, *Incomparable*, 424, 425–27, 442.

123. Nine Federalists voted "pro-Washington City" (Arnett, *Incomparable*, 437). In these days of "all or nothing" political rhetoric, these Federalists must have had powerful motivations in standing with the enemy. Significantly, the bill that kept the capital in Washington City passed by a majority of nine votes.

124. Green, *Washington: Village*, 59, 67; Arnett, *Incomparable*, 442; Huntingdon, "Heiress," 96; Klaus, "Smartest," 24. On the eve of the attack, the local families, not Congress, paid for the defense of Washington City (Green, *Washington: Village*, 59).

125. Green, *Washington: Village*, 41–42. See also Jacob, *Elites*, 28; Klaus, "Smartest," 33.

126. Green, *Washington: Village*, 70–71.

127. Crowninshield, *Letters*, 15–16.

128. Anthony, *Dolly*, 234.

129. As always, subtle influence is hard to measure, but in a poem written by Thomas Law shortly after the invasion, female figures—"Liberty" and "Columbia"—led the reconstruction (Thomas Law, untitled verses, n.d., Thomas Law Papers, DLC).

130. "Thirty-Four Years Ago: A Reminiscence," undated newspaper clipping (probably from the *National Intelligencer*), Cutts-Madison Collection, MHS. See also Ellet, *Court Circles*, 94.

131. Rosebush, *Public Wife*, 54; Truman, *Group Portrait*, 27; Hurd, *Cavalcade*, 50; Goodwin, *Dolly Madison*, 188; Furman, *Profile*, 72; Arnett, *Incomparable*, 194.

132. Twentieth-century women's historians used the public/private rhetoric to create a "separate spheres" paradigm that seemed to explain much about how women and men actually lived their lives. Beginning with Linda K. Kerber in 1988, many women's historians have questioned the rigidity of the public/private dichotomy, and new studies have uncovered "political women" hitherto invisible, as well as exploring the gendered dimension of politics. See Kerber, "Separate Spheres"; Kerber et al., "Beyond Roles"; Ginzberg, *Benevolence*; Ryan, *Women in Public*; Zagarri, "Manners"; Brown, "Brave New Worlds"; Basch, "Morals"; Lewis, "Blessings"; Lewis, "Of Every Age, Sex, and Condition"; Edwards, *Angels in the Machinery*; Wood, "Woman"; Zagarri, "First Party"; Gilmore, *Gender and Jim Crow*; Varon, *"Mean to Be"*; Lewis, "Ambivalence"; Coryell, "Woman Politico."

3. WASHINGTON WOMEN IN PUBLIC

1. THH to PGH, 29, 30 Nov. 1817, THH Papers, DLC.

2. Charles Bulfinch to Hannah Bulfinch (wife), 7 Feb. 1817, Bulfinch Collection, MHS. Green entitled her chapter 3 "Phoenix on the Potomac, 1812–1817" (*Washington: Village*, 56).

3. Green, *Washington: Village*, 71–72; Eliza Parke Custis Law to David Baillie Warden, MS 871, David Baillie Warden Papers, Maryland Historical Society.

4. Earman, "Boardinghouses," 11; CAM to MAM, 10 Nov. 1808, CAM Papers; Green, *Washington: Village*, 72; Thomas Law, untitled verses, n.d., Thomas Law Papers, DLC.

5. MBS to JBK, 13 March 1814, MBS Papers. James Sterling Young presented Washington City as "government at a distance and out of sight" (*Washington Community*, 253); cf. Earman, "Boardinghouses," 140.

6. Lewis, "Ambivalence," 123–24; Thomas Law, untitled verses, n.d., Thomas Law Papers, DLC.

7. MBS, "Inaugurations—1806," 532; Lewis, "Ambivalence," 123; James Kirke Paulding to Henry Breevort, Jr., 25 Sept. 1815, Paulding Letters, NYHS.

8. For the new grandeur, see "Temple," 16–18; Stanford Canning, cited in Willson, *Friendly Relations*, 113.

9. Furman, *Profile*, 76–77.

10. Young, *Washington Community*, 191; White, *Jeffersonians*, 38.

11. Cunningham, *James Monroe*, 188.

12. From 1800 to 1830 seats in the House rose from 106 to 213 and in the Senate from 32 to 48 (Earman, "Boardinghouses," 34; Young, *Washington Community*, 198, 194).

13. Young, *Washington Community*, 193, 195–96.

14. Ibid., 196–97, 188; White, *Jeffersonians*, 44.

15. Young, *Washington Community*, 202.

16. For the 1,447 representatives and senators sent by states to Washington between 1800 and 1830, the simple average was 2.5 terms; if onetimers are excluded, the simple average rises to 3.5 terms, or seven years in office, "a significant period of time" in a productive adult life (Earman, "Boardinghouses," 34, 74, 155–83, 2, 32).

17. Ibid., 34.

18. Ibid., 36, 76; Young, *Washington Community*, 97–98, 102–7, 123–25. See also Bogue and Marlaire, "Mess and Men," 207, 221–22, 225–26; Earman, "Boardinghouses," 2, 142.

19. THH to PGH, 17 Dec., 26 Nov. 1818, THH Papers, DLC.

20. CAM to MAM, 8 April 1806, CAM Papers; Sung, "Letters," 171–72; 173–74.

21. For these provincial complaints, see Bushman, *Refinement*, 219–22; Earman, "Boarding-houses," 118–19.

22. Bushman, *Refinement*, 165, 167.

23. Carson, *Ambitious Appetites*, 88; Kasson, *Rudeness*, 132.

24. CAM to MAM, 21 Nov. 1811, 19 Dec. 1808, CAM Papers; THH to PGH, 6 Feb. 1818, THH Papers, DLC.

25. Trollope, *Domestic Manners*, 35–36, 97–98, 161. For the gradual movement of women into the public sphere elsewhere, see Ryan, *Women in Public*; Ginzberg, *Benevolence*.

26. Job Durfee to Judith Borden Durfee (wife), 6 Jan. 1822, Job Durfee Papers, DLC; Louis McLane to Kitty McLane (wife), 19 Dec. 1817, Louis McLane Papers, DLC.

27. Job Durfee to Judith Borden Durfee, 6 Jan. 1822, Job Durfee Papers, DLC; Duncan McArthur to (wife), 6 Feb. 1824, Duncan McArthur Papers, DLC; CAM to MAM, 21 Nov. 1811, CAM Papers; Willie Person Mangum to Charity Alston Mangum (wife), 1826, Willie Person Mangum Papers, DLC. See also HGO to Sophia Otis (daughter), 26 Feb. 1817, HGO Papers.

28. Bushman, *Refinement*, 41–42; Halttunen, *Painted Women*, 113–14.

29. Teute, "Wild," 51–52; Watterston, *L—— Family*, 34–49, 68–79, 92–107; Bowling, *Creating*, 78. See also Boydston, "Free Men and Masterless Women."

30. Cooley, *Etiquette*, 52–53; MBS to JBK, 13 March 1814, MBS Papers; CAM to MAM, 19 Dec. 1808, CAM Papers. See also JWR, "Autobiography," 59, WCR Papers, DLC; Lewis, "Ambivalence," 134–45.

31. MBS to Anna Maria Smith (sister-in-law), Jan. 1819, to JBK, 13 March 1814, MBS Papers.

32. See Poor, *Perley's*, 46–47. See also Young, *Washington Community*, 72. Jan Lewis questions the usefulness of "separate spheres" theory in describing the halls of Congress during this era ("Ambivalence," 145–51).

33. Sophia May, Diary, 28 Jan. 1807, Sophia May Papers, AAS; MBS to MBB, 20 April 1829, MBS Papers.

34. MBS to Anna Maria Smith (sister-in-law), Jan. 1819, MBS Papers.

35. Seaton, "Diary," in Seaton, *William Winston*, 147. See also CAM to MAM, 1 Dec. [no year], 11 Jan. 1811, 27 June 1812, CAM Papers.

36. THH to PGH, 23 Dec. 1817, THH Papers, DLC; CAM to MAM, 3 April 1806, CAM Papers; Grund, *Aristocracy*, 231; MBS to JBK, 13 March 1814, MBS Papers.

37. CAM to MAM, 13 Dec. 1811, CAM Papers; MBS, *First Forty*, 146.

38. CAM to MAM, 19 Dec. 1808, CAM Papers. See also MBS to Anna Maria Smith (sister-in-law), 12 Nov. 1818, MBS Papers; CAM to MAM, 3 April 1806, CAM Papers; Brown, *Plumer's Memorandum*, 479–80.

39. CAM to MAM, 12 Feb. 1809, 13 Dec. 1811, CAM Papers.

40. For instance, Catharine Akerly Mitchell was privy to the secret debates around the War of 1812 by virtue of the discussions at her boardinghouse table (ibid., 27 June 1812).

41. Mary P. Ryan champions retaining the concept of "public" while rejecting its gender correlate (*Banners*, 4).

42. HGO to SFO, 3, 5, 21 Feb. 1819, HGO Papers.

43. Charles Bulfinch to Hannah Bulfinch, 22 March 1818, Bulfinch Papers, MHS; CAM to MAM, 19 Dec. 1808, CAM Papers.

44. Cooley, *Etiquette*, 37–39; Lombardo, "Calling Cards," 4; Kasson, *Rudeness*, 173–74. For more on these visits, see Davidoff, *Best Circles*, 44.

45. Carson, *Ambitious Appetites*, 103, 105.

46. Davidoff, *Best Circles*, 46. Ironically, the rebuffed persons had to be genteel enough to recognize that they were being rejected. See Halttunen, *Painted Women*, 112–13.

47. Davidoff, *Best Circles*, 44–45. See Bushman, *Refinement*, 50, for gentry obsessions with intruding and being intruded upon.

48. Cooley, *Etiquette*, 34–35; Lombardo, "Calling Cards," 4. For further card customs, see Cooley, *Etiquette*, 36; Davidoff, *Best Circles*, 42; Kasson, *Rudeness*, 173; Lombardo, "Calling Cards."

49. MBS to JBK, 27 Nov. 1829, 9 Dec. 1831, MBS Papers; Cooley, *Etiquette*, 36.

50. Nimrod, *Fudge*, 41; THH to PGH, 8 Dec. 1817, THH, DLC; Job Pierson to Clarissa Bulkeley Pierson (wife), 22 Dec. 1831, to Sarah Pierson (daughter), 31 May 1832, Job Pierson Papers, DLC.

51. MBS to JBK, 1 Jan. 1814, MBS Papers; Job Pierson to Clarissa Bulkeley Pierson, 10 Dec. 1831, Job Pierson Papers, DLC; CAM to MAM, 3 April 1806, CAM Papers; THH to PGH, 20 (?) Nov. 1818, THH Papers, DLC.

52. Cooley, *Etiquette*, 37, 76. See also Job Pierson to Clarissa Bulkeley Pierson (wife), 15 Jan. 1832, Job Pierson Papers, DLC.

53. THH to PGH, 21 (?) Jan. 1818, THH Papers, DLC.

54. HGO to SFO, 22 Nov. 1818, 27 Feb. 1817, 31 Dec. 1818, HGO Papers; William Wirt to Catherine Gamble Wirt (wife), 17 Nov. 1817, William Wirt Papers, Maryland Historical Society.

55. HGO to SFO, 22 Nov. 1818, 30 Dec. 1820, HGO Papers; THH to PGH, 14 Jan. 1818, THH Papers, DLC.

56. William Wirt to Catherine Gamble Wirt, 17 Nov. 1817, William Wirt Papers, Maryland Historical Society. See also Cooley, *Etiquette*, 41.

57. Samuel Latham Mitchill used the phrase "in [your] sovereign and political capacity" in a letter to Catharine (Samuel Latham Mitchill to CAM, 8 Dec. 1804, CAM Papers).

58. See Colley, "Female Elite," 9.

59. For examples, see JWR to WCR, 4 April 1828, WCR Papers, DLC, and letters by Eliza Bancroft Davis, John Davis Papers, AAS, and Phebe Guernsey Hubbard, THH Papers, DLC.

60. Young, *Washington Community*, 158; Job Pierson to Clarissa Bulkeley Pierson (wife), 8 June 1832, Job Pierson Papers, DLC. See also ibid., 7 Dec., 14 June 1832.

61. WCR to JWR, 13 Dec. 1826, WCR Papers, DLC.

62. CAM to MAM, 28 Jan. 1812, CAM Papers.

63. Ibid.; ibid., 21 Feb. 1812. According to the *Congressional Directory* for 1811–12, fourteen legislators lived in Akerly Mitchill's boardinghouse, so she influenced thirteen votes (Sung, "Letters," 185).

64. CAM to MAM, 21 Feb. 1812, CAM Papers. See also U.S. Congress, *American State Papers*, Class IX: Claims (1790–1823), 414.

65. See Wood, *Radicalism*, 80–81, 174–79, 263–64. On early Republican politicians' fear of the fusion of the personal and the political, as in "political friendships," see Freeman, "Slander," 40.

66. Young, *Washington Community*, 175–78; White, *Jeffersonians*, 43.

67. Wood, *Radicalism*, 361; Ellis, *American Sphinx*, 197.

68. Banning, *Persuasion*, 59, 69.

69. On patronage and the building of a loyal aristocracy, see Elias, *Civilizing*, 193–97, 223–24, 267; Landes, *Public Sphere*, 17–18, 27, 36; Goodman, *Republic*, 53–54, 74–76, 89; Wood, *Creation*, 52–53, 418.

70. See Ryan, *Cradle,* 184–85; Bledstein, *Professionalism,* 4–6, 13–21. Only 5 percent of this government elite was appointed directly from private life, without previous public service (White, *Jeffersonians,* 83).

71. MBS to JBK, 24 Nov. 1831, MBS Papers.

72. John Smith to ?, 10 March 1808, John Smith Collection, DLC; Harriet Otis, Diary, 13 April 1812, HGO Papers. A customary number of men required for a troop was forty.

73. MBS to JBK, 15 Dec., 24 Nov. 1831, MBS Papers. See also ibid., 15 Feb. 1832.

74. MBS to Susan H. Smith (sister-in-law), 19 March 1821, ibid.

75. Louis McLane to Kitty McLane (wife), 24 Jan. 1818, McLane Papers, DLC.

76. Later in the century middle-class women used their family alliances more aggressively to act politically. See Coryell, "Woman Politico."

77. For Bayard Smith's benevolence work among the poor, see Teute, "Wild," 54–55; MBS, *Winter,* 236–45.

78. For the development of benevolent and charitable associations in nineteenth-century America, see Ginzberg, *Benevolence;* Hewitt, *Women's Activism;* Ryan, *Cradle;* Scott, *Natural Allies.* For the later influence of the political skills and techniques developed by the women, see Baker, *Moral Frameworks,* xvi–xvii, 89. For a contention that southern women framed their political work (as did male Whig rhetoricians) as disinterested benevolence, rather than religious reform, see Varon, *Mean to Be,* 2–3, and her chaps. 1 and 2.

79. See Brekke, "Martha Jefferson Randolph."

80. MBS to MBB, 24 Oct. 1828, Martha Jefferson Randolph to MBS, 5 Oct. 1828, MBS Papers.

81. MBS to MBB, 24 Oct. 1828, ibid. For Martha Jefferson Randolph's grateful acknowledgment of Bayard Smith's services, see her letter to MBS, 10 Nov. 1828, ibid. Many thanks to Margaret Bayard Smith biographer Rose Barquist and to Mary Wolfskill, Head of the Reading Room, Manuscript Division, DLC, for locating the crucial letters for me.

82. MBS to Letitia B. Porter, 25 Oct. 1828, MBS Papers.

83. MBS to JBK, 24 Nov. 1831, ibid.

84. Bayard Smith herself was more likely to have seen herself as Eleanor Parke Custis Lewis did: "The fear of refusal will never deter me from attempting to serve my friends, I have no idea of that kind of pride. We must risk something, before we can be certain of success in anything" (Lewis to Elizabeth Bordley Gibson, 19 March 1826, in Brady, *Beautiful Nelly,* 174).

85. MBS to JBK, 25 Sept. 1826, MBS Papers.

86. Ibid., 2 July 1815.

87. Ibid., 29 Jan. 1814.

88. Foot, "Gender Dimension," 621; Enloe, *Bananas,* 97.

89. DPTM to Samuel Todd, 31 March 1809, DM Papers, DLC; MBS to JBK, 15 Dec., 24 Nov. 1831, MBS Papers.

90. Carson concurs; see *Ambitious Appetites,* 87. I would go further and question the strictness of separation between work or family life.

91. MBS to JBK, 20 Dec. 1831, MBS Papers.

92. JBK to MBS, 22 Sept. 1816, ibid.

93. Non-kin petitioners also played on the trope of mothers and motherly concerns in their requests for intercession. Phebe Morris, Dolley's "adopted" daughter, approached her patron with a request for a foreign appointment for her father, on the grounds that his health demanded a change of scene.

94. See, for instance, Aronson, *Status and Kinship in the Higher Civil Service.*

95. MBS to JBK, 16 Sept. 1816, MBS Papers.

96. Ibid., undated but clearly written later in Bayard Smith's career.

97. Davidoff and Hall argue that all business or economic enterprises are family businesses, though roles within them are deeply gendered (*Family Fortunes,* 25, 32, 200–211, 215–25, 272–75, 279–89).

4. LOUISA CATHERINE ADAMS CAMPAIGNS
FOR THE PRESIDENCY

1. Boller, *Wives,* 49–51; Caroli, *First Ladies,* 18–19; Truman, *Group Portrait,* 27–29; Sarah Gales Seaton, cited in Jacob, *Elites,* 18; MBS to JBK, 23 Nov. 1817, MBS Papers.

2. Anthony, *Saga,* 102; Boller, *Wives,* 50; Caroli, *First Ladies,* 18; Truman, *Group Portrait,* 27–29; Young, *Washington Community,* 171; JQA, Diary, 7 Nov. 1817, in Adams, *Memoirs* 4:16–17. Some contemporaries of Kortright Monroe's claimed the chief illness she suffered was "queen fever" (Anthony, *Saga,* 98). The sources make it clear that she suffered from severe epilepsy, once almost perishing by falling into a fire (ibid., 102–3).

3. Abner Lacock, former senator from Pennsylvania, loved the idea of canceling the levees (Lacock to James Monroe, 4 June 1821, cited in Cunningham, *James Monroe,* 134–35). The guards were John Quincy Adams's idea (JQA, Diary, 31 Dec. 1819, in Adams, *Memoirs* 6:493–94).

4. Seaton, *William Winston,* 137.

5. There were actually two etiquette wars—in December 1817 and December 1819. During the first, the diplomatic corps complained to James Monroe about issues of diplomatic receiving during levees. President Monroe called a cabinet meeting to discuss the situation and decided to receive the foreign ministers and their families half an hour before the "general company"; then he dispatched John Quincy Adams to inform the ministers. The second etiquette war, the subject of this examination, was among the various branches of the U.S. government. Although it erupted in 1819, the issues and trouble had been brewing since the Monroes took office.

6. JQA, Diary, 5 Jan. 1818, in Adams, *Memoirs* 4:34–35.

7. Ibid., 22 Jan. 1818, pp. 45–46

8. Ibid., 11, 12, 15 Dec. 1818, 16 and 23 Dec. 1819, pp. 188, 189, 192, 479, 487; Seaton, "Diary," Dec. 1819, in Seaton, *William Winston,* 144–45.

9. JQA, Diary, 20 Dec. 1819, in Adams, *Memoirs* 4:481. The two state papers are JQA to James Monroe, 25 Dec. 1819, and JQA to Daniel D. Tompkins, 29 Dec. 1819, ibid., 483–86, 487–91; Louisa Catherine also notes the state papers in her journal (LCA, Journal, 20 Dec. 1819, APM, 265).

10. JQA to James Monroe, 25 Dec. 1819, in Adams, *Memoirs* 4:485.

11. THH to PGH, 14 Jan. 1822, THH Papers, DLC; Seaton, "Diary," in Seaton, *William Winston,* 137.

12. JQA, Diary, 15 Dec. 1818, in Adams, *Memoirs* 4:192; LCA, Journal, 22 Dec. 1819, APM, 265; John Adams to LCA, 13 Jan. 1820, 29 Dec. 1818, APM, 124, 123.

13. See Richard Clough Anderson, Diary, 29 April 1821, Richard Clough Anderson Papers, DLC.

14. LCA, Journal, 29 Nov. 1820, APM, 265; Shepherd, *Cannibals,* 206.

15. Schlesinger, *Political Parties* 1:267. On the role of Congress as kingmaker, see Shepherd, *Cannibals,* 208–9.

16. Watson, *Liberty,* 75, 79.

17. JQA, Diary, 3 Feb. 1819, in Adams, *Memoirs* 4:242; Ames, "Political Newspaper," 76–78.

18. LCA, Journal, 2 March 1821, APM, 265.

19. Young, *Washington City*, 123, 95, 63.

20. Louis McLane to Kitty McLane (wife), 8 Feb. 1822, Louis McLane Papers, DLC; THH to PGH, 14 Dec. 1822, THH Papers, DLC. See also LCA, Journal, 3 May 1820, APM, 265.

21. Peterson, *Triumvirate*, 118.

22. MBS to JBK, 13 Jan. 1825, 13 [June, July, or Aug.] 1820, MBS Papers.

23. MBS to MBB, 14 Jan. 1824, ibid.

24. LCA, Journal, 20 Dec. 1819, APM, 265.

25. Young, *Washington Community*, 217–18; JQA, Diary, 1 March 1819, in Adams, *Memoirs* 4:279–80. See also JQA, Diary, 20 Jan. 1820, p. 509, where John Quincy estimated that he spent a quarter of his time in the "round of receiving and returning visits."

26. Merrill Peterson links socializing with business, and Young calls it a "chore" (Peterson, *New Nation*, 87; Young, *Washington Community*, 47). See also John Adams to LCA, 25 Dec. 1822, APM, 124, where John Adams gracefully commiserated with Louisa Catherine about "so much ceremony."

27. Like many others, Thomas Hubbard was always "swearing off" parties but continued to attend (see THH to PGH, 31 Dec. 1818, 6 Feb. 1819, 23 Nov., 2 Dec. 1821, 5 Jan. 1822, THH Papers, DLC). Margaret Bayard Smith later gave another reason for constant attendance, reporting that Mrs. Clay "is obliged to go to other people's parties, sick or well, for fear of giving offense, a thing more carefully avoided now than ever" (MBS to Susan H. Smith [sister-in-law], Feb. 1828, MBS Papers).

28. For Louisa Catherine Johnson Adams's early years, see Challinor, "Price," which is especially notable for psychological insights into the Johnson home and the anxiety and tension engendered by the family's social ambitions and financial instability. Challinor states that "Louisa could neither live with ambition nor stifle its imperious demands." Challinor presents Louisa Catherine as a woman whose life was ruled by her ambition to marry well, and having achieved that, she took on her husband's ambition (ibid., 9–11). See also Challinor, "Mis-Education."

29. See Ellis, *Passionate Sage*, 44–46.

30. LCA, Journal, 4 March, 29 Nov. 1820, 3 Feb. 1824, 9 Feb. 1820, APM, 265.

31. LCA to JQA, 4 July 1796, JQA to LCA, 31 Jan. 1797, APM, 382, 383. See also Challinor, "Mis-Education," 44.

32. Challinor, "Price," 484–88.

33. JQA, Diary, 17 Dec. 1818, in Adams, *Memoirs* 4:193. See also LCA, Journal, 12 Feb. 1819, APM, 264.

34. W. H. Lyttleton to Charles Bagot, 22 Jan. 1827, cited in Dangerfield, *Era*, 7; Rufus Choate's remark cited in Paullin, "British Diplomats," 251.

35. JQA cited in Shepherd, *Chronicles*, 267–68. John Quincy blamed his "dear mother" for his backwardness in the art of conversation (JQA, Diary, 15 July 1820, in Adams, *Memoirs* 5:165).

36. Cited in Bashkina et al., *Relations*.

37. Margaret Bayard Smith also vetted Louisa Catherine approvingly, as "a woman of fine talents" (MBS to JBK, 28 Dec. 1818, MBS Papers).

38. For Louisa Catherine Johnson Adams's work in the Russian court, see Allgor, "LCA in Russia," 15–43; Butterfield, "Dragon-Killer," 171; Shepherd, *Cannibals*, 212–13.

39. Louisa Catherine's childhood memories comprise a large part of her memoir "Record of My Life," unpaginated, APM, 265.

40. LCA, Journal, 12 Feb. 1819, APM, 264; Shepherd, *Cannibals*, 207.

41. See also Anthony, *Saga*, 107; Jacob, *Elites*, 34–35; Parsons, "Louisa," 89.

42. JQA, Diary, 27 Dec. 1819, in Adams, *Memoirs* 4:493; Young, *Washington Community*, 175.

43. JQA, Diary, 20 Dec. 1819, in Adams, *Memoirs* 4:481.

44. JQA to James Monroe, 25 Dec. 1819, and to Daniel D. Tompkins, 29 Dec. 1819, ibid., 483–86, 487–91.

45. JQA to Daniel D. Tompkins, 29 Dec. 1819, ibid., 488.

46. See Butterfield, "Dragon-Killer," 165, 170–72. Butterfield was an early and appreciative admirer of Louisa Catherine's political efforts. See also Challinor, "Price," 268–72, 290–92; Corbett, "Anguished," 75–76, 79; Shepherd, *Cannibals*, 207–15; Anthony, *Saga*, 106–8, 109–11; Boller, *Wives*, 57; Caroli, *First Ladies*, 20–24, 279; Parsons, "Louisa," 83, 86–87, 89–92; Truman, *Group Portrait*, 280.

47. LCA, Journal, 14 Dec. 1819, APM, 265; ibid., 1823, cited in Shepherd, *Cannibals*, 239.

48. JQA, Diary, 25 Feb. 1821, in Adams, *Memoirs* 5:297–98.

49. Shepherd, *Cannibals*, 226; LCA to JQA, 28 June 1822, JQA to LCA, 10 and 15 July 1822, cited in ibid.

50. Joseph Hopkinson to LCA, Jan. 1823, in Adams, *Memoirs* 6:130–32.

51. JQA to Joseph Hopkinson, 23 Jan. 1823, ibid., 132–37.

52. LCA, Journal, 22 Dec. 1819, APM, 265.

53. Ibid., 20 Dec. 1819, 19 Feb. 1819, 24 Dec. 1819, APM, 265, 264, 265.

54. Ibid., 23 Jan. 1821, APM, 265.

55. Ibid., 25 March 1819, 3 Feb. 1820, 7 Jan., 8 March 1821, APM, 265.

56. Cunningham, *James Monroe*, 136–37; LCA, Journal, 14 Dec. 1819, APM, 265.

57. John Adams, among others, thought it "not strange to say that your evenings are made party questions for everything relative to you and yours must be" (Adams to LCA, 13 Jan. 1820, APM, 124).

58. THH to PGH, 21[?] Jan. 1818, THH Papers, DLC. When Louisa Catherine attended the French minister's ball, she made it clear that she and Mr. Adams went "as guests, it being impossible for us to be subscribers" (LCA, Journal, 26 Feb. 1819, APM, 264). See also Louis McLane to Kitty McLane, 1 Jan. 1822, Louis McLane Papers, DLC.

59. Harrison Otis mentions her Tuesdays as regular events (HGO to SFO, 29 Nov. 1820, HGO Papers).

60. WCR to JWR, 17 Dec. 1824, WCR Papers, DLC; John Adams to LCA, 29 Dec. 1818, APM, 123. For the role of specialized etiquette skills and entertaining and eating rituals in the creation of a ruling elite, see Elias, *Civility*, 306–7.

61. Rosalie Stier Calvert to Isabelle Stier van Havre, 5 Nov. 1806, in Callcott, *Riversdale*, 150; HGO to SFO, 5 Dec. 1818, HGO Papers. See also Margaret Hall to her sister, 19 Jan. 1828, Margaret Hall Papers, DLC.

62. LCA to JQA, 10 June 1804, cited in Shepherd, *Cannibals*, 194. See also John Davis to Eliza Bancroft Davis (wife), 15 Dec. 1825, John Davis Papers, MHS; THH to PGH, 26 Dec. 1822, THH Papers, DLC.

63. Louisa Catherine insisted her husband decline an invitation to dine with William Crawford on a Tuesday night but was willing to preside alone under certain circumstances, such as when "Mr. A." dined at the president's (LCA, Journal, 17 Jan. 1820, 20 Dec. 1819, APM, 265).

64. This description of John Quincy is part of a longer description from Louisa Cather-

ine's play, written in the White House, "The Metropolitan Kaleidoscope, or Varieties of Winter Etchings," by "Rachel Barb," 18 Dec. 1827, APM 274.

65. Teute, "Roman Matron," 111. See also Schneider, "Adams's Ball," 12–13.

66. Truman, *Governmental Process*, 265. Richard L. Bushman discussed "personal sociability" as one of the qualifications in the "right to rule" enjoyed by the privileged in his lecture at Historic Deerfield, 6 July 1995.

67. Louis McLane to Kitty McLane, 4 Jan. 1822, Louis McLane Papers, DLC; WCR to JWR, 17 Dec. 1823, WCR Papers, DLC.

68. LCA, Journal, 21 Nov. 1820, 12 March 1821, APM, 265.

69. Ibid., 24 March 1821, 29 Jan. 1820, 7 Feb. 1823.

70. Ibid., 10 Feb., 23 Jan. 1823.

71. Ibid., 20 Feb. 1819. This was the Transcontinental Treaty of 1819.

72. Examples from John Quincy's diary: 19 Dec. 1817, 22 Jan., 11 April, 9, 10, 11, 12, Dec. 1818, 18 March 1819, APM, 33; LCA, Journal, 23 Jan. 1823, APM, 265; JA to LCA, 13 Jan. 1820, APM, 124.

73. LCA, Journal, 13 Feb., 23 Dec. 1823, 21 May, 5 Dec. 1820, APM, 265.

74. Young, *Washington Community*, 226; LCA, Journal, 13 Dec. 1820, 3 Jan. 1824, APM, 265; Stephen Pearse to wife, 9 Dec. 1824, Everett-Peabody Papers, MHS. In 1822 William Lee noted that "Mr. Adams is rising greatly" (cited in Mann, *Yankee*, 203).

75. Louisa Catherine Adams began her 1818 journal with the slight paraphrase from William Shakespeare's *As You Like It* 2.7.139–40. The quotation appears repeatedly in much correspondence from Washington City to the homefolks.

76. John Adams to LCA, 17 Dec. 1822, APM, 124; LCA, Journal, 4 Dec. 1823, APM, 265.

77. LCA, Journal, 6 Dec. 1823, APM, 265.

78. Ibid., 19 Dec., 20 Dec. 1823.

79. Schneider, "Adams's Ball," 2. One of Louisa Catherine's nieces, Abigail Adams, was visiting during this time and helped with preparations for the Jackson Ball. Her diary, since lost, furnished material for an 1871 article in *Harper's Bazaar* and the discussion in Anne Hollingsworth Wharton's *Social Life in the Early Republic.* Edith P. Mayo of the Smithsonian Institution helped me find a copy of Schneider, "Adams's Ball."

80. Sophia Otis to SFO (mother), 6 Jan. 1820, HGO Papers.

81. Among many others, Benjamin Ruggles discussed the possibility that the election would go to the House (Ruggles to Thomas Worthington, 20 Jan. 1823, Thomas Worthington Collection, Ohio Historical Society).

82. JQA, Diary, 6 Jan. 1824, in Adams, *Memoirs* 6:228.

83. LCA, Journal, 13 Dec. 1827, APM, 265. Scholars differ on the number of invitations sent, because of confusion over how many people were included on a single invitation. Louisa Catherine indicated that "five hundred were struck off" at the printers (ibid., 20 Dec. 1823). Most scholars agree on the final count of about a thousand actual attendees.

84. Ibid., 22 Dec. 1823; Schneider, "Adams's Ball," 5–6. For the involvement of guests and hosts as both performers and audience, all engaged in the task of presenting the most gracious, pleasing self, see Bushman, *Refinement*, 51–58.

85. Kasson, *Rudeness*, 169; Bushman, *Refinement*, 132. See also Kasson, *Rudeness*, 50, 93–96, for houses and objects as social stabilizers.

86. LCA, Journal, 28 Feb. 1823, APM, 265; Charles Francis Adams, Diary, 4 and 6 Jan. 1824, in DiPace and Donald, *Diary of C. F. Adams*, 33–34; Wharton, *Social Life*, 212.

87. Charles Francis Adams, Diary, 4 and 6 Jan. 1824, in DiPace and Donald, *Diary of C. F. Adams*, 32, 33; LCA, Journal, 27 Dec. 1823, APM, 265.

88. LCA, Journal, 8 Dec., 28 Feb. 1823, APM, 265; Wharton, *Social Life*, 212; Schneider, "Adams's Ball," 9. Harrison Gray Otis reported John Quincy Adams's waltzing ability to his wife, but he did not see John Quincy on the floor; Louisa Catherine told him about it (HGO to SFO, 11 Dec. 1818, HGO Papers).

89. John Ogg, *Washington Republican*, 4 Jan. 1824.

90. Schneider, "Adams's Ball," 10; John Clagett Proctor, "John Quincy Adams Was Brilliant in the Social Sphere," *Sunday Star* (Washington), 28 June 1936 (citing as his source a local newspaper); LCA, Journal, 23 Jan. 1824, APM, 265.

91. Charles Francis Adams, Diary, 8 Jan. 1824, in DiPace and Donald, *Diary of C. F. Adams*, 34; Wharton, *Social Life*, 212.

92. Charles Frances Adams, Diary, 8 Jan. 1824, in DiPace and Donald, *Diary of C. F. Adams*, 34; Phoebe Morris to DPTM, 19 Jan. 1824, cited in Cutts, *Life*, 169–70; *Harper's*, "Mrs. John Quincy," 166–67. Schneider contends that "steel provided a discreet replacement for the twinkle of diamonds, which had become dangerous in Revolutionary times" (Schneider, "Adams's Ball," 9–10).

93. LCA, Journal, 8 Jan. 1824, APM, 265; Shepherd, *Cannibals*, 244.

94. Guests left with stomachs full of delicacies and memories of the Adamses standing together on the threshold (Schneider, "Adams's Ball," 12).

95. LCA, Journal, 8 Jan. 1824, APM, 265.

96. Lockwood, *Yesterdays*, 204; Schneider, "Adams's Ball," 12.

97. Schneider, "Adams's Ball," 8–9, 13.

98. Carson, *Ambitious Appetites*, 59.

99. One example among many, William Rives declared "it almost certain that Mr. Adams will be elected" (WCR to JWR, 31 Jan. 1825, WCR Papers, DLC).

100. Dangerfield, *Era*, 336; Remini, *American Freedom*, 83.

101. See Dangerfield, *Era*, 336; Remini, *American Freedom*, 83.

102. Shepherd, *Cannibals*, 251; MBS to JBK, 25 Feb. 1825, MBS Papers; Dangerfield, *Awakening*, 227.

103. Dangerfield, *Era*, 342.

104. MBS to JBK, 25 Feb. 1825, MBS Papers.

105. Dangerfield, *Era*, 332–35.

106. JQA, Diary, 9 and 29 Jan. 1825, 31 Aug. 1824, APM, 38. See also Bemis, *JQA and the Union*, 33–34; Dangerfield, *Era*, 344–45; Remini, *American Freedom*, 85–86.

107. Nagel, *Descent*, 144.

108. Van Rensselaer was a guest at an Adams dinner party and attended Tuesday soirees as well (LCA, Journal, 9 Jan. 1823, APM, 265).

109. Young, *Washington Community*, 135.

110. See Oliver, *Portraits*, 94, 108–11, 102–4; Shepherd, *Chronicles*, 272; Shepherd, *Cannibals*, 215.

111. Shields and Teute, "Court."

5. THE FALL OF ANDREW JACKSON'S CABINET

1. Shepherd, *Cannibals*, 253–55, 258–59.

2. See ibid., 259–69. Louisa Catherine had predicted that her husband's election would "put me in a prison" (LCA, Journal, 19 Feb. 1823, APM, 265).

3. See Watson, *Liberty*, 73–95; Remini, *Election*.

4. Watson, *Liberty*, 93, 104; Challinor, "Price," 249; Shepherd, *Cannibals*, 302–3. See also Miles, "President Adams' Billiard Table."

5. Cited in Watson, *Liberty,* 91.

6. "John Quincy Adams's Message to Congress, 1825," cited in ibid., 83–84.

7. Everett, "Conduct," 5; Henry Clay, cited in Ward, *Symbol,* 187; Watson, *Liberty,* 91–92; Niven, *Calhoun,* 131.

8. Watson, *Liberty,* 92. See also Basch, "Morals"; Owsley, "Marriages of Rachel Donelson."

9. Watson, *Liberty,* 94–95.

10. MBS to J. Bayard H. Smith (son), 25 Feb. 1829, MBS Papers. The "fear-ants'" worries turned out to be overrated (Watson, *Liberty,* 103–4; see also Aronson, *Status*).

11. Cited in Marszalek, *Affair,* 57; Daniel Webster to Ezekiel Webster (brother), 23 Feb. 1829, cited in ibid., 58.

12. MBS to JBK, 12 Jan. 1829, MBS Papers.

13. For the background of Jackson's cabinet, see Wood, "Woman," annotated draft version.

14. John Floyd, governor of Virginian and Calhoun partisan, cited in Watson, *Liberty,* 101. "Millennium of minnows" was a phrase coined by a disappointed newspaper reporter (MBS to MBB, 15 March 1829, MBS Papers).

15. ME, *Autobiography,* 209–10. In her autobiography, published fifty-two years after her death, Margaret spelled her birth name "O'Neil." Though her editors may have made the change (John F. Marszalek attributes it to a printer's error, uncorrected before Margaret's death [*Affair,* 245 n. 7]), Margaret might indeed have wanted to adopt this Anglicized version in her desire to appear upper class and not Irish. I use the spelling "O'Neale" because the name appears that way in two deeds signed by her father in the office of the Recorder of Deeds of the District of Columbia. She is known to history as "Peggy Eaton," but neither name is suitable for her designation here. Using Eaton by itself is ahistorical, especially because she had different surnames at other points in her life. "Peggy," too, is a dilemma. In her autobiography she insisted that no one ever called her that; the only nickname she recalled was an occasional use of "Madge," by her mother. But Margaret's memory and interpretation of events in this work prove selective; because her goal was to present herself as a refined member of a rising upper class (and, once again, not Irish), she might have been lying about the frequency of the usage of Peggy. But a subject's personal preference is important, and because she was legally Margaret, no matter which last name she used, Margaret she is here. Her latest biographer, John F. Marszalek, has also made the choice to render her Margaret, based on her stated preference. He also contends that "calling her Peggy played into the preconceptions of the events of which she was a part" (Marszalek, *Affair,* xi–xii).Indeed, the only uses of Peggy I have encountered among the primary sources are derogatory and dismissive, and I agree that the name plays into stereotypes of class, gender, ethnicity, and occupation.

16. ME, *Autobiography,* 11, 13–17.

17. Poore, *Perley's* 1:122. See also Pollack, *Democracy's,* 271–75; ME, *Autobiography,* 20–22.

18. John Eaton's first wife was Myra Lewis Eaton, the sister of Jackson adviser and promoter William B. Lewis and adoptive daughter to Rachel Jackson.

19. AJ to Rachel Jackson, 21 Dec. 1823, AJ Papers; AJ to Ezra Stiles Ely, 23 March 1829, cited in Parton, *Life* 3:186–91.

20. Pollack, *Democracy's,* 59; MBS to JBK, Jan. 1829, MBS Papers. For Timberlake's illnesses and cutting of his own throat, see Marszalek, *Affair,* 42–43; ME, *Autobiography,* 37–38.

21. John Eaton to AJ, 7 Dec. 1828, cited in Remini, *Election,* 162.

22. ME, *Autobiography,* 70; MBS to JBK, Jan. 1829, MBS Papers; Churchill Cambreleng to

Martin Van Buren, 1 Jan. 1829, Martin Van Buren Papers, DLC; Louis McLane to James A. Bayard, 19 Feb. 1829, Bayard Papers, DLC. The household implement in question was a chamberpot.

23. "Narrative by Major William B. Lewis," 25 Oct. 1859, cited in Parton, *Life* 3:160–61; ME, *Autobiography*, 83.

24. MBS, "Inaugurations," 116.

25. Ibid., 116–17. For the eyewitness version, see MBS to JBK, 11 March 1829, MBS Papers. See also Henry Clay's description, cited in Dangerfield, *Era*, 424.

26. Levi Woodbury to Elizabeth Woodbury (wife), quoting Virgil Maxcy, 29 Nov. 1829, Levi Woodbury Collection, DLC.

27. Ezra Stiles Ely to AJ, 18 March 1829, cited in Marszalek, *Affair*, 78.

28. AJ to Ezra Stiles Ely, 23 March 1829, cited in Parton, *Life* 3:186–91. See also AJ to Richard K. Call, 5 July 1829, AJ Papers.

29. AJ to Ezra Stiles Ely, 3 Sept. 1829, AJ Papers; Parton, *Life* 3:203–6.

30. Van Buren, *Autobiography*, 352–54; Bowers, *Party*, 121–22; Miller, *Scandals*, 122.

31. Farrell, "Bellona," 479; JQA, Diary, 6 Feb. 1830, in Adams, *Memoirs* 8:185–86; "eyewitness account" cited in Furman, *Profile*, 108.

32. John Davis to Eliza Bancroft Davis, 23 Dec. 1829, John Davis Papers, AAS.

33. Pollack, *Democracy's*, 112.

34. Nevin, "To the President," 94–96.

35. For Richard M. Johnson's own domestic situation, which certainly sensitized him to sticky situations, see Marszalek, *Affair*, 116.

36. "Memorandum in Jackson's Handwriting," 29 Jan. 1830, in Bassett, *Correspondence*, 4:123–24; AJ to Andrew Jackson Donelson, 5 Aug. 1829, cited in ibid., 323–26; Phillips, *Eaton*, 72, 84, 95–97; Watson, *Liberty*, 102.

37. Warren Dutton to Elizabeth Lowell Dutton, 21 Feb. 1831, Russell Family Papers, MHS.

38. Marszalek, *Affair*, 124.

39. Benjamin Williams Crowninshield to Henry Dearborn, 4 Jan. 1830, Benjamin Williams Crowninshield Papers, DLC.

40. JQA, Diary, 6 Feb. 1830, in Adams, *Memoirs* 8:185; James Gordon Bennett, cited in Pollack, *Democracy's*, 122.

41. From the *New York Courier*, cited in *Niles' Register* 40 (7 May 1831): 165.

42. Van Buren, *Autobiography*, 348–50.

43. ME, *Autobiography*, 91, 65.

44. John C. Calhoun, "Reply to Mr. Eaton," was widely printed, see among others: *National Daily Intelligencer* (Washington), 31 Oct. 1831; Van Buren, *Autobiography*, 250.

45. Van Buren, *Autobiography*, 407–8.

46. Calhoun, "Reply."

47. Bushman, *Refinement*, 412–13.

48. Carson, *Ambitious*, 16; John Varnum to Leverett Saltonstall, 12 Jan. 1826, Varnum Family Papers II, MHS.

49. John Varnum to Leverett Saltonstall, 12 Jan. 1826, Varnum Family Papers II, MHS; Bushman, *Refinement*, 237.

50. Richard L. Bushman, lecture at Historic Deerfield, 6 July 1995.

51. Willie Person Mangum to Charity Mangum (wife), 11 Dec. 1825, Willie Person Mangum Papers, DLC.

52. WCR, Journal, 3, 5 Jan. 1817, WCR to JWR, 10 Dec. 1827, WCR Papers, DLC.

53. *Niles' Register* 15 (16 Jan. 1819): 387.

54. *Metropolitan* (Washington), 29 Feb. 1820.

55. Cooley, *Etiquette*, 21.

56. *Metropolitan* (Washington), 29 Feb. 1820.

57. Nimrod, *Fudge*, 44. For John Randolph's story of a "four pronged silver fork," see LCA, Journal, 30 March 1820, APM, 265; for the meanings of forks, see Carson, *Ambitious*, 65–73; for Andrew Jackson's four-pronged silver forks and two-pronged steel forks, see Ellet, *Court Circles*, 148.

58. *Metropolitan* (Washington), 29 Feb. 1820; Nimrod, *Fudge*, 4.

59. WCR to JWR, 10 Dec. 1827, 12 April 1828, WCR Papers, DLC. See also ibid., 30 April 1828.

60. John Davis to Elizabeth Bancroft Davis (wife), 8 Dec. 1825, John Davis Papers, AAS; WCR to JWR, 14 Dec. 1824, WCR Papers, DLC.

61. John Varnum to Leverett Saltonstall, 2 Feb. 1827, Varnum Family Papers II, MHS.

62. WCR to JWR, 7 Dec. 1828, WCR Papers, DLC; MBS to MBB, 20[?] Dec. 1828, MBS Papers.

63. MBS to MBB, Spring 1829, MBS Papers.

64. Marszalek, *Affair*, 112; MBS to JBK, 26 Jan. 1830, MBS Papers.

65. On gossip, see Spacks, *Gossip*; Demos, *Entertaining*; Kamensky, *Governing the Tongue*; Norton, "Defamation"; Freeman, "Slander"; Dunbar, *Grooming*.

66. Spacks, *Gossip*, 3, 19.

67. Ibid., 5, 8, 13, 207, 261. See also ibid., 20; Demos, *Entertaining*, 305–6; Freeman, "Slander," 36; Gelles, *Portia*, 72; Elias, *Civility*, 304.

68. See Freeman, "Slander," 29–30; Spacks, *Gossip*, 6, 262; Gelles, *Portia*, 82; Shields and Teute, "Jefferson," 6; see also Shields and Teute, "Court."

69. Spacks, *Gossip*, 6, 15, 21–22; Freeman, "Slander," 49, 57.

70. Gelles, *Portia*, 83; Spacks, *Gossip*, 11, 262, 123–24.

71. Spacks, *Gossip*, 15, 22, 34; Norton, "Defamation," 6, 36; Gelles, *Portia*, 79. See also Janeway, *Powers of the Weak*; Scott, *Weapons of the Weak*.

72. Spacks, *Gossip*, 50; Norton, "Defamation," 37.

73. The *Baltimore American* sternly upheld the stricture against printing female names(cited in *Niles' Register* 5 [April 1828]: 34, 100).

74. John Wallace Barry to Susan Taylor, 19 April 1831, cited in Marszalek, *Affair*, 163; *Niles' Register* 40 (23 April 1831): 142; *Providence (R.I.) Journal*, cited in *Daily National Intelligencer* (Washington), 5 May 1831.

75. *Norfolk (Va.) Herald*, cited in *Daily National Intelligencer* (Washington), 5 May 1831; *National Journal* (Washington), 26 July 1831.

76. Bradley N. Cummings, Journal, 25, 28 June 1831, Bradley N. Cummings Papers, MHS; *New York Commercial Advertiser*, cited in *National Journal* (Washington), 24 June 1831.

77. *Norfolk Herald*, cited in *Daily National Intelligencer* (Washington), 5 May 1831; Andrew Jackson Donelson to John Branch, 29 May 1831, cited in Marszalek, *Affair*, 177.

78. See Wood, "Woman."

79. *National Journal* (Washington), 10, 28 June 1831; *Rhode Island American and Gazette* (Providence), 9 Aug. 1831, cited in Marszalek, *Affair*, 181; John Branch's letter published in *National Journal* (Washington), 20 May 1831.

80. Rousseau, cited in Pateman, "Disorder," 20, 25.

81. *National Journal* (Washington), 17 June 1831. See also ibid., 10, 21 June 1831.

82. AJ to Andrew Jackson Donelson, 10 July 1831, cited in Bassett, *Correspondence* 4:311;

Rhode Island American and Gazette (Providence), 9 Aug. 1831, cited in Marszalek, *Affair*, 181; Wood, "Woman," 27.

83. Samuel D. Ingham to Editor, *Nashville Republican*, 26 Aug. 1831; John C. Calhoun, cited in Wood, "Woman," 27; Duff Green to Andrew Jackson Donelson, 15 July 1830, cited in Marszalek, *Affair*, 150.

84. MBS to JBK, 26 Jan. 1830, MBS Papers.

85. Pollack, *Democracy's*, 195; ME, *Autobiography*, 146. See also Wood, "Woman," 28.

86. Marszalek, *Affair*, 178.

87. Ibid., 169; Samuel D. Ingham to Editor, *Niles' Register*, 28 May 1831; *Nashville Republican*, 22 Aug., 16 Sept. 1831; *Washington Globe*, 14, 25 July 1831; Bassett, *Correspondence* 4:163–64.

88. *National Daily Intelligencer* (Washington), 23 July 1831.

89. Ellet, *Court Circles*, 164–65.

90. For court customs, favors, and notions of individual "worth," see Elias, *Civility*, 271.

91. *Born to Command: King Andrew the First*, in Hess and Kaplan, *Ungentlemanly*, pl. II–23, p. 68; *National Daily Intelligencer* (Washington), 27 June 1831.

92. Elkanah Hogg (pseud.), *The Lay of the First Minstrel, or The Court of King Andrew the First* (New York: Sampson Veto, Printer to His Majesty, 1834), 6–7, 13, 44–47 (the publication information is part of the joke); Botsford, *Reign of Reform* (published a year and a half or so before the Eaton affair was publicly discussed).

93. For Rachel Robards Jackson's situation, see Basch, "Morals," 892–93. See also Marszalek, *Affair*, 181.

94. "Exhibition of Cabinet Pictures," item number E98, Political Cartoon Collection, AAS. The titles of the "Pictures" include "She Would If She Could," "Innkeeper's Daughter," "Beware a Bad Name," "Provoked Husband," "Family Quarrels," "School for Husbands," "Love's Frailties," "Fraternal Discord," and "Guilty or Not Guilty."

95. Another cartoon which scholars often mention in connection with "Peggy Eaton" is one called "The Celeste-al Cabinet" (item number C392, Political Cartoon Collection, AAS), which depicts a popular French dancer of the day, Madame Celeste, performing before Jackson's cabinet. But this cartoon dates from 1836, long after the Eaton affair, and probably only serves to illuminate the characters of the men watching, especially Van Buren, who stood for president that year. See also Reilly, *Political Prints*, 79–81.

96. Halttunen, *Painted Women*, 191; Grund, *Aristocracy*, 54.

97. Trollope, *Domestic Manners*, 194–95, 133; Carson, *Ambitious*, 11; Martin, *Common Courtesy*, 4.

98. MBS, *Gentility*, 140.

99. A gentleman, *Laws of Etiquette*, 9–11.

100. Bushman, *Refinement*, xv.

101. Wood, "Woman," 15–16.

102. Bushman, *Refinement*, 208.

103. MBS to JBK, 29 Aug. 1831, MBS Papers; newspapers and eyewitness accounts cited in Marszalek, *Affair*, 107–8.

104. MBS to JBK, 27 Nov. 1829, MBS Papers.

105. Kasson, *Rudeness*, 7; Davidoff, *Best Circles*, 17.

106. Marszalek, *Affair*, 52.

107. MBS to JBK, 29 Aug. 1831, MBS Papers. John Marszalek agrees that people fell in with the boycott not because they necessarily believed the rumors but because they obeyed "proper societal procedure" (*Affair*, 101).

108. Eliza Johnston to Henry Clay, 12 Dec. 1829, in Hopkins, *Henry Clay* 8:135.

109. Pollack, *Democracy's*, 211.

110. MBS to JBK, 29 Aug. 1831, 11 Nov. 1830, 20 March 1831, MBS Papers. See also Ellet, *Court Circles*, 170, 196–97, for contrasting exclusiveness and democracy at the Jackson White House.

111. LCA, Journal, 30 Nov. 1823, APM, 265; Wood, "Woman," 48; MBS, *First Forty*, 327. For the role of "disinterested women" in party politics and the development of nationalism, see Waldstreicher, *Fetes*, 232–42, and Rosemarie Zagarri's *Petticoat Government: Women and American Politics, 1789–1828* (forthcoming).

112. Emily Donelson, cited in Wood, "Woman," 23.

113. Teute, "Roman Matron," 116.

114. Jacob, *Elites*, explores how the postwar Washington community fulfilled that potential.

CONCLUSION

1. Grund, *Aristocracy*, 300.

2. Mickey Edwards, interview, "All Things Considered," National Public Radio, 14 Feb. 1997.

3. Varon, "Tippecanoe," 517–18, 519; Varon, *Mean to Be*, 77–78, 99. On the power of the everyday in creating global forces, see Holt, "Marking," 7–8, 10.

4. Fox-Genovese, "Placing Women's History in History," 14–15; Kelly-Gadol, "Social Relations of the Sexes"; Scott, "Gender," 48, 49.

5. Foot, "Gender Dimension," 621. See also Rosenberg, "Gender," 124. On moving politics beyond voting, see Gilmore, *Gender and Jim Crow*.

6. Ulrich, *Midwife's Tale*, 9. For recent examinations of Bayard Smith's papers, fiction, and professional writings, see Teute, "Wild," 51; Teute, "In 'the Gloom of Evening.'" In addition, two full-length studies are forthcoming by Teute and Rose Barquist.

7. Ellet, *Court Circles*, iii.

8. LCA, "Adventures," APM, 269.

Bibliography

PRIMARY SOURCES

Manuscripts

Adams Family Papers Project, Massachu-
  setts Historical Society, Boston
Adams Papers Manuscript on microfilm
American Antiquarian Society, Worcester,
  Massachusetts
  John Davis Papers
  Sophia May Papers
Dumbarton House, Washington, D.C.
  Dolley Madison Collection
Library of Congress, Manuscript Division
  (District Branch), Washington, D.C.
  Richard Clough Anderson Papers
  Bayard Papers
  Benjamin Williams Crowninshield
    Papers
  Cutts Collection
  Cutts Family Miscellany
  Job Durfee Papers
  Augustus John Foster Papers
  Margaret Hall Papers
  Thomas Hubbard Collection
  Andrew Jackson Papers
  Thomas Law Papers
  Duncan McArthur Papers
  Louis McLane Papers
  Dolley Madison Papers
  James Madison Papers
  Willie Person Mangum Papers
  Milnor Papers

Catharine Akerly Mitchill Papers
Job Pierson Papers
William Plumer Papers
Sarah Ridg Papers
William Cabell Rives Papers
John Smith Collection
Margaret Bayard Smith Papers
Martin Van Buren Papers
Levi Woodbury Collection
Maryland Historical Society, Baltimore
  David Baillie Warden Papers
  Wirt Family Papers
Massachusetts Historical Society, Boston
  Bulfinch Collection
  Bradley N. Cummings Papers
  Cutts-Madison Collection
  Dwight-Howard Collection
  Everett-Peabody Papers
  Harrison Gray Otis Family Papers
  Russell Family Papers
  Varnum Family Papers II
New-York Historical Society, New York
  Albert Gallatin Papers
  Benjamin Latrobe Papers
  Paulding Letters
New York Public Library, New York
  Benjamin Latrobe Papers
Ohio Historical Society, Columbus
  Thomas Worthington Collection

PUBLISHED PRIMARY SOURCES

Books and Pamphlets

Adams, Charles Francis. *The Diary of Charles Francis Adams, 1820–1829.* Ed. Aida DiPace and
  David Donald. Cambridge, Mass., 1964.

Adams, John Quincy. *Memoirs of John Quincy Adams*. Ed. Charles Francis Adams. Philadelphia, 1875.

——. *The Writings of John Quincy Adams*. Ed. Worthington Chauncey Ford. New York, 1917.

Calvert, Rosalie Stier. *Mistress of Riversdale: The Plantation Letters of Rosalie Stier Calvert*. Ed. and trans. Margaret Law Callcott. Baltimore, 1991.

Clay, Henry. *The Papers of Henry Clay*. Ed. James F. Hopkins et al. Lexington, Ky., 1959–.

Crowninshield, Mary Boardman. *Letters of Mary Boardman Crowninshield*. Ed. Francis Boardman Crowninshield. Cambridge, Mass., 1935.

Cutts, Lucia B. *Memoirs and Letters of Dolly Madison, Wife of James Madison, President of the United States*. Boston, 1886.

Eaton, Margaret. *The Autobiography of Peggy Eaton*. New York, 1932.

Everett, Alexander H. *Conduct of the Administration*. Pamphlet reprinted from the Boston *Daily Advertiser and Patriot*. American Antiquarian Society.

Gerry, Elbridge, Jr. *Diary of Elbridge Gerry, Jr.* New York, 1927.

Grund, Francis J. *Aristocracy in America: From the Sketchbook of a German Nobleman*. New York, 1959.

Hamilton, Alexander. *The Papers of Alexander Hamilton*. Ed. Harold C. Syrett and Jacob E. Cooke. New York, 1961–87.

Jackson, Andrew. *The Correspondence of Andrew Jackson*. Ed. John Spencer Bassett. Washington, D.C., 1926–33.

Jefferson, Thomas. *The Anas of Thomas Jefferson, 1791–1809*. Ed. Franklin B. Sawvel. New York, 1903.

——. *Autobiography*. In *The Complete Jefferson*. Ed. Saul K. Padover. New York, 1943.

——. *The Family Letters of Thomas Jefferson*. Ed. Edwin Morris Betts and James A. Bear. Columbia, Mo., 1966.

——. *Notes on the State of Virginia*. In *The Life and Selected Writings of Thomas Jefferson*. Ed. Adrienne Koch and William Peden. New York, 1944.

——. *Papers of Thomas Jefferson*. Ed. Julian P. Boyd et al. Princeton, N.J., 1950–.

——. *The Portable Thomas Jefferson*. Ed. Merrill D. Peterson. New York, 1984.

——. *The Writings of Thomas Jefferson*. Ed. Paul Leicester Ford. New York, 1892–99.

King, Rufus. *The Life and Correspondence of Rufus King*. Ed. Charles R. King. New York, 1897.

Lee, William. *A Yankee Jeffersonian: Selections from the Diary and Letters of William Lee of Massachusetts*. Ed. Mary Lee Mann. Cambridge, Mass., 1958.

Lewis, Eleanor Parke Custis. *George Washington's Beautiful Nelly: The Letters of Eleanor Parke Custis Lewis to Elizabeth Bordley Gibson, 1794–1851*. Ed. Patricia Brady. New York, 1991.

Madison, James. *The Papers of James Madison: Presidential Series*. Ed. Robert A. Rutland et al. Charlottesville, Va., 1984–.

Melish, John. *Travels through the United States of America*. Philadelphia, 1812.

Moore, Thomas. *Epistles, Odes, and Other Poems*. Philadelphia, 1806.

——. *Memoirs, Journal, and Correspondence*. Ed. Lord John Russell. London, 1853–56.

Plumer, William. *William Plumer's Memorandum of Proceedings in the United States Senate, 1803–1807*. Ed. Everett S. Brown. New York, 1969.

Poore, Ben. Perley. *Perley's Reminiscences of Sixty Years in the National Metropolis*. Philadelphia, 1886.

Smith, Margaret Bayard. *The First Forty Years of Washington Society*. Ed. Gaillard Hunt. New York, 1906.

Story, William W., ed. *Life and Letters of Joseph Story*. Boston, 1851.

Trumbull, John. *The Autobiography of Colonel John Trumbull, Patriot-Artist, 1756–1843*. Ed. Theodore Sizer. New Haven, 1953.

United States Congress. *American State Papers*. Washington, D.C., 1832–61. Class IX: Claims. 1st Congress, 2d session–17th Congress, 5 Feb. 1790–3 March 1823.

Washington, George. *The Writings of George Washington.* Ed. John C. Fitzpatrick. Washington, D.C., 1931–44.

Articles

Bagot, Mary. "'Exile in Yankeeland': The Journal of Mary Bagot, 1816–1819." Ed. David Hosford. *Records of the Columbia Historical Society of Washington* 51 (1984): 30–50.

Bigelow, Abijah. "Letters of Abijah Bigelow, Member of Congress to His Wife, 1810–1815." *American Antiquarian Society Proceedings* 40 (15 Oct. 1930): 305–406.

Crowninshield, Mary Boardman. "Some Letters of Mary Boardman Crowninshield." Ed. Margaret Pardee Bates. *Essex Institute of Historical Collections* 83 (1947): 112–42.

Few, Frances. "The Diary of Frances Few." Ed. Noble E. Cunningham, Jr. *Journal of Southern History* 29 (Feb–Nov. 1963): 345–61.

Mitchill, Catharine. "Catharine Mitchill's Letters from Washington, 1806–1812." Ed. Carolyn Hoover Sung. *Quarterly Journal of the Library of Congress* 34:3 (July 1977): 171–89.

Mitchill, Samuel Latham. "Dr. Mitchill's Letters from Washington, 1801–1813." *Harper's New Monthly Magazine* 58:347 (April 1879): 740–55.

Ogg, John. In *Washington Republican,* 4 Jan. 1824. Massachusetts Historical Society.

Newspapers and Periodicals and Political Cartoons

Metropolitan. Washington, D.C. American Antiquarian Society.

Nashville (Tenn.) Republican. American Antiquarian Society.

National Intelligencer. Washington, D.C. American Antiquarian Society and Massachusetts Historical Society.

National Journal. Washington, D.C. American Antiquarian Society.

Niles' Register. Vols. 5, 15, 16, 24, 28, 37, 40. American Antiquarian Society and Massachusetts Historical Society.

Sunday Star. Washington, D.C. American Antiquarian Society.

Washington (D.C.) Globe. American Antiquarian Society.

Washington (D.C.) Republican, 4 Jan. 1824. Massachusetts Historical Society.

Political Cartoons Collection, American Antiquarian Society.
   "The Celeste-al Cabinet." Item no. C392.
   "Exhibition of Cabinet Pictures." Item no. E98.
   "Rats leaving a falling house." Item no. R233.
   ".00001 The value of a unit with four cyphers going before it." Item no. V214.

SECONDARY WORKS

Books

Adams, Henry. *History of the United States during the Administration of Thomas Jefferson.* New York, 1930.

———. *John Randolph.* Boston, 1898.

———. *Life of Albert Gallatin.* Philadelphia, 1879.

Anderson, Benedict. *Imagined Communities: Reflections of the Origin and Spread of Nationalism.* London, 1991.

Anthony, Carl Sferrazza. *First Ladies: The Saga of the President's Wives and Their Power, 1789–1961.* New York, 1990.

Anthony, Katharine. *Dolly Madison: Her Life and Times.* Garden City, N.Y., 1949.

Arnebeck, Bob. *Through a Fiery Trial: Building Washington, 1790–1800.* Lanham, Md., 1991.

Arnett, Ethel Stephens. *Mrs. James Madison: The Incomparable Dolley.* Greensboro, N.C., 1972.

Aronson, Sidney H. *Status and Kinship in the Higher Civil Service: Standards of Selection in the Administrations of John Adams, Thomas Jefferson, and Andrew Jackson.* Cambridge, Mass., 1964.

Baker, Paula. *The Moral Frameworks of Public Life: Gender, Politics, and the State in Rural New York, 1870–1930.* New York, 1991.

Banning, Lance. *The Jeffersonian Persuasion: Evolution of a Party Ideology.* Ithaca, N.Y., 1978.

Bashkina, Nina N., et al., eds. *The United States and Russia: The Beginning of Relations, 1765–1815.* Washington, D.C., 1980.

Bemis, Samuel Flagg. *John Quincy Adams and the Union.* New York, 1956.

Bledstein, Burton. *The Culture of Professionalism: The Middle Class and the Development of Higher Education in America.* New York, 1976.

Boller, Paul F., Jr. *Presidential Wives: An Anecdotal History.* New York, 1988.

Botsford, Margaret. *The Reign of Reform, or Yankee Doodle Court.* Philadelphia, 1829.

Bowers, Claude G. *The Party Battles of the Jackson Period.* Boston, 1922.

Bowling, Kenneth R. *Creating the Federal City, 1774–1800: Potomac Fever.* Washington, D.C., 1988.

Brant, Irving. *James Madison: Secretary of State.* Indianapolis, 1953.

———. *James Madison: The President, 1809–1812.* Indianapolis, 1959.

Brooks, Geraldine. *Dames and Daughters of the Young Republic.* New York, 1901.

Brown, Rita Mae. *Dolley: A Novel of Dolley Madison in Love and War.* New York, 1994.

Buel, Richard, Jr. *Securing the Revolution: Ideology in American Politics, 1789–1815.* Ithaca, N.Y., 1972.

Burstein, Andrew. *The Inner Jefferson: Portrait of a Grieving Optimist.* Charlottesville, Va., 1993.

Burt, Nathaniel. *First Families: The Making of an American Aristocracy.* Boston, 1970.

Busey, Samuel C. *Pictures of the City of Washington in the Past.* Washington, D.C., 1898.

Bushman, Richard L. *The Refinement of America: Persons, Houses, Cities.* New York, 1992.

Cable, Mary. *The Avenue of the Presidents.* Boston, 1969.

Caroli, Betty Boyd. *First Ladies.* New York, 1987.

Carson, Barbara. *Ambitious Appetites: Dining, Behavior, and Patterns of Consumption in Federal Washington.* Washington, D.C., 1990.

Clark, Allen C. *Life and Letters of Dolly Madison.* Washington, D.C., 1914.

Colley, Linda. *Britons: Forging the Nation, 1707–1837.* New Haven, 1992.

Cooley, E. M. *A Description of the Etiquette at Washington City.* Philadelphia, 1829.

Cott, Nancy F. *The Bonds of Womanhood: "Woman's Sphere" in New England, 1780–1835.* New Haven, 1977.

Cunningham, Noble E., Jr. *The Jeffersonian Republicans: The Formation of Party Organizations, 1789–1801.* Chapel Hill, N.C., 1957.

———. *The Presidency of James Monroe.* Lawrence, Kans., 1996.

Dangerfield, George. *The Awakening of American Nationalism, 1815–1828.* New York, 1965.

———. *The Era of Good Feelings.* New York, 1952.

Davidoff, Lenore. *The Best Circles: Women and Society in Victorian England.* Totowa, N.J., 1974.

Davidoff, Lenore, and Catherine Hall. *Family Fortunes: Men and Women of the English Middle Class, 1780–1859.* Chicago, 1987.

Dean, Elizabeth Lippincott. *Dolly Madison: The Nation's Hostess.* Boston, 1928.

Demos, John Putnam. *Entertaining Satan: Witchcraft and the Culture of Early New England.* New York, 1983.

DePauw, Linda Grant, and Conover Hunt. *"Remember the Ladies": Women in America, 1750–1815.* New York, 1976.

Dunbar, Robin. *Grooming, Gossip, and the Evolution of Language.* Cambridge, Mass., 1997.

Edwards, Rebecca. *Angels in the Machinery: Gender in American Party Politics from the Civil War to the Progressive Era.* New York, 1997.

Elias, Norbert. *The History of Manners.* Vol. 1 of *The Civilizing Process.* Trans. Edmund Jephcott. New York, 1978.

——. *Power and Civility.* Vol. 2 of *The Civilizing Process.* Trans. Edmund Jephcott. New York, 1982.

Elkins, Stanley, and Eric McKitrick. *The Age of Federalism: The Early American Republic, 1788–1800.* New York, 1993.

Ellet, Elizabeth. *The Court Circles of the Republic.* Hartford, 1869.

Ellis, Joseph J. *American Sphinx: The Character of Thomas Jefferson.* New York, 1993.

——. *Passionate Sage: The Character and Legacy of John Adams.* New York, 1993.

Enloe, Cynthia. *Bananas, Beaches, and Bases: Making Feminist Sense of International Politics.* Berkeley, Calif., 1990.

Fee, Walter R. *Transition from Aristocracy to Democracy in New Jersey, 1789–1829.* Somerville, N.J., 1933.

Formisano, Ronald P. *The Birth of Mass Political Parties, Michigan, 1827–1861.* Princeton, N.J., 1971.

Foster, Augustus John. *Jeffersonian America: Notes on the United States of America.* Ed. Richard Beale Davis. San Marino, Calif., 1954.

Furman, Bess. *White House Profile.* New York, 1951.

Gelles, Edith B. *Portia: The World of Abigail Adams.* Bloomington, Ind., 1992.

A Gentleman. *The Laws of Etiquette; or Short Rules and Reflections for Conduct in Society.* Philadelphia, 1839.

Gerson, Noel Bertram. *The Velvet Glove.* Nashville, 1975.

Gilmore, Glenda Elizabeth. *Gender and Jim Crow: Women and the Politics of White Supremacy in North Carolina, 1896–1920.* Chapel Hill, N.C., 1996.

Ginzberg, Lori. *Women and the Work of Benevolence: Morality, Politics, and Class in the Nineteenth Century United States.* New Haven, 1990.

Goodman, Dena. *The Republic of Letters: A Cultural History of the French Enlightenment.* Ithaca, N.Y., 1994.

Goodwin, Maud Wilder. *Dolly Madison.* New York, 1896.

Green, Constance McLaughlin. *Washington: Village and Capital, 1800–1878.* Princeton, N.J., 1962.

Griswold, Rufus Wilmot. *The Republican Court, or American Society in the Days of Washington.* New York, 1855.

Hall, Florence Howe. *Social Usages at Washington.* New York, 1906.

Halttunen, Karen. *Confidence Men and Painted Women: A Study of Middle-Class Culture in America, 1830–1870.* New Haven, 1982.

Hess, Stephen, and Milton Kaplan. *The Ungentlemanly Art: A History of American Political Cartoons.* New York, 1968.

Hewitt, Nancy A. *Women's Activism and Social Change: Rochester, New York, 1822–1872.* Ithaca, N.Y., 1984.

Hofstadter, Richard. *The Idea of a Party System: The Rise of Legitimate Opposition in the United States, 1780–1840.* Berkeley, Calif., 1969.

Hogg, Elkanah [pseud.]. *The Lay of the First Minstrel, or The Court of King Andrew the First.* New York, 1834.

Holloway, Laura C. *Ladies of the White House, or In the Home of the Presidents.* Philadelphia, 1881.

Hunt, Gaillard. *As We Were: Life in America, 1814.* 1914. Rept., Stockbridge, Mass., 1993.

Hunt, Lynn. *Politics, Culture, and Class in the French Revolution.* Berkeley, Calif., 1984.

Hunt-Jones, Conover. *Dolley and the "Great Little Madison."* Washington, D.C., 1977.

Hurd, Charles. *Washington Cavalcade.* New York, 1948.

——. *The White House: A Biography.* New York, 1940.

Ingersoll, Charles J. *History of the Second War between the United States and Great Britain.* Philadelphia, 1852.

Jacob, Kathryn Allamong. *Capital Elites: High Society in Washington, D.C., after the Civil War.* Washington, D.C., 1995.

Jaeger, Stephen. *The Origins of Courtliness: Civilizing Trends and the Formation of Courtly Ideals, 939–1210.* Philadelphia, 1985.

Jaher, Fredric Cople. *The Urban Establishment: Upper Strata in Boston, New York, Charleston, Chicago, and Los Angeles.* Urbana, Ill., 1982.

Jones, Vivien, ed. *Women in the Eighteenth Century: Constructions of Femininity.* London, 1990.

Kamensky, Jane. *Governing the Tongue: The Politics of Speech in Early New England.* New York, 1997.

Kasson, John F. *Rudeness and Civility: Manners in Nineteenth-Century Urban America.* New York, 1990.

Kerber, Linda. *Women of the Republic: Intellect and Ideology in Revolutionary America.* Chapel Hill, N.C., 1980.

Klapthor, Margaret Brown. *The First Ladies Cookbook.* New York, 1969.

Landes, Joan B. *Women and the Public Sphere in the Age of the French Revolution.* Ithaca, N.Y., 1988.

Lester, Malcolm. *Anthony Merry Redivivus: A Reappraisal of the British Minister to the United States, 1803–6.* Charlottesville, Va., 1978.

Lipset, Seymour Martin. *The First New Nation: The United States in Historical and Comparative Perspective.* New York, 1963.

Lloyd, Alan. *The Scorching of Washington: The War of 1812.* West Vancouver, B.C., n.d.

Lockwood, Mary Smith. *Yesterdays in Washington.* Rosslyn, Va., 1915.

Malone, Dumas. *Jefferson the President: First Term, 1801–1805.* Boston, 1970.

Marszalek, John F. *The Petticoat Affair: Manners, Mutiny, and Sex in Andrew Jackson's White House.* New York, 1997.

Martin, Judith. *Common Courtesy in Which Miss Manners Solves the Problem That Baffled Mr. Jefferson.* New York, 1985.

Martineau, Harriet. *Retrospect of Western Travel.* 1838. Rept. New York, 1969.

Mayo, Edith P., and Denise Meringolo. *First Ladies: Political Role and Public Image.* Washington, D.C., 1994.

McLaughlin, Jack. *Jefferson and Monticello: The Biography of a Builder.* New York, 1988.

Means, Marianne. *The Woman in the White House: The Lives, Time, and Influence of Twelve Notable First Ladies.* New York, 1963.

Miller, Hope Ridings. *Scandals in the Highest Office.* New York, 1973.

Muller, Charles G. *The Darkest Day: 1814, the Washington-Baltimore Campaign.* Philadelphia, 1963.

Nagel, Paul C. *Descent from Glory: Four Generations of the John Adams Family.* New York, 1983.

Nimrod, Harry, ed. *The Fudge Family in Washington.* Baltimore, 1820.

Niven, John. *John C. Calhoun and the Price of Union: A Biography.* Baton Rouge, La., 1988.

Okin, Susan Miller. *Women in Western Political Thought.* Princeton, N.J., 1979.

Oliver, Andrew. *Portraits of John Quincy Adams and His Wife.* Cambridge, Mass., 1970.

Parton, James. *The Life of Andrew Jackson.* New York, 1861.

Peterson, Merrill D. *The Great Triumvirate: Webster, Clay, and Calhoun.* New York, 1987.

——. *Thomas Jefferson and the New Nation: A Biography.* New York, 1970.

Phillips, Leon [Noel Bertram Gerson]. *That Eaton Woman: In Defense of Peggy O'Neale Eaton.* Barre, Mass., 1974.

Pocock, J. G. A. *Virtue, Commerce, and History.* Cambridge, Mass., 1985.

Pollack, Queena. *Peggy Eaton: Democracy's Mistress.* New York, 1931.

Randolph, Sarah N. *The Domestic Life of Thomas Jefferson.* 1871. Rept. Charlottesville, Va., 1978.

Reilly, Bernard F., Jr. *American Political Prints, 1766–1876: A Catalog of the Collections in the Library of Congress.* Boston, 1991.

Remini, Robert V. *Andrew Jackson and the Course of American Freedom, 1822–32.* New York, 1981.

———. *The Election of Andrew Jackson.* Philadelphia, 1963.

Rives, William Cabell. *Biography of James Madison.* Boston, 1878.

Rosebush, James S. *First Lady, Public Wife: A Behind-the-Scenes History of the Evolving Role of First Ladies in American Political Life.* Lanham, Md., 1987.

Rousseau, Jean-Jacques. *Emile; or On Education.* Ed. and trans. Alan Bloom. New York, 1979.

Ryan, Mary P. *Cradle of the Middle Class: The Family in Oneida County, New York, 1790–1865.* Cambridge, Mass., 1981.

———. *Women in Public: From Banners and Ballots, 1825–1880.* New York, 1990.

Schlesinger, Arthur M. *Learning How to Behave: A Historical Study of American Etiquette Books.* New York, 1947.

Schlesinger, Arthur, Jr., ed. *History of U.S. Political Parties.* New York, 1973.

Scott, Anne Firor. *Natural Allies: Women's Associations in American History.* Urbana, Ill., 1991.

Seale, William, *The President's House: A History.* Washington, D.C., 1986.

Seaton, Josephine. *William Winston Seaton and the National Intelligencer.* Boston, 1871.

Sharp, James Roger. *American Politics in the Early Republic: The New Nation in Crisis.* New Haven, 1993.

Shepherd, Jack. *The Adams Chronicles: Four Generations of Greatness.* Boston, 1975.

———. *Cannibals of the Heart: A Personal Biography of Louisa Catherine and John Quincy Adams.* New York, 1980.

Sisson, Daniel. *The American Revolution of 1800.* New York, 1974.

Smelser, Marshall. *The Democratic Republic, 1810–1815.* New York, 1968.

Smith, Margaret Bayard. *What Is Gentility?* Washington, D.C., 1828.

———. *A Winter in Washington; or Memoirs of the Seymour Family.* New York, 1824.

Smith, Marie. *Entertaining in the White House.* Washington, D.C., 1967.

Spacks, Patricia Meyer. *Gossip.* New York, 1985.

Tayloe, Benjamin Ogle. *Our Neighbors on La Fayette Square.* 1872. Rept. Washington, D.C., 1982.

Trollope, Frances. *Domestic Manners of the Americans.* 1832. Rept. Ed. John Lauritz Larson. St. James, N.Y., 1993.

Truman, David. *The Governmental Process: Political Interest and Public Opinion.* New York, 1960.

Truman, Margaret. *First Ladies: An Intimate Group Portrait of White House Wives.* New York, 1995.

Ulrich, Laurel Thatcher. *A Midwife's Tale: The Life of Martha Ballard, Based on Her Diary, 1785–1812.* New York, 1990.

Van Buren, Martin. *The Autobiography of Martin Van Buren.* Ed. John C. Fitzpatrick. Washington, D.C., 1920.

Varon, Elizabeth R. *"We Mean to Be Counted": White Women and Party Politics in Antebellum Virginia.* Chapel Hill, N.C., 1998.

Waldstreicher, David. *In the Midst of Perpetual Fetes: The Making of American Nationalism.* Chapel Hill, N.C., 1997.

Ward, John William. *Andrew Jackson: Symbol for an Age.* New York, 1962.

Warden, David Baillie. *A Chorographical and Statistical Description of the District of Columbia.* Paris, 1816.

Warner, Michael. *The Letters of the Republic: Publication and the Public Sphere in Eighteenth-Century America.* Cambridge, Mass., 1990.

Warren, Mercy Otis. *History of the Rise, Progress, and Termination of the American Revolution.* Boston, 1805.

Watson, Harry L. *Liberty and Power: The Politics of Jacksonian America.* New York, 1990.

Watterston, George. *The L—— Family in Washington; or, A Winter in the Metropolis.* Washington, D.C., 1822.

Wharton, Anne Hollingsworth. *Social Life in the Early Republic.* Philadelphia, 1902.

White, Leonard. *The Jeffersonians.* New York, 1951.

Willson, Beckles. *Friendly Relations: A Narrative of Britain's Ministers and Ambassadors to America (1791–1930).* London, 1934.

Wood, Gordon S. *The Radicalism of the American Revolution.* New York, 1992.

Woodham-Smith, Cecil. *The Reason Why.* New York, 1954.

Young, James Sterling. *The Washington Community, 1800–1828.* New York, 1966.

Zagarri, Rosemarie. *The Politics of Size: Representation in the United States, 1776–1850.* Ithaca, N.Y., 1989.

Chapters and Articles

Allgor, Catherine. "'A Republican in a Monarchy': Louisa Catherine Adams in Russia." *Diplomatic History* 21:1 (Winter 1997): 15–43.

Ames, William E. "The *National Intelligencer:* Washington's Leading Political Newspaper." *Records of the Columbia Historical Society,* 1966–68, 71–83.

Basch, Norma. "Manners, Morals, and Politics in the Election of 1828." *Journal of American History* 80:3 (Dec. 1993): 890–918.

Bloch, Ruth. "The Gendered Meanings of Virtue in Revolutionary America." *Signs* 13 (Autumn 1987): 37–59.

Bogue, Allan G., and Mark Paul Marlaire. "Of Mess and Men: The Boardinghouse and Congressional Voting, 1821–1842." *American Journal of Political Science* 19 (May 1975): 207–30.

Boorstin, Daniel J. "Roles of the President's House." In *The White House: The First Two Hundred Years,* ed. Frank Freidel and William Pencak, 3–15. Boston, 1994.

Brown, Kathleen M. "Brave New Worlds: Women's and Gender History." *William and Mary Quarterly,* 3d ser., 50 (April 1993): 245–67.

Bryan, W. B. "The Name White House." *Records of the Columbia Historical Society* 33–34 (1932): 306–8.

Butterfield, Lyman H. "Tending a Dragon-Killer: Notes for the Biographer of Mrs. John Quincy Adams." *Proceedings of the American Philosophical Society* 118 (April 1974): 165–78.

Callan, Hilary. "The Premiss of Dedication: Notes toward an Ethnography of Diplomats' Wives." In *Perceiving Women,* ed. Shirley Ardener. London, 1975.

Cameron, Vivian. "Political Exposures: Sexuality and Caricature in the French Revolution." In *Eroticism and the Body Politic,* ed. Lynn Hunt. Baltimore, 1991.

Caroli, Betty Boyd. "The First Lady's Changing Role." In *The White House: The First Two Hundred Years,* ed. Frank Freidel and William Pencak, 170–85. Boston, 1994.

Challinor, Joan Ridder. "The Mis-Education of Louisa Catherine Johnson Adams." *Proceedings of the Massachusetts Historian Society* 98 (1987): 21–48.

Cohen, Lester. "The Politics of Language and the Aesthetics of Self." *American Quarterly* 35 (1983): 481–98.

Corbett, Katharine T. "Louisa Catherine Adams: The Anguished 'Adventures of a Nobody.'" In *Woman's Being, Woman's Place: Female Identity and Vocation in American History,* ed. Mary Kelley. Boston, 1979.

Coryell, Janet. "The Woman Politico: Women and Partisan Politics in Mid-Nineteenth-Century America." In *Women and the Unstable State in Nineteenth-Century America,* ed. Alison M. Parker and Stephanie Cole. College Station, Tex., 2000.

Deneys, Anne. "The Political Economy of the Body in the *Liaisons dangereuses* of Choderlos de Laclos." In *Eroticism and the Body Politic*, ed. Lynn Hunt. Baltimore, 1991.

Farrell, Brian. "Bellona and the General: Andrew Jackson and the Affair of Mrs. Eaton." *History Today* 8:7 (July 1958): 474–84.

Foot, Rosemary. "Where Are the Women? The Gender Dimension in the Study of International Relations." *Diplomatic History* 14 (Fall 1990): 615–22.

Fox-Genovese, Elizabeth. "Placing Women's History in History." *New Left Review* 133 (May–June 1982): 5–29.

Freeman, Joanne B. "Dueling as Politics: Reinterpreting the Burr-Hamilton Duel." *William and Mary Quarterly*, 3d ser., 53:2 (April 1996): 289–317.

———. "Slander, Poison, Whispers, and Fame: Jefferson's 'Anas' and Political Gossip in the Early Republic." *Journal of the Early Republic* 15:1 (Spring 1995): 25–57.

Gillette, Howard, Jr. "Introduction." In *Southern City, National Ambition: The Growth of Early Washington, D.C.*, ed. Howard Gillette, Jr. Washington, D.C., 1995.

Holt, Thomas C. "Marking: Race, Race-making, and the Writing of History." *American Historical Review* 100:1 (Feb. 1995): 1–20.

Howe, Daniel Walker. "European Sources of Political Ideas in Jeffersonian America." *Reviews in American History* 10 (Dec. 1982): 28–44.

———. "Why the Scottish Enlightenment Was Useful to the Framers of the American Constitution." *Comparative Studies in Society and History* 31 (July 1989): 572–87.

Howe, John R. "Republican Thought and the Political Violence of the 1790s." *American Quarterly* 19 (Summer 1967): 148–65.

Hunt, Lynn. "Introduction." In *Eroticism and the Body Politic*, ed. Lynn Hunt. Baltimore, 1991.

———. "The Many Bodies of Marie Antoinette: Political Pornography and the Problem of the Feminine in the French Revolution." In *Eroticism and the Body Politic*, ed. Lynn Hunt. Baltimore, 1991.

Huntingdon, Frances Carpenter. "The Heiress of Washington City: Marcia Burnes Van Ness, 1782–1832." *Records of the Columbia Historical Society* 69–70 (June 1971): 80–101.

Kelly-Gadol, Joan. "The Social Relations of the Sexes: Methodological Implications of Women's History." In *The Signs Reader: Women, Gender, and Scholarship*, ed. Elizabeth Able and Emily K. Able. Chicago, 1983.

Kerber, Linda K. "Separate Spheres, Female Worlds, Woman's Place: The Rhetoric of Women's History." *Journal of American History* 75:1 (June 1988): 9–39.

Kerber, Linda K., et al. "Beyond Roles, Beyond Spheres: Thinking about Gender in the Early Republic." *William and Mary Quarterly*, 3d ser., 46:3 (June 1989): 565–85.

Klapthor, Margaret Brown. "Benjamin Latrobe and Dolley Madison Decorate the White House, 1809–1811." *United States National Museum Bulletin 241: Contributions from the Museum of History and Technology*, paper 49 (1965): 153–64.

Klaus, Susan L. "'Some of the Smartest Folks Here': The Van Nesses and Community Building in Early Washington." *Washington History* 3:2 (Fall/Winter 1991–92): 22–45.

Lerche, Charles O., Jr. "Jefferson and the Election of 1800: A Case Study in the Political Smear." *William and Mary Quarterly*, 3d ser., 5:4 (Oct. 1948): 467–91.

Lewis, Jan. "'The Blessings of Domestic Society': Thomas Jefferson's Family and the Transformation of American Politics." In *Jeffersonian Legacies*, ed. Peter S. Onuf. Charlottesville, Va., 1993.

———. "'Of Every Age, Sex, and Condition': The Representation of Women in the Constitution." *Journal of the Early Republic* 15:3 (1995): 359–87.

———. "Politics and the Ambivalence of the Private Sphere: Women in Early Washington,

D.C." In *A Republic for the Ages: The United States Capitol and the Political Culture of the Early Republic*, ed. Donald R. Kennon. Charlottesville, Va., 1999.

———. "The Republican Wife." *William and Mary Quarterly*, 3d ser., 44 (Oct. 1987): 689–721.

Lombardo, Daniel. "A Look Back: Calling Cards Used for Social Reasons." *Amherst Bulletin* 27 (28 April 1995): p. 4.

Mannix, Richard. "Albert Gallatin in Washington, 1801–1813." *Records of the Columbia Historical Society*, 1971–72, 60–80.

Maza, Sarah. "The Diamond Necklace Affair Revisited (1785–1786): The Case of the Missing Queen." In *Eroticism and the Body Politic*, ed. Lynn Hunt. Baltimore, 1991.

McCormick, John H. "The First Master of Ceremonies of the White House." *Records of the Columbia Historical Society* 7 (1904): 170–94.

McGerr, Michael. "Political Style and Women's Power, 1830–1930." *Journal of American History* 77:3 (Dec. 1990): 864–85.

Miles, Edwin A. "President Adams' Billiard Table." *New England Quarterly* 45 (1972): 31–43.

"Mrs. John Quincy Adams' Ball, 1824." *Harper's Bazaar*, 18 March 1871, 166–67.

Nevin, David. "To the President, Peggy Eaton Was Chaste Indeed." *Smithsonian* 23 (May 1992): 84–97.

Norton, Mary Beth. "Gender and Defamation in Seventeenth-Century Maryland." *William and Mary Quarterly*, 3d ser., 44:1 (Jan. 1987): 3–39.

Owsley, Harriet Chappell. "The Marriages of Rachel Donelson." *Tennessee Historical Quarterly* 36 (Winter 1977): 479–92.

Parsons, Lynn Hudson. "Louisa (Catherine Johnson) Adams." In *American First Ladies: Their Lives and Legacy*, ed. Lewis L. Gould. New York, 1996.

Pateman, Carole. "'The Disorder of Women': Women, Love, and the Sense of Justice." *Ethics* 91 (Oct. 1980): 20–34.

Paullin, Charles O. "Early British Diplomats in Washington." *Records of the Columbia Historical Society* 44–45 (1942–43): 241–67.

Raley, Robert L. "Interior Designs by Benjamin Henry Latrobe for the President's House." *Antiques* 75 (June 1958): 568–71.

Rosenberg, Emily. "Gender." *Journal of American History* 77 (June 1990): 116–24.

Santiago, Denise-Marie. "Domestic Goddess Dissed." *Philadelphia Inquirer*, 2 July 1997, D-12.

Shulman, Holly Cowan. "Dolley (Payne Todd) Madison." In *American First Ladies: Their Lives and Their Legacy*, ed. Lewis L. Gould. New York, 1996.

Smelser, Marshall. "The Federalist Period as an Age of Passion." *American Quarterly* 10 (Winter 1958): 391–419.

Smith, Margaret Bayard. "Presidential Inaugurations." *Ladies' Magazine and Literary Gazette* 4:12 (Dec. 1831): 529–37.

Teute, Fredrika J. "In 'the Gloom of Evening': Margaret Bayard Smith's View in Black and White of Early Washington Society." *Proceedings of the American Antiquarian Society* 106:1 (1996): 37–58.

———. "Roman Matron on the Banks of Tiber Creek: Margaret Bayard Smith and the Politicization of Spheres in the Nation's Capital." In *A Republic for the Ages: The United States Capitol and the Political Culture of the Early Republic*, ed. Donald R. Kennon. Charlottesville, Va., 1999.

———. "'A Wild, Desolate Place': Life on the Margins in Early Washington." In *Southern City, National Ambition: The Growth of Early Washington, D.C., 1800–1860*, ed. Howard Gillette, Jr. Washington, D.C., 1995.

Varon, Elizabeth R. "Tippecanoe and the Ladies, Too: White Women and Party Politics in

Antebellum Virginia." *Journal of American History* 82:2 (Sept. 1995): 494–521.

Wood, Kirsten E. "'One Woman So Dangerous to Public Morals': Gender and Power in the Eaton Affair." *Journal of the Early Republic* 17:2 (Summer 1997): 237–75. Annotated draft in my possession.

Zagarri, Rosemarie. "Gender and the First Party System." In *Federalists Reconsidered*, ed. Doron Ben-Atar and Barbara Oberg. Charlottesville, Va., 1998.

——. "Morals, Manners, and the Republican Mother." *American Quarterly* 44 (June 1992): 192–215.

MANUSCRIPTS, CONFERENCE PRESENTATIONS,
AND PUBLIC LECTURES

Boydston, Jeanne. "Free Men and Masterless Women: Gender, Labor, and the Discourse on Prostitution in the Early Republic, 1790–1830." Paper presented at the Berkshire Conference on the History of Women, June 1996.

Brekke, Linzy. "Martha Jefferson Randolph and the Politics of Family in the Early Republic." Senior thesis, Mount Holyoke College, 1998.

Bushman, Richard L. Public lecture at Historic Deerfield, 6 July 1995.

Carson, Barbara. "Complicating Categories: Women, History, and Historic Preservation/ Material Culture in the United States," Paper presented at the Berkshire Conference for Women in History, June 1996.

Challinor, Joan Ridder. "Louisa Catherine Johnson Adams: The Price of Ambition." Ph.D. diss., American University, 1982.

Colley, Linda. "The Female Elite in Unreformed Britain." Paper presented at Brown University, April 1995.

Earman, Cynthia Diane. "Boardinghouses, Parties, and the Creation of a Political Society: Washington City, 1800–1830." M.A. thesis, Louisiana State University at Baton Rouge, 1992.

Freeman, Joanne B. "Affairs of Honor: Political Combat and Political Character in the Early Republic." Ph.D. diss., University of Virginia, 1997.

——. "Affairs of Honor: Political Combat and Political Character in the Early Republic." Paper presented at Yale University, February 1997.

——. "Aristocratic Murder and Democratic Fury: Honor and Violence in Early National New England." Paper presented at the American Historical Association, January 1997.

——. "Jefferson and Political Combat." Paper presented at "New Horizons in Jefferson Scholarship" at the International Center for Jefferson Studies, Charlottesville, Va., Oct. 4–5, 1996.

Jacob, Kathryn Allamong. "High Society in Washington during the Gilded Age: Three Distinct Aristocracies." Ph.D. diss., The Johns Hopkins University, 1986.

Kern, Susan. Paper presented at "New Horizons in Jefferson Scholarship" at the International Center for Jefferson Studies, Charlottesville, Va., Oct. 4–5, 1996.

Schneider, Gretchen. "Mrs. Adams' Ball: A Political and Social Arena in Early Nineteenth-Century America." Paper presented at "Traditional Dance in the Twentieth Century," Honolulu, August 1978.

Shields, David S., and Fredrika J. Teute. "Jefferson in Washington: Domesticating Manners in the Republican Court." Paper presented at the Institute of Early American History and Culture, June 1997.

——. "The Republican Court and the Historiography of a Women's Domain in the Public Sphere." Paper presented at Society for Historians of the Early Republic, July 1993.

Simon, Amy, "'She Is So Neat and Fits So Well': Garment Construction and the Millinery Business of Eliza Oliver Dodd, 1821–1833." M.A. thesis, University of Delaware, 1993.

Smith, Rogers, "The Attractions of Exclusion." Paper presented at roundtable on "Nationalism, Loyalties, and Identities in the Era of the Early Republic," at the Society for Historians of the Early Republic Conference, July 1997.

Zagarri, Rosemarie, "Petticoat Politicians and Concurrent Patriots." Paper presented at the American Antiquarian Society, November 1996.

Museum Exhibitions and Catalogs

Dolley at Dumbarton: The First Lady Took Shelter from the British in a House with Many Family Ties. Washington, D.C., 1996. Exhibition catalog, Dumbarton House, 26 March through 2 Nov. 1996.

Temple of Liberty: Building the Capitol for a New Nation. Washington, D.C., 1995. Exhibition catalog, Library of Congress, Madison Gallery, 24 Feb. through 24 June 1995.

Miscellaneous Media

Edwards, Mickey, Interview, "All Things Considered," National Public Radio, 14 Feb. 1997.

Sondheim, Stephen. *Pacific Overtures.* Revelation Music Publishing Corporation and Rilting Music, Inc., 1975, 1976.

Acknowledgments

Undertaking this project about the centrality of social events and personal relations in building a political structure, I have been struck by the conjunction of life and art, how we model our projects on our lives. The process of researching and writing this book has, in many important ways, resembled attending a wonderful party.

When you throw a great party, someone has to pick up the tab. Many thanks to those who catered this affair with their financial support. My greatest debt is to Yale University and the Jacob K. Javits Fellowship Program, which supported my entire graduate career. I am also grateful for the Mary E. Woolley Fellowship (Mount Holyoke College), the John F. Enders Dissertation Grant (Yale), the Kate B. and Hall J. Peterson Dissertation Fellowship (American Antiquarian Society), the Andrew W. Mellon Dissertation Fellowship (Massachusetts Historical Society), the Whiting Fellowship in the Humanities (Yale), the Joseph A. Skinner Fellowship (Mount Holyoke College), and the Fund for Research (Simmons College).

Many librarians, archivists, and library-based scholars have transformed me from a scullery scholar to Cinderella, the belle of the ball: at the American Antiquarian Society, Ellen S. Dunlap, John Hench, Caroline F. Sloat, Joanne D. Chaison, Laura E. Wasowicz, "Team Misc-Pam" (who brought me every single box of Miscellaneous Pamphlets), and the late, treasured Joyce Tracy; at the Massachusetts Historical Society, Conrad E. Wright, Len Travers, Peter Drummey, Brenda Lawson, Celeste Walker, and the staff of the Adams Papers, Virginia Smith and her team of detectives; at the Library of Congress (Manuscript Division), Fred W. Bauman, Ernest J. Emerich, Jeffrey M. Flannery, Michael J. Klein, Kathleen C. McDonough, all led by the intrepid Mary M. Wolfskill; at the Library of Congress, Gerard W. Gewalt and John McDonough; at the Historical Society of Washington, D.C., Bonnie Hedges and Jane Freundel Levey; at the New England Historic Genealogical Society, Gary Boyd Roberts; at the Papers of James Madison, David Mattern and J. C. A. Stagg; at the Mount Holyoke College Library, Susan Perry and her whole staff; and at the Simmons College Library, Patricia Durisin and the reference librarians.

When I arrived at the party, I found already there a gracious group of welcoming women, at first strangers, then friends and colleagues. The profession wonders what difference having women in the academy will make; these women have made scholarship a collaborative (rather than a competitive) effort: Susan Branson, Martha Burns, Barbara Carson, Janet Coryell, Cynthia Diane Earman, Edith Gelles, Kathryn Jacob, Laurie F. Newby, Susan Randomsky, Emily S. Rosenberg, Elizabeth Varon, Rosemarie Zagarri. I am especially grateful for those who shared "their women" with me: Frederika J. Teute, Sarah Booth Conroy, Rose Barquist, Joan Ridder Challinor, Carolyn Sung Hoover, Holly Cowan Shulman, and Kirsten Wood.

I am extremely grateful to the throng of friends and colleagues who brought food, read, listened, and cared: Kay Althoff, Susanna Blumenthal, Jo Ben-Atar, Linzy Brekke, Stephen Bullock, Andrew Burstein, Leslie Butler, Lisa Cardyn, Catherine Corman, Ellen Curtis, Carolyn Dietel, Julia Ehrhardt, Rob Forbes, Gianna Gifford, Barbara Goren, Ann and Joe Grochmal, Catherine Gudis, Jack Hitt, Allegra and Andrew Hogan, Eric Jones, Geoffrey Kabaservice, Jane Kamensky, Kavita Khory, Catherine Lawrence and Eric Papenfuse (who actually gave me primary sources), Marie McHugh, Chandra Miller, Marina Moskowitz, Christopher Pyle, Janet Richards and Stuart Kirsch, Lori Rotskoff, Holly Sharac, Alexandra Shepherd, Diane Simon, John Stauffer, David Waldstreicher, Rachel Wheeler. In particular, Joanne B. Freeman has epitomized the highest standards of generosity, scholarship, and joyful engagement with my work and with me.

In addition to old friends, every good party brings new and fascinating people, in this case the Washington crowd who lent glamour to the occasion: Edith P. Mayo, Claudia Brush Kidwell, Robert Selim (Smithsonian Institution); Kenneth R. Bowling, Donald R. Kennon (United States Capitol Historical Society); Donald Ritchie, Lucinda Robb (National Archives); Don Hawkins (Historical Society of Washington, D.C.); Douglas L. Wilson and his staff (International Center for Jefferson Studies); Judith Frank; Anthony Pitch; Kym Rice; and all of the staff at the Octagon House, the Anacostia Museum, and Dumbarton House.

My teachers at Yale have stood out from the crowd as guides, supporters, and inspirations: Jon Butler, Linda Colley, David Brion Davis, Glenda Gilmore, Cynthia Russett, Robin Winks. Senior faculty at other institutions have also been generous with their time, encouragement, and suggestions: Elaine Forman Crane, Ann Fabian, Linda Kerber, John Marszalek, Anne Firor Scott. My new colleagues at Simmons College in Boston lent support and illumination at the dissertation-into-a-book stage: Keith Phelan Gorman and Laura Prieto. Indeed, thanks to the whole Simmons community who have cheered this project on to completion. Two conference opportunities have played a significant role in the intellectual development of this project, and I thank the audiences and participants of the symposium on "New Horizons in Jefferson Scholarship" at the International Center for Jefferson Studies (1996) and of the panel on "'Politicos' and Perfect Hostesses: Elite White Women and Early Republican Politics" at the Society for the Historians of the Early American Republic Conference (1997).

Richard Holway of the University Press of Virginia was an early supporter of my work, and I am so pleased that our first lunch has taken us so far. He, Nancy Essig, Ellen Satrom, and Ellie Goodman have carefully and imaginatively brought the book to life. I am grateful, too, for the generosity of all who read this work as a manuscript and commented so usefully. In particular, Jan Lewis's wisdom and her willingness to share it changed this project in myriad ways. The final product is all the better for her suggestions.

No lady would dream of arriving at a party unescorted. During my journey to this occasion, I have been squired by some extraordinary beaux: Jacques Fabert, who told me I had a brain; John Mack Faragher, who told me to be a historian; and my treasured friend Joseph J. Ellis, who asked me who I was. Once I arrived at Yale, Doron Ben-Atar dared me to study political women, losing bet after bet with untiring grace. And most especially John Demos, who let me dance and dance.

Dolley Madison taught me that every good party has a hostess, a tactful, gracious presence who is watchful but never controlling, who intervenes to smooth the way before any disaster or faux pas can happen. Nancy F. Cott has subjected my ideas and my prose to her razor-sharp intellect and proved the perfect mentor, someone who led me as we worked side by side. Nancy, thank you for a lovely time.

My party metaphor falls apart when it comes to my family. Deepest gratitude to Clifford and Mary Allgor, who prayed me through it; Esther Lipman, who loved, laughed, listened, and always contributed; Avi and Mia Lipman, who have never known me when I wasn't doing this and like me anyway; and my siblings Elizabeth, Patrick and Amanda, Chris and Corrie who, though far away, kept me laughing and kept me going. Special love to Nick Procaccino, Peggy Maybach, and Emily Longhi, who have loved me all the way through. I dedicate this book to my beloved partner, Jonathan, who has been my model for the life of the mind and of the everyday.

Portions of chapter 3 are reprinted by permission of the publisher from *Women and the Unstable State in Nineteenth-Century America*, ed. Alison M. Parker and Stephanie Cole (College Station: Texas A&M University Press, 2000).

The index was prepared by Marilyn J. Rowland, and Cynthia Diane Earman conceived the jacket design.

Finally, I must acknowledge the warmth, guidance, and support of the many museum curators, historical house guides, clubwomen, and docents who enthusiastically responded to my project. These women, who present history to the public and live history on the ground, have always known the power of the quotidian and the interconnectedness of politics and life, even though their insights have not always received serious attention from the academic world of history. I hope this book affirms and extends their lives' work and tells them (and us) that they were correct all along.

Index

Jeffersonian America

Jan Ellen Lewis and Peter S. Onuf, editors
Sally Hemings and Thomas Jefferson: History, Memory, and Civic Culture

Peter S. Onuf
Jefferson's Empire: The Language of American Nationhood

Catherine Allgor
Parlor Politics: In Which the Ladies of Washington Help Build a City and a Government